TRADER VIC II

WILEY FINANCE EDITIONS

FINANCIAL STATEMENT ANALYSIS
Martin S. Fridson

DYNAMIC ASSET ALLOCATION
David A. Hammer

INTERMARKET TECHNICAL ANALYSIS
John J. Murphy

INVESTING IN INTANGIBLE ASSETS
Russell L. Parr

FORECASTING FINANCIAL MARKETS
Tony Plummer

PORTFOLIO MANAGEMENT FORMULAS
Ralph Vince

TRADING AND INVESTING IN BOND OPTIONS
M. Anthony Wong

THE COMPLETE GUIDE TO CONVERTIBLE SECURITIES WORLDWIDE
Laura A. Zubulake

MANAGED FUTURES IN THE INSTITUTIONAL PORTFOLIO
Charles B. Epstein, Editor

ANALYZING AND FORECASTING FUTURES PRICES
Anthony F. Herbst

CHAOS AND ORDER IN THE CAPITAL MARKETS
Edgar E. Peters

INSIDE THE FINANCIAL FUTURES MARKETS, 3RD EDITION
Mark J. Powers and Mark G. Castelino

RELATIVE DIVIDEND YIELD
Anthony E. Spare

SELLING SHORT
Joseph A. Walker

TREASURY OPERATIONS AND THE FOREIGN EXCHANGE CHALLENGE
Dimitris N. Chorafas

THE FOREIGN EXCHANGE AND MONEY MARKETS GUIDE
Julian Walmsley

CORPORATE FINANCIAL RISK MANAGEMENT
Diane B. Wunnicke, David R. Wilson, Brooke Wunnicke

MONEY MANAGEMENT STRATEGIES FOR FUTURES TRADERS
Nauzer J. Balsara

THE MATHEMATICS OF MONEY MANAGEMENT
Ralph Vince

THE NEW TECHNOLOGY OF FINANCIAL MANAGEMENT
Dimitris N. Chorafas

THE DAY TRADER'S MANUAL
William F. Eng

OPTION MARKET MAKING
Allen J. Baird

TRADING FOR A LIVING
Dr. Alexander Elder

WILEY FINANCE EDITIONS

TRADER VIC II—
Principles of Professional Speculation

Victor Sperandeo

Wiley Finance Edition
JOHN WILEY & SONS, INC.
New York • Chichester • Brisbane • Toronto • Singapore

This text is printed on acid-free paper.

Copyright © 1994 by Victor Sperandeo
Published by John Wiley & Sons, Inc.

Library of Congress Cataloging-in-Publication Data:

Sperandeo, Victor.
    Trader Vic II—principles of professional speculation /
Victor Sperandeo.
      p.   cm. — (Wiley finance editions)
    Includes index.
    ISBN 0-471-53577-X
    1. Investment analysis. 2. Speculation. 3. Stocks. I. Title.
II. Series.
HG4529.S63   1994
332.63'22—dc20   93-29227

Printed in the United States of America

10 9 8 7 6 5 4 3 2 1

This book is dedicated to the greatest leaders in the history of the world, represented by one woman and one man:

Elizabeth I   Queen of England (reigned 1558–1603). When she ascended to the throne, Elizabeth inherited numerous debts. Her genius was in the method she chose to raise revenue to pay those debts, which was unique in tax policy: She made taxation voluntary! Her words: "To tax and to be loved is not given to man. I will end as I began with my subjects, with love." Within 15 years she had a surplus, and was loved deeply.

Thomas Jefferson   Writer of the Declaration of Independence and third president of the United States, Jefferson's leadership philosophy was written in the Declaration's Preamble: "We hold these truths to be self evident, that all men are created equal, that they are endowed by their Creator with certain inalienable Rights, that among these are Life, Liberty and the pursuit of Happiness." (Please note "the pursuit of happiness" was originally "property.")

Acknowledgments

I want to thank the people who have provided critical help in producing this book. Certainly Douglas Kent, who was mainly responsible for editing, correcting, and advising me on where I was unclear, inconsistent, or wrong on a point I was portraying. Doug has been with me for eight years and knows all my principles deeply, and whatever comes from this book, it would do better to thank him rather than me since I could not have produced it without him.

Sally Mulroy, a highly successful professional trader in her own right, has helped me immensely in reviewing, editing, and general reading and advising. She gave me a professional perspective about several chapters where I was unsure or questioned what would appeal to other professionals. Her time and effort are much appreciated and will not be forgotten. I'd also like to thank Terry Brown for providing the foundation for this book.

The people at John Wiley & Sons were terrific in their patience, since this book is long overdue. I thank Karl Weber and, more recently, Myles Thompson, who worked diligently with me to complete this project. It is a fine publisher, with fine people, and I would work with them again any time. Their support was greatly appreciated.

VICTOR SPERANDEO

Short Hills, NJ
February 1994

Contents

PART FOUR   A TRADER'S PSYCHOLOGY   245

Introduction

In *Trader Vic—Methods of a Wall Street Master,* I introduced the basic principles of speculation for the amateur or professional trader. The purpose of this book is to go a step further and provide detailed analytical tools for market analysis and forecasting. It is a user's manual, if you will, for the established pro. Its message is directed at professional traders, those who wish to be professional traders, and those who love the markets as a passionate hobby, in lieu of golf or other time-consuming activities. The purpose is simple: to help improve your trading and, as a result, to help you make more money.

To achieve any level of success in trading requires a significant investment in time and effort. All markets are the same in one important aspect: They constantly change. Keeping on top of everything takes discipline, research, attention to detail, and continuous study. But what is the best approach for that study? With all there is to master, what is the *best* way to decide what to buy and sell?

DEFINING A PERSONAL PHILOSOPHY

To answer those questions, you need to develop a philosophy of trading and investing. A philosophy is a particular view of life and the world that you believe is "the truth." When you understand my philosophy of trading, you will have a solid, unchanging foundation from which to make day-to-day decisions.

My trading philosophy rests on some fundamental principles that I will describe shortly. Those principles grew out of my years of studying and thinking about economics.

Now there's a funny thing about economics. It's an area in which a great many highly educated people have developed many theories and strongly held opinions, and have produced mountains of research to support their theories and opinions—and they seldom agree with one another. Because economics is an inexact science, the study of it includes a large measure of subjectivity, of personal philosophy. Anyone who thinks or writes about economics will, to some degree, incorporate the influence of personal values and beliefs, and I am no exception.

What you will be reading in this book is my own vision of economic "truth," developed from 28 years in this business. I describe some of the common theories held by the experts, and tell which ones I disagree with, and why. From my perspective, some of them are fallacies and distortions that have badly muddled investment decisions. If you already agree with me, fine. If you don't, I hope you will proceed with an open mind. Economically I believe in the Austrian School of Economics; philosophically I am an Objectivist, the philosophy of Ayn Rand.

THREE GUIDING PRINCIPLES

The one overriding principle that governs my philosophy is this: In general, movements in the market are the result of fundamental economic forces, which in turn are the consequence of political actions and decisions. A current example (summer 1993) is the debate over national health care. Congress, in some way, is going to put further controls on the medical industry (political decision), which in turn will lower profits for medical companies (economic consequences). The price movement in this example is the sell-off in medical stocks; as a group, they have dropped more than 30 percent from February 1992 to February 1993.

The second principle is a corollary to the first: In past events we can see what will happen in the future, if we know how to look. The best way to understand how to apply your philosophy to any current event is to go as far back in time as there is factual data, and construct a history of what occurred and why. By integrating and studying the fundamental causes, we can generally predict what is likely to happen in the future.

Never blindly accept what "an expert" tells you. As a trader, you should prove, by historical example, all opinions and viewpoints you decide to believe in and speculate on. Research history, and examine each opinion, until you are confident that you have uncovered the truth, and proved it with objective factual data.

Finding the truth is critical because analyzing mistakes is fundamental to growth in all life's challenges. In the markets, moreover, you can be right for the wrong reasons, and wrong even though you made a great odds-on investment. The reason is subtle but simple: The markets are not consistently objective. At times, they are emotional, subjective, and psychological.

The third principle is closely allied with contrarian thinking. Being a contrarian doesn't mean being stubborn. It means having the intellectual independence not to be swept along with the crowd. The key to making money is to recognize the existence of a false belief, monitor its progress, and act decisively just *before* everyone else wakes up.

All three types of thinking are presented in this book, along with actual examples of what I went through—both when I was right and when I was wrong.

The overarching theme of this book is the use of historical events to predict the future; the accent is on discovering the truth behind all theories and events by underscoring historical facts. In the coming chapters I describe my experience with various historical studies that have proven to be successful.

OVERVIEW OF THE BOOK

The need for principles is nowhere more apparent than in the fields of financial forecasting, market analysis, and professional speculation. It is a world so complex, so full of details, facts, and figures, that any attempt to trade in it without understanding the principles by which it operates is tantamount to gambling on a coin toss. A few traders may be fortunate enough to make money through sheer luck for a period of time, but most of us have to sift through countless facts and figures, separate the grain from the chaff, form a judgment as to what the future will bring, and put money on the line according to that judgment.

Principles act as the screens for an intellectual threshing process, separating the essential from the irrelevant and making sound market analysis and forecasting possible. As with a grain thresher, intellectual screens must be placed in a stepwise, hierarchical order: The first one holds back the stalks and passes through the seed and chaff; the second holds back smaller bits of stem and chaff and passes through seed and dust; the third separates the seed even more finely; and so forth, until finally, just pure grain is left, ready for processing.

Too small a screen at the top will clog your mind, denying it the information necessary to form a good judgment. Too large a screen at the bottom will allow too much information through and bury your mind under a pile of details too large to process. The analytical process must be fitted with the right set of principles positioned in the right order if you are to maintain any degree of accuracy in predicting future market behavior.

PART ONE: ECONOMIC FUNDAMENTALS

Any attempt at market analysis must start with goal setting. In the context of professional speculation, my goal has always been to build wealth, and consequently, my trading philosophy rests on a foundation of three principles: (1) preservation of capital, (2) consistent profitability, and (3) pursuit of superior returns. I describe this philosophy in Chapter 1.

After establishing basic goals, the next step is to develop systematized knowledge to make achieving the goals possible. Just as a person who wishes to become a doctor must endure premed training in math, chemistry, and biology before entering the rigors of medical school, so a would-be professional trader, speculator, or investor must learn the basic principles of market analysis before moving on to a higher order knowledge. I will present what I believe to be the hierarchical principles necessary to accurately sift through the bounty of information available, form reasonable market forecasts, and place trades according to them.

Unfortunately, being reasonable with respect to making forecasts doesn't necessarily translate into being correct in your predictions or profitable in your trades. Because the market comprises millions of people making choices, it is impossible to forecast market behavior with absolute certainty. The best you can do is to use your mental thresher to identify the most likely forthcoming scenario and trade only when the odds favor success. If you can do that, you'll stay way ahead of the pack.

But how do you develop the most likely forthcoming scenario? You begin with a fundamental premise, one we have met before:

> The market is governed by fundamental economic forces, which are affected by the current state of the political system, which in turn is constantly being changed by politicians.

This is simply a restatement of the law of cause and effect as it applies to the marketplace. It refers to the fact that there is a cause-and-effect relationship between human action and economic growth or decline, regardless of the numbers of people involved. In essence, economic activity is a process of production and trade. Production, the reformation of nature's resources for human use and consumption, is a prerequisite for survival. Trade, the free exchange of surpluses (savings), is a prerequisite for economic expansion and true growth. Whether in a small tribe or a massive industrial nation, the principles are the same, and traders must understand them to accurately project forthcoming economic events. Analyzing basic economic relationships and forecasting the future based on the results of such analysis are the province of fundamental analysis, which I describe in detail in the rest of Part One.

Fundamental analysis alone, however, only gives you a broad preview of the future; it is insufficient in scope to provide enough information on which to trade in anything except the long term (a period lasting months to years). This is because fundamental analysis does not concern itself with precise timing. The fundamental approach tells you *what* is likely to occur, but it cannot tell you *when.*

PART TWO: TECHNICAL ANALYSIS

A market is composed of individual human beings, each pursuing values defined within that person's unique context. In considering the stock market, or any market, as a whole, change will occur only when the predominance of market participants believe change is occurring or is forthcoming. This is the second fundamental premise:

> The predominant psychology of market participants determines the direction of price movements and thus the timing of changes.

Therefore, to predict trend changes in the market accurately, you must have some way to gauge the predominance of opinion.

The only accurate and reliable way I know to measure the predominance of opinion is by monitoring the placement of assets in the market, which is reflected by watching the patterns of price movements. Since few situations are so unique as to create an entirely new economic environment, it is possible to correlate patterns of economic behavior with patterns of price movements. This is the province of technical analysis, which I discuss in variant forms in Chapters 7 through 11.

So we have two sets of tools associated with two basic premises: fundamental analysis, associated with the axiom that economic forces drive the market; and technical analysis, associated with the axiom that the predominant psychology of market participants determines the timing of trend changes.

The two premises are inseparably linked. The economic forces reflect the basic requirements of human survival, but how and when those requirements are implemented depend on how each human being decides to place his or her assets, and those decisions in turn are affected by government incentives and regulations. Individuals must adjust their decisions to this process. When a predominance of market participants, as measured by the cumulative placement of their assets, pursue a similar course, a trend is established. When most market participants decide they are on the wrong course, the trend reverses. Therein lies the link between fundamental and technical analysis.

Many investors utilize either fundamental *or* technical analysis to evaluate the potential of their trades. This is a grave error. By combining fundamental and technical analysis into your overall analytical approach to speculation, you can grasp not only what is most likely to occur in the future, but when it will likely occur. Thus, you have the power to put the odds in your favor. Moreover, you can refine your knowledge and work for precision timing in your market decisions, moving in and out of the intermediate (weeks to months) trend to maximize profits. Once you develop a knack for precision timing, you are ready to enter the world of options and pursue exceptionally superior returns.

PART THREE: OPTIONS TRADING

Trading options, discussed in Chapters 12 and 13, is the most difficult of the speculator's tasks. Options are difficult to trade because they require you to project the what, when, and how of a price trend with a high degree of accuracy, something that numerous studies have shown few people can do. On the positive side, however, many options strategies allow you to place an absolute limit on risk while offering the potential for superior returns. By combining fundamental and technical analysis in a systematic way, options can become the best way to maximize profits.

Even if you don't trade options, it is essential to understand them and pay close attention to the options markets, especially the stock and stock index options markets. Since 1980, large institutions have built themselves into a position of market dominance. A single institutional money manager can control billions of dollars in market assets. As a result, a small number of men and women can largely determine the direction of the price trend in the short-to-intermediate term.

PART FOUR: A TRADER'S PSYCHOLOGY

The market is, by its nature, a most merciless judge. Every day, the efficiency of your judgment goes on trial, and when the gavel comes down with the closing bell, your sentence is automatically reflected on your ledger sheets. If your judgment is good, then you'll consistently make money. But if your judgment is bad, then your survival depends on lady luck who, at best, will usually serve you for only a little while.

Being under such relentless and continual pressure can be an enormous psychological and emotional burden. The constant stress and tension of trading can take a tremendous toll on you, both physically and emotionally. But only if you let it. To avoid paying the price of mental and/or physical exhaustion requires an exceptional level of integrity in thought, emotions, and actions.

EPILOGUE

Finally, I close the book with a highly personal essay on a subject that few people are willing to look at openly: the morality of wealth. Before we get bogged down in data and detail, it behooves us all to remember what trading is all about: making money. Trading is hard work—about the hardest thing I know. Those who work that hard deserve their success; no apology is necessary.

To those of you who read my first book, let me thank you for making it a success. Let me also apologize for any redundancies that you may find in this book. The principles outlined here are designed to be an extension of those in the first book. At the same time, however, for this book to stand on its own, some repetition was essential.

Although this book provides a great deal of knowledge and information, trading the markets is still an art rather than a science. Even though my contributions will give you a big edge in achieving superior returns, nothing can guarantee success all the time; you must accept that as part of this business.

PART ONE
ECONOMIC FUNDAMENTALS

1

The Fundamental Principles of a Sound Investment Philosophy

Using the term *philosophy* in a book about speculation may sound a little pedantic, especially if the word makes you recall the arcane, impractical posturings of your college class in philosophy. I relate to the older school that gave philosophy its original meaning: "love of wisdom or knowledge." This makes philosophy very real, and makes it a search for the truth. If we don't know enough, if we can't define goals and pursue them by obtaining knowledge and applying it successfully, then the real world, like a giant garbage disposal, will chew us up and send us down the drain of failure. The same applies to speculating or investing in the financial markets.

A philosophy, in a more limited context, is defined (*Webster's New Universal Dictionary,* 1979) as "the general principles or laws of a field of knowledge, activity, etc." In the field of investment, three fundamental principles make up its philosophy. Stated in order of importance, they are:

1. Preservation of capital.
2. Consistent profitability.
3. The pursuit of superior returns.

With these three integrating principles serving as both cornerstones and guideposts, the remaining elements of a complete approach to professional speculation and investment are easier to construct.

PRESERVATION OF CAPITAL

Sam Bass's first rule of making money is: "Don't lose any." From the standpoint of speculation, I agree, provided you have money in the first place. But for those of us who did not inherit money, the first rule of making money is: Produce something. It is an inescapable fact that human beings must produce in order to survive. But to prosper and grow, we must be able to produce more than we require and save the surplus either for consumption at a later time or for investment in other endeavors. Savings slated for investment is, by definition, capital savings, or more simply, capital.

To trade, you must have capital, either yours or someone else's; and every time you make a trade, you put that capital at risk. To survive as a market professional, you must be right at least often enough to consistently cover your expenses without consuming your investment capital. In other words, at minimum, you must *preserve capital* to stay in business. While this may seem self-evident, it has implications that may be all too easy to overlook.

The principle of preservation of capital implies that before you consider any potential market involvement, *risk* should be the prime concern. Only within the context of the potential risk should the potential reward become the determining factor in taking a position. This is the true meaning of risk/reward analysis. Properly applied, it sets the standard for evaluating not only whether to be involved in a trade or investment, but also to what degree. Thus, preservation of capital—"Don't lose any"— becomes the basis for prudent money management.

Approaching market participation with risk as your prime concern forces you to look at performance from an absolute standpoint rather than a relative one. For many investors and money managers, this is not the case. Their goal is to "outperform the averages." If the market is down 15 percent, but their portfolio is down only 10 percent, they think they are a success. Not only is this approach a poor excuse for bad performance, it distorts the money manager's ability to engage in appropriate risk management.

In terms of performance, there is only one valid question: "Have I made money, or not?" If so, then it is appropriate to increase the percentage of capital at risk. If not, then it is time to cut back. Any other approach will ultimately lead to capital consumption.

As a general rule, I use a 3:1 reward-to-risk ratio as a minimum requirement for involvement in any trade. In other words, I enter a position only if the odds, determined by a combination of fundamental analysis and the measures discussed in Chapter 9, point to a minimum upside potential three times greater than the maximum downside potential. In addition, in the early stages of a new accounting period, I risk only a small fraction, at most 2 or 3 percent, of available capital in any position, regardless of the reward potential. Assuming I risk 3 percent of capital and lose on three trades in a row, and assuming I am right on the fourth trade and hit the expected three-bagger, then my account is net down only about ½ percent, as demonstrated in Table 1.1.

If you can successfully limit your trades to those in which the risk/reward ratio is at least 1:3, and if you properly limit the amount of capital you put at risk, you need be correct only once in every three trades (not one in four) to be profitable.

CONSISTENT PROFITABILITY

If you consistently apply the principle of preservation of capital as a basis for money management, you are led naturally to consistent profitability. Thus principle number 2 is a natural outgrowth of applying principle number 1. But considered as a principle in itself, consistent profitability

Table 1.1 Preservation of Capital at Work

Trade No.	Capital Available	Capital at Risk (3%)	Win/Lose	Capital Made/Lost	% Performance
1	100.00	3.00	Lose	(3.00)	−3.00
2	97.00	2.91	Lose	(2.91)	−5.91
3	94.09	2.82	Lose	(2.82)	−8.73
4	91.27	2.74	Win	8.22	−0.51
5	99.49				

leads you to refinements in money management and asset allocation decisions that will both preserve capital and ensure profitability. Capital isn't a static quantity—it is either gained or lost. To gain capital, you have to be consistently profitable, but to be consistently profitable, you have to preserve gains and minimize losses. Therefore, you must constantly balance the risks and rewards of each decision, scaling your risk according to accumulated profits or losses, thereby increasing the odds of *consistent* success.

For example, assume that you apply the minimum 1:3 risk/reward criterion and are successful in every third trade. You start by risking 3 percent of your *initial* capital, and proceed on each consecutive trade by risking 3 percent of *available* capital. Then, every time you bring your portfolio from the red into the black, you bank 50 percent of the gain, making it untouchable for that accounting period. Based on these assumptions, your trading record might closely resemble that presented in Table 1.2.

If you extrapolate this trading record through an entire year, and assume that you make just 30 trades that year, then you will end up with an annual return of 27.08 percent, while never risking more than 3 percent of available capital in any one trade.

Table 1.2   Applying the Principle of Consistent Profitability

Trade No.	Capital Available[a]	Capital at Risk (3%)	Win/Lose	Capital Made/Lost	Total % Performance[b]	Cum. Gains Retained
1	100.00	3.00	Lose	−3.00	−3.00	0.00
2	97.00	2.91	Lose	−2.91	−5.91	0.00
3	94.09	2.82	Win	+8.47	+2.56	1.28
4	101.28	3.04	Lose	−3.04	−0.48	1.28
5	98.24	2.95	Lose	−2.95	−3.43	1.28
6	95.29	2.86	Win	+8.58	+5.15	3.85
7	101.29	3.04	Lose	−3.04	+2.11	3.85
8	98.25	2.95	Lose	−2.95	−0.84	3.85
9	95.30	2.86	Win	+8.58	+7.74	7.72
10	100.01					

[a]Capital Available = Initial Capital +/− (Gains/Losses) − Gains Retained.
[b]Total % Performance = (Total Gains < Losses >)/(Initial Capital) × 100%.

Although this is a highly oversimplified example, it illustrates the principles of preservation of capital and consistent profitability very well. In the real world, you may lose on three trades in a row, make money on the next two, lose money on the next five, and then make money on three of the next five. But if you apply this kind of money management approach and are correct in just 33 percent of your trades, the results will be similar.

Notice the stability of the capital available column in Table 1.2. The greatest drawdown is 5.91 percent, and as long as you win one in three, that will be the maximum loss. Also notice that, going into the tenth trade, your available investment capital is only slightly more than you started with, but only because you are attempting to lock in a measure of your profits while simultaneously preserving capital.

Even if you don't win one in three, by limiting the amount of capital at risk, you will always have some left to build with. Assuming, for example, that you limit your risk to a maximum of 3 percent of available capital, you could lose 30 consecutive times and still have 40.1 percent of your original capital left to trade with. That's a lot better than losing everything.

Now notice the total performance column. Although the returns alternate between positive and negative within each three-trade cycle, on each consecutive cycle, the minuses become smaller and the pluses become larger. With a minimum 1-in-3 success rate, if you continue to manage your capital this way, then eventually your total returns will consistently remain positive. Assuming reasonably accurate market calls, a well-managed portfolio should build, at minimum, in just such a way.

By banking 50 percent of total returns each time you go from a negative to a positive return within your measuring period, you both increase the amount of available capital after each gain and increase the probability that you will remain profitable. In actual practice, you might decide to bank 50 percent of the net from each profitable trade as long as your performance was positive, but the results would not be substantially different. The basic idea is to never put all your profits at risk. It is fine to double up on a profitable position, but not if it means putting all your gains at risk.

There are tax consequences to consider, but the principle is still valid. Limit your risk, retain a portion of each gain, and profits will accrue. Once you reach a comfortable level of profitability, you can begin to pursue superior returns.

THE PURSUIT OF SUPERIOR RETURNS

Any time you put on a trade, superior returns are possible. What you think is probably going to be a 3-to-1 return may turn into a 5-to-1 or even a 10-to-1 return. That is good fortune, but it is not what I'm referring to. The pursuit of superior returns involves more *aggressive* risk taking, and only with a portion of profits, never initial trading capital.

Most people might think aggressive risk taking involves altering the basic risk/reward criterion. To the contrary, it is foolish ever to ignore or underweigh potential risk. Profits, once accrued, are essentially the same as capital, and must be preserved. But once you have achieved a comfortable level of profits, it is appropriate to increase the *size* of positions by risking a portion of profits. If you win, you dramatically increase your returns. If you lose, you are still profitable, and can continue to pursue consistent profitability until you reach a higher risk plateau once more.

My favorite way to pursue superior returns is with options. As I will explain in detail in Chapter 12, options allow you to absolutely limit your downside risk and, in many cases, have extremely favorable upside potential, especially in a potentially volatile market. A personal example will illustrate the idea, although sadly, it ended up as an opportunity loss.

On Thursday, November 14, 1991, I sent clients for whom I act as a consultant a fax bulletin in response to the Senate proposal to put a cap on revolving interest rates. This is what I told them:

> Yesterday, the Senate, in a last-minute attachment to the banking bill, approved by a 74–19 vote a measure that would place an upper limit on revolving credit interest rates. Alleging that the banks and other large card-issuing institutions are "gouging consumers," the measure's chief sponsor, Senator Alfonse D'Amato, proposed that the upper limit should be set to float 4 percent above the interest penalty charged by the IRS. Currently, the cap would be 14 percent, well below the average rate of 18.94 percent, and by D'Amato's estimates, up to $7.5 billion in interest payments could be saved by the consumer.
>
> Politicians are arguing that this will have a stimulant effect. I think just the opposite. In fact, if the bill passes in the House, I believe the October 9th lows will be taken out. . . .
>
> My reasoning is as follows:
>
> 1. Time and again throughout history, usury laws, like all price limits, have led to a scarcity of supply. The last thing this economy needs right now is more credit contraction.

2. Banks and other institutions will lose approximately 26 percent of their margin on what is currently among the most profitable segments of their business—revolving credit interest income.

3. Without this income, banks and other card-issuing institutions will be forced to increase reserves against loan losses. In addition, they will reduce credit limits and more carefully scrutinize those to whom they issue new cards. Many cardholders who have been borrowing from Peter to pay Paul will be forced into bankruptcy, and the card issuers will have to eat the losses.

4. As a result, consumer debt will contract at an accelerated rate, having a dramatic impact on consumer spending. The recovery will stall, and stock prices will fall *if not plummet.*

This morning, bank stocks gapped down on the news of the D'Amato measure. Advanta, a company that insures credit-card debt, fell from 38½ to 29½. [This company insures savings, credit card debt, and credit card insurance, in addition to issuing credit cards itself.] I think these moves are a portent of more to come if the bill is passed. It may be enough to pop the OTC speculation bubble that has been building.

In response to my own advice, when the market started looking weak on Thursday afternoon (one day before an option expiration), I bought 150 November OEX 370 puts (the OEX was at 371) at $125 per. Unfortunately, I had to leave on a trip to Miami that afternoon. During my flight, the market rallied 15 points in Dow terms. When I got to Miami, I checked and saw it had closed much stronger than I expected it to. Knowing I wouldn't be able to monitor the position closely, I left instructions to close the position if the S&P Futures opened up the next morning. The S&Ps did in fact open up—two ticks, which was the high for the day. Even though the rest of the market was opening down, my assistant carried out my instructions religiously and closed the position at a $50 per contract loss. To my dismay, I checked the market often enough during the day to know that had I been in front of my screens, I would have held the position and watched. Prices plummeted all day Friday. The puts I had owned went to $1,500 per contract before expiring that day, and I lost $206,250 in income potential. In that sense, my trip to Miami was expensive as hell. Fortunately, I had bought the December puts for all my clients, which I held for them and made money for them. But on my own account . . . zilch.

I use this as a sort of example in reverse. I wasn't in a pursuit-of-superior-returns mode. I looked at the opportunity as a normal trade: The risk/reward was good, but I didn't want to lose my entire investment, so I liquidated via a rule that usually works, but had I been in a more aggressive mode, I would have given the puts more time, I would have been willing to endure a greater risk, and in this case, I would have achieved an 1100 percent return on my investment. Oh well.

CONCLUSION

Preservation of capital, consistent profitability, and the pursuit of superior returns are three simple principles that collectively act as the starting point and general guideline for making profits in the financial markets. They are hierarchical—preservation of capital leads to consistent profitability that makes the pursuit of superior returns possible.

But to put these principles into practice, we need much more information. For example, preserving capital requires us to temper the lure of potential rewards by making risk the prime concern. But what is risk, and how can it be measured? To answer this and the many other questions involved in a detailed approach to market analysis, we must understand as many of the principles that govern market behavior as possible. In Chapter 2, you will learn the most basic information of all: the fundamental economic principles of market forecasting.

2
The Economic Principles of Market Forecasting

George Soros has been a powerhouse of performance in the investment world. Just recently, I learned his secret. In a speech before the Committee for Monetary Research and Education, former *Barron's* reporter John Liscio summed it up with the following Soros quote:

> Economic history is a never-ending series of episodes based on falsehoods and lies, not truths. It represents the path to big money. The object is to recognize the trend whose premise is false, ride that trend, and step off before it is discredited.

What an incredibly sad statement. One of the best investment minds in the world states openly that the best way to make money is to cash in on trends based on lies and falsehoods.

As cynical as this approach sounds, I cannot disagree with its essence. In order to identify false premises, you have to discredit them with the truth. But in order for most investors to act on a falsehood, they must accept it as the truth. So what Mr. Soros implies in his statement is that if you want to make big money, you have to understand the basic truths of economics, look around you and identify trends denying those truths, ride them, and get out when it appears that the predominance of market participants are about to realize they've been conned.

This is a restatement of the two fundamental principles of market analysis and forecasting that I stated in the Introduction:

1. The market is governed by fundamental economic forces that are affected by the current state of the political system, which in turn is constantly being changed by politicians.
2. The predominant psychology of market participants determines the timing of changes in the direction of price movements.

I have understood these principles implicitly for a long time, and yet, especially in 1990 and 1991, one of my greatest weaknesses has been to focus too much on the first premise and too little on the second. For example, on April 10, 1991, the *New York Times* reported that 70 percent of the country's leading economists were predicting that the recession would soon turn. I don't know what the other 30 percent were saying, but I was extremely confident that the 70 percent majority of "experts" was wrong. I *knew* the economy would achieve slow growth at best in 1991, and stated so in an editorial in *Barron's* on May 13.

My reasoning was that the government's policy of high taxation in a recessionary environment, coupled with stringent regulatory restrictions on bank lending, would result in either continued recession or economic stagnancy, regardless of Fed policy with respect to interest rates. Lower short-term interest rates alone, I argued, would not bring long-term rates down—the prerequisite for any significant credit expansion. I said that any attempt at economic stimulus by easing monetary policy would stimulate inflationary fears in the bond market, keeping upward pressure on long-term rates. I combined many other arguments to conclude:

> All of these elements will contribute to slow growth, if any, in 1991. None justifies current levels in stock prices. . . . Although I understand the thinking that has driven stock prices to current heights, I am skeptical that the type of recovery the market so obviously expects will occur. We will see a recovery . . . eventually, but it will probably come later rather than sooner; even then, it will be halting.

As of this writing, Bush is out and Clinton is in, and the number one issue on everybody's mind is the economy. The Fed has cut short rates more than 24 times since April 1989, bringing the Fed Funds rate down from 9.75 percent to around 3.0 percent at one point. During the same period, long bond yields have dropped only slightly, hovering between 7.5 and 8.0 percent, and bank lending is still very tight. Just months ago, consumer confidence was lower than it was at the depths of the 1982 recession. Congress is debating not whether to stimulate the economy, but how and when, thus completely reversing their thinking of 1991, which focused on controlling the deficit (they never have admitted they were wrong, of course). There is a predominant fear that the recession will continue. In other words, my projections were right.

My economic projections were right, but I haven't made much money in stocks. My reasoning was that stock prices, on average, were "overpriced," so I was disinclined to participate on the long side in any significant way. But in not participating, I missed achieving some excellent gains, especially in the OTC market. I felt strongly that the appreciation in the OTC market was a bubble, one of the "lies" Soros referred to. But unlike Soros, I didn't go into the stock-picking mode and take advantage of the falsehood being accepted by the market. In retrospect, I should have.

It reminds me of a scene from a great old movie called *The Cincinnati Kid,* starring Steve McQueen and Edward G. Robinson. Both men are professional gamblers—poker players. Robinson, known simply as "the man," is the established number one player—the man to beat. McQueen plays an up-and-comer whose utmost goal is to become number one. Near the end of the movie, McQueen is finally at the table with Robinson. After hours of play, everyone else is out, and it's down to the last hand.

The game is five-card stud, in which one card is dealt down and one up, followed by a round of betting, then another card is dealt face up, followed by more betting, then another, and so forth until there is one card down and four up on the final bet. After three cards have been dealt, the Cincinnati Kid has a pair of tens showing, while the man has a queen and king of diamonds showing. The kid's pair bets, but then the man bets heavily, indicating that he has at least a king or queen in the hole—a better pair than the kid. The kid calls him and the next card is dealt—an ace for the kid, and the ten of diamonds for the man. Again, the betting is heavy, but now it appears that the man is working a flush, and possibly a straight flush. A straight flush by the way, is the rarest hand in poker.

When the fourth up card is dealt, the kid gets another ace and the man gets the ace of diamonds. The kid now has two pair showing, while the man has a ten, queen, king, ace of diamonds showing. As a man with some knowledge of poker myself, I felt the tension deeply. You see, the man had no odds on his side in betting after the third up card. He was beat by what the kid had showing, and the odds of his having pulled cards that could win were highly against him: 1 in 649,700!

The betting continues, back and forth, until finally the kid calls him. They turn over their cards. The kid has an ace in the hole, giving him an ace-high full house. But the man has a jack of diamonds in the hole, giving him a royal straight flush—the highest hand in poker and the only hand in that particular game that could beat the kid.

As the man gets up from the table, he looks at the kid and says, "That's down to what it's all about kid, making the wrong move at the right time."

From virtually every standpoint, it was a bad bet to buy the market in early 1991. Nevertheless, those who did, made money. As for me, I feel like the Cincinnati Kid—I made the right bet, but at the wrong time.

The purpose of this chapter is to lay the necessary groundwork so that you will be able to identify when to make the wrong bet at the right time; that is, how to identify economic falsehoods that create money-making opportunities on both the upside and downside. But the prerequisite to identify an economic falsehood is to understand the inexorable economic forces that govern market behavior. Unfortunately, that's not always easy.

The most dangerous of all economic falsehoods is a misunderstanding of the study itself. Economics has been reduced almost solely to the study of government economic management; which means the study of how much and from whom the government should expropriate private resources and distribute them to other individuals and economic sectors.

In his so-called new economics, Keynes formalized and gave quasi-scientific status to economic fallacies that are as old as civilized human beings—the falsehoods that Soros refers to. Keynes provided a rationalization for government intervention into free markets, for government control of the supply of money and credit, for policies of irresponsible deficit spending, and for inflationary expansionism. With few exceptions, the intellectual community has taken his fallacies as axiomatic principles and expanded them into a hopelessly complex system of terms and mathematical equations that confuse the most obvious, fundamental, and important of economic issues.

ECONOMICS DEFINED

Economics is the study of a branch of human action. According to economist Ludwig von Mises, "It is the science of the means to be applied for the attainment of ends chosen. . . . [It] is not about things and tangible material objects; it is about men, their meanings and actions."[1] In other words, economics is the study of the instruments, methods, and actions available to human beings for attaining their goals.

Ludwig von Mises has written approximately 20 books on economics. However, you will almost never see his name in college textbooks. Some exceptions are those used at Auburn University in Alabama and the University of Nevada, both of which expound on the Austrian School of Economics. von Mises' most famous book, *Human Action,* is over 900 pages long and not very easy to read. His most famous student was Frederick von Hayak, who won a Nobel Prize in economics. The Austrian School of Economics stands for freedom of the individual, totally free markets, use of the gold standard, and the subjective nature of value, but these are only a few of its principles. The Austrian School is the most accurate view of how the world works in the short run and, more importantly, the long run, that I have ever encountered.

The single, most fundamental goal of all is survival. For most living things, the process of survival is substantially automatic, and life or death is predominantly a matter of circumstance, not choice. But for human beings, survival depends on the conscious exercise of the mind, and furthermore, on the *choice* to pursue values that further life. We must not only discover and choose *what* we need to survive (what von Mises refers to as "ends") but also *how* to obtain it (what von Mises calls "means").

Key in von Mises' definition is the word "chosen." Human beings must choose to learn, survive, and prosper. All people, unless they choose to be a parasite, must learn to provide for their own individual survival by evaluating the ends and means available, making choices, and acting effectively.

No matter what an individual's personal economic philosophy may be, any view of economics always requires certain fundamental processes:

- Evaluation.
- Production.
- Saving.
- Investment.

- Innovation.
- Exchange.

I believe that all these processes happen first on the individual level, and then on the level of the society as a whole. As I wrote in *Trader Vic— Methods of a Wall Street Master:*

> Consider, for example, Daniel Defoe's character Robinson Crusoe. . . . Stranded on an island . . . , Crusoe first devised a method of acquiring more food than he immediately needed and storing it so that he could redirect his efforts towards achieving other necessities. He used the time he saved to build shelter, provide for his defense against the natives, and manufacture clothing. Then through industry, ingenuity, and management of time, he simplified the process of acquiring essentials and went on to produce other luxuries as time allowed.
>
> The keys to the process of increasing his standard of living were *evaluation, production, saving, investment, and innovation.* He *evaluated* the ends and means available to him and chose the alternatives that best addressed his needs. The *value* of each thing that he sought was set by his judgment according to his perception of what was most needed, the means available to obtain it, and what it would cost him to get it relative to the alternatives. He *produced* the essentials necessary for survival and *saved* enough of them so that he could *invest* his energy into developing other products that he needed or desired. The *price* he paid at each step was the time and energy he spent according to his own evaluation of his needs. What he gained on balance in the exchange was his *profit.* If he made mistakes, and his efforts were futile, then he suffered a *loss.* His actions were a matter of *exchange,* the exchange of a less desirable state for a more desirable one. At every step, he managed his time; he made choices based on the consequences of his options in the short, intermediate, and long term. As he became more and more sophisticated through *technological innovation,* the cost of essentials (in terms of time and energy spent to achieve them) diminished and he could afford to spend more time in the pursuit of "luxuries."[2]

Just as one person on a desert island must act according to fundamental economic principles in order to survive, so must a complex industrial society. It is a grave fallacy ever to assume that these processes exist apart from those required of an individual human being. For an economic principle to be valid, it must apply first and foremost to the individual. Only then can it be accurately extrapolated and applied to a larger group or to a society as a whole. The principles of evaluation, production, saving, investment, innovation, and exchange are prerequisites of individual human survival. Understood in this context, they form the basis of economic analysis on any scale.

THE PRIMACY OF PRODUCTION

Mainly as a result of Keynesian thinking, government now largely chooses what means are to be applied to what ends, and thus, economics has been reduced to the study of government intervention in the marketplace. In Keynesian terms, the driving force behind production, and therefore the driving force of humankind's economic advancement, is aggregate demand—the desire to consume, as measured by dollars and cents of disposable income. To increase production, Keynes said, just have government carefully place a few extra paper dollars in everyone's hand to increase aggregate demand. In response, businesses will produce more, people will consume more, and the wealth of the nation, as measured by the gross domestic product (GDP), will increase.

In my view, the premise that aggregate demand determines the level of production is grossly misleading. One person, acting alone, cannot generate wealth simply by demanding more or consuming more. In fact, everything else being equal, if a man on a desert island starts demanding more and meets the demand by consuming more than normal, he is pursuing a path of self-destruction, diminishing his ability to produce more in the future. The same is true of an "aggregate," regardless of its size or complexity.

There is an inviolable chain from which economic growth arises, and the first link is production—the basic requirement for human survival. But production alone won't lead to growth; growth requires savings.

SAVINGS, INVESTMENT, AND TECHNOLOGICAL INNOVATION

It is not the employer who pays wages, he only handles the money. It is the product who pays wages.

Henry Ford

For growth to occur, there must be production; enough production not only to provide for the immediate needs of survival, but also to provide the seed stock for future production. In other words, before economic growth can occur, *surpluses* must be generated for the purpose of *savings*. Savings take two forms: plain savings, which is the setting aside of unconsumed goods for future use; and capital savings, which is an allotment of saved goods for direct use in the future production process. Both types of savings must precede economic growth.

Plain savings are a hedge against nature, whether it be mother nature or human nature. On a simple level, plain savings might involve the canning of fruits and vegetables to make surviving the winter possible. On a more advanced level, plain savings might consist of the retained earnings of a corporation, which allow it to survive during periods of diminished sales of its product(s). In both cases, plain savings are a material means of saving time that can be spent pursuing other ends in the future.

Capital savings proceed from plain savings and consist of surpluses allotted for investment in the future production process. A simple example of capital savings is grain set aside for next year's planting. On a more complex level, earnings set aside for the purchase of new machinery are capital savings.

No matter what the level of analysis, capital savings involve another key economic factor of production, *technological innovation.* Before savings can be allotted for the process of future production, before they can become capital savings, two preconditions must exist: First, enough plain savings must exist to allow investing time in other ventures; and second, the means of future production must exist. Assuming that enough plain savings exist, developing the means of future production requires technological innovation.

In our modern-day setting, we think of technology in terms of computer chips and advanced electronic components. But in fact, technological innovation is any form of newly applied knowledge, that is, any new method of applying capital savings. From a fishhook to the Space Shuttle, every material human advancement has been the result of a combination of technological innovation and capital savings. In other words, we are now building on the savings and innovations of our ancestors.

At each stage of economic development and advancement, someone had to figure out how to recombine and rearrange natural and manufactured elements to create new products or make the production of existing products more efficient. But just knowing how is not enough, the question of *with what* must also be answered and resolved. The *with what* is capital savings. In this sense, capital savings and investment capital are identical.

This is the case with all new production. An entrepreneur develops a concept of how to utilize resources for future production. Then, that person or another individual or group *invests* savings, whether in the form of time or material, to make the concept reality. In so doing, they take a risk. If they are successful, then they bring new products and services into existence, reaping the benefits, or *profits,* as a result of putting their savings at risk. If they fail, they suffer a *loss,* the loss of previous production; that is, savings are consumed.

Notice that I have used most of the common terms associated with economics and finance without ever using the words *money* or *credit.* Considered as fundamental economic principles, production, savings, investment, capital, profit, and loss have nothing to do with money and credit. Money and credit are nothing more than technological innovations that make the chain of production and economic growth more efficient, manageable, and measurable.

Unfortunately, many economists equate money with wealth, and credit with the source of new wealth. While it is true that money and credit are necessary for an economic system to reach the degree of complexity that ours has attained, it is not true that they are prerequisites for economic growth. Money is a prerequisite for accounting, evaluation, and trade in a complex market economy. Credit is a means of trading accumulated savings in a complex economy. I'll discuss both in more detail in Chapter 3.

I have, however, left out of the current discussion two vital principles of economic analysis: evaluation and exchange.

EVALUATION AND EXCHANGE

Why do we produce? How do we decide what to produce? Why do we trade? What do we trade? How do we decide when to consume versus save and/or invest? The answers to these questions are complex, but they are vital.

For a person alone on a deserted island, the answers are more obvious. Faced with the problem of physical survival, Robby Crusoe has two major alternatives: produce or die. Once he makes the basic choice to produce, he must first identify his most important needs. That's easy: food and shelter, in order of importance. Then his alternatives start becoming slightly more complex. Does he try to catch fish first, or does he look for edible plants? Once he finds food, should he stockpile some so he can have time to build a shelter, or should he spend half of each day gathering food and the other half building a shelter? Once he builds a shelter, he can start constructing tools. Should he make a fishing pole, or a net? Should he dry his fish in the sun, or build a smoker for them? And so forth.

At each step, Robby must *evaluate* the means and ends available to him and choose those that best suit his needs *as he perceives them.* The choice he makes is the exchange, the trade. In effect, Robby makes a deal with himself, deciding to exchange a less desirable state for a more desirable one. His thinking process might follow these lines:

> Well, producing is hard, but it's better than dying, so I'll trade producing for dying. Well, the plants taste better when they're picked fresh, but I'm tired of waking up freezing cold or half buried in sand. So I guess I'll spend a couple of days stockpiling enough food so I can devote an entire day to building a shelter. Well, a fishing pole is easier to make, but I'll catch a lot more fish with a net, so I guess I'll exchange the extra effort for the chance at more fish.

With each choice, he takes a risk and either reaps a profit or suffers a loss.

Without a single other individual to contend with, without a market, without currency, Robby must live according to the basic principles of economics. He must identify alternatives, place a value on them, choose what to pursue, how much to spend or invest, and put his time and/or savings at risk; all for a trade—the exchange of a more desirable state for a less desirable one. Extrapolate Robby's choices to a complex market and nothing changes. The basic processes of evaluation, production, savings, investment, innovation, and exchange are the same. The more advanced and complex the economic environment, the more essential it becomes to remember that value is ultimately subjective—depending on the unique context and the process of evaluation each market participant employs.

Markets are composed of individuals, and individuals are required by their nature to use the same process that Robby employs on his desert island. Like Robby, all of them are fallible; they can make mistakes both individually and as a group. What drives an individual or a group of individuals to act, to exchange one state for another, is the *perception* of value.

THE SUBJECTIVE NATURE OF VALUE

Value is not stored in the goods to be exchanged or in the object under question for investment. Value is instead a subjective measurement, and it falls into one of two categories. *Consumer value* is a psychological relationship between a person's conception of his or her wants and conceptions of how well the goods in question will satisfy those wants. *Investment value* is a psychological relationship between a person's conception of what is cheap and what is dear, based on the subjective view of what is important in the appreciation of the price of the given object.

Risk is measurable; *uncertainty* is not! Risk is the ratio of the probability of an event occurring versus the probability it will not occur. To be successful, a trader must be able to differentiate between the two.

As a professional speculator or investor, when you know that the bulk of market participants are wrong in their perceptions, it creates what I'll coin a "Soros opportunity," something that with your fundamental economic wisdom you can cash in on, but only in the context of understanding the tenor of the predominance of opinion.

For example, throughout 1991, the economic environment was highly tenuous. Stocks like IBM were below their 1987 crash lows, trading at 10 to 12 times earnings. At one point, Mobil was yielding 5 percent, but because oil prices were dropping, it too was trading at 11 times earnings. At the same time, the so-called growth stocks were yielding less than 2 percent, but were trading at 30, 40, or even higher price/earnings ratios (PEs). Merck, for example, traded at 37 times earnings, was yielding about 1.5 percent, and was near its all-time highs. Simultaneously, Amgen was losing money and traded at *minus* 1500 times earnings. There are many more examples, but the point is made. Market participants were buying the biotechs, the drug stocks, any stock that demonstrated earnings growth or potential earnings, with virtual disregard for the PE or yield.

This trend has shifted to some degree as the market's perception of value changed. If the market tumbles, then the perception will change completely, and the high PE stocks will be the hardest hit. Consider, for example, the case of PSE & G shown in Figure 2.1. In 1928, PSE & G stock reached a high of 137.5, earned $3.93 per share (PE = 35), and paid a $3.40 dividend. In 1932, it earned $3.46 per share, paid a $3.30 dividend, and sold at $28 per share. The company didn't change substantially,

FIGURE 2.1   Public service electric and gas company special chart.

earnings didn't change substantially, but the market's perception of value changed dramatically.

There are two lessons here. First, any time an analyst places a "fair market value" on a stock, remember that the only true measure of value is what the market says it is. Value is subjective and constantly changing. What is important is whether the market believes the analyst's assessment, nothing else. Second, if you believe a stock or a group of stocks are "overpriced," be sure you factor the predominance of market opinion into your analysis. Charles DeGaulle said, "Treaties are like roses and young girls, they last while they last." Substitute "Trend" for Treaties, and you have an excellent truism. The old trading rule that says "When nothing changes, nothing changes" is absolutely true. Don't get snagged by being too far ahead of the market. Take Soros's advice. Ride the tide of falsehood and get off before the truth be known.

THE NATURE OF ECONOMIC VALUE

Many misconceptions and errors arise from the failure to recognize that value is subjective. One of the most common and damaging is the notion that "one person's profit is another person's loss." Aside from the fact that if this were true, it would be impossible for economic growth to occur, this fallacy totally ignores the very essence of what wealth is. In *Trader Vic: Methods,* I wrote:

> The fact that value is subjective—that people value things differently— both drives people to trade and makes it possible for both sides to profit.[3] The farmer who has excess corn but not enough meat values his surplus corn less than the rancher who needs corn to fatten his cattle—the opportunity for a trade exists. As more and more people associate and get involved in the process of *exchanging their surpluses,* trading becomes more complex. The interaction of numerous individuals, the social device of production and trade through free association, is called a market.

In its true meaning, profit originates not in trade, but in the production of surpluses recognized by the market as *economic values,* or economic goods. Trade is the mechanism by which profits are maximized, but it is not their source. An economic value is anything that fulfills a perceived need, is recognized by the market as such, and is attainable; this includes both commodities and services. Wealth is an accumulation of *unconsumed* economic values, in whatever form they may take; it is the principal source of savings, and therefore, of economic growth.[4]

You may be wondering how I, as a professional speculator, can possibly declare that, strictly speaking, profits do not originate in trade. After all, my business is to make profits solely by trading, and in many cases, my profit is indeed someone else's loss. But the kind of profits I make occur consequent to the production of surpluses; that is, I could not achieve them unless profits, as previously defined, had already been achieved. Reduced to the economic nuts and bolts of it, my task as a speculator is to correct other people's mistakes by guiding capital toward its best use as determined by the law of supply and demand.

In March 1992, for example, I thought the predominance of opinion was on the verge of changing with respect to the "growth" stocks, especially the drugs and the biotechs mentioned earlier. I shorted them in size, and sure enough, they eroded consistently until November 1992. In effect, I earned control of misplaced capital to put it to more productive use (i.e., they were wrong; I was right, in this case). In essence, I purchased, at a discount, the savings lost by those who took a bad investment risk. Of course, when I am wrong, the reverse is the case.

Interestingly, the drugs and the biotechs started to rally after Clinton won the presidential election. At the risk of dating the material in this book, I want to make a prediction: Drugs will rally only to suffer under the Clinton administration, the result of Clinton's and a Democratic-controlled Congress's bias against the "rich" drug companies. The biotechs will do better due to an opposite bias for "smaller, entrepreneurial" companies.

CONCLUSION

The purpose in outlining these fundamental principles of economic analysis is to lay the groundwork for identifying economic truths and falsehoods that underlie market trends. In my view, the best approach to analyzing market behavior is from the top down; that is, to look first at the economic fundamentals driving the overall business cycle; then to look at the derivative trends such as those in the stock, bond, and commodities markets considered as a whole; and finally to examine individual stocks, bonds, and futures.

Equipped with the economic fundamentals outlined in this chapter, it is now possible to identify the cause-and-effect relationships underlying the cyclical periods of booms and busts we have become accustomed to in modern history.

3
Money, Credit, and the Business Cycle

At this writing, the bulk of the U.S. citizenry is optimistic that our leadership on Capitol Hill will "do something" to bring the U.S. economy out of the doldrums. But there is much uncertainty about what that "something" should be. With Clinton at the helm and Democratic majorities in both houses, speculation is rampant as to what form the tax cuts and tax increases will take. Some Democrats are advocating "taxing the rich." Others are crying for more government support and/or incentive programs. Still others are blaming the sluggishness of the economy on Fed policy and think that even lower interest rates are the key to recovery.

It is a sad irony that we expect the legislators in Washington, DC, to cure our economic woes, for I would venture a guess that not 1 in 50 of our elected officials has a clear concept of what actually causes economic recession. In the current debate, I haven't heard one of them allude to basic economic principles in advocating a recovery package. Instead, they speak in abstract bromides that simultaneously appeal to the emotions of their constituency and blame the political opposition for our current economic crisis. And as they continue to squabble, the economy continues to slug along.

The irony of it all is that the business cycle is a direct outgrowth of the monetary and fiscal policy defined by our leaders in Washington. It is their feeble attempts to manage the economic activity of the nation that leads to booms and busts. As von Mises puts it:

> The wavelike movement affecting the economic system, the recurrence of periods of boom which are followed by periods of depression [recession], is the unavoidable outcome of the attempts, repeated again and again, to lower the gross market rate of interest by means of credit expansion.[1]

If you understand the full meaning of this quote, then go on to the next chapter. But if you don't, read on, for in analyzing von Mises' statement, I hope to equip you with knowledge that will empower you to predict the *what* of future economic activity with a high degree of accuracy. And once you know the what, you can start focusing your attentions on figuring out the *when* within the context of probability.

It may sound arrogant to say it is possible to predict the economic future with a high degree of certainty. And indeed there are many specifics you can never know. You can, however, know the basic shape of things if you pay attention. Let me illustrate with an example from my own experience.

In 1979, we were in the middle of the "oil crisis." The Middle East had a stranglehold on oil prices. Carter had imposed price controls on domestic oil production and a tax on imports, which immediately created shortages. Oil stocks performed phenomenally, while the other industrial stocks appreciated at a lower rate. The Fed was ticking up interest rates but let the money supply expand at an accelerating rate. In other words, higher petroleum product prices were being monetized by an expansion in the money supply, that is, inflation.

Then, two things happened. First, on October 12, 1979, Volcker announced that the Fed would shift its policy toward targeting money supply growth rather than interest rates, which meant the beginning of the end of a decade of inflationary expansionism. Second, presidential candidate Ronald Reagan announced that, if elected, he would deregulate oil prices.

Once convinced that Ronald Reagan would gain the nomination and beat Carter, I knew the end of the era of climbing interest rates and high-priced oil stocks was near at hand. I also knew as oil prices dropped, the other industrial stocks would benefit, at least until the piper had to be paid for a decade of inflationary expansionism. So, coming into the November 1980 election, I shorted the oils in size. Sure enough, the S&P 500 (heavily weighted to the oils), topped in November. Oil prices topped in January. The Dow Industrials appreciated through April, while the S&P sold off. In July, the Dow confirmed the end of a bull market. It was time to pay the piper, and I started playing the short side.

As I said before, economic activity is governed by forces that are influenced by government policy. Every economic action taken by human beings has a predictable consequence. When economic action takes place on a massive scale in the form of government monetary and fiscal policy, the consequences on the economy as a whole are relatively easy to predict with a high degree of certainty. The only wild card is the ingenuity and innovation of individuals who, through their ceaseless efforts to produce more, can dampen negative governmental action.

The key in economic forecasting is never to lose sight of the simple principles outlined in Chapter 2. Combine those principles with knowledge of the nature of money and credit (including interest rates) in the context of human action, and the tremendously complex subject of the business cycle becomes relatively easy to understand.

In the preceding chapter, I stated that money and credit are not primary elements, but outgrowths, of the basic principles of economics. An individual on a desert island employs fundamental economic principles but has no use for money and credit. Nor would money and credit be necessary to a tribal community producing only the basic requirements for survival. Before the need for money and credit can arise, the members of an economic community must be engaged in the active exchange of their surpluses; they must have established a market. The need for money arises only when the members of the marketplace have achieved a high level of productivity and long-term control over their lives. The same is true for credit.

In a complex market economy, money and credit become absolute and vital links in the chain of evaluation, production, saving, investment, innovation, and exchange. As an economic activity grows more and more complex, money and credit become prerequisites for economic progress and growth, but only if understood and implemented according to their basis in human action. If improperly understood and implemented, they lead to periodic booms and busts—the business cycle.

THE LESSON OF PIERRE AND SASSON

One of my favorite stories illustrates the essential mechanism of the business cycle very well. It goes like this:

Once there were two Cajun farmers down in Louisiana named Pierre and Sasson. One day, Pierre is over at Sasson's farm admiring his horse. "Sasson, mon ami," said Pierre, "that ees a beautiful horse. I must buy that horse."

"Ah Pierre," replied Sasson, "I cannot sell eet. I have owned thees horse for a long time and am very fond of eet."

"But ah will geev you ten dolaire for eet," says Pierre.

"Ooo la la," says Sasson, "zen reluctantly, I agree," and they wrote up a contract.

About a week later, Sasson comes over to Pierre's farm and says, "Ah Pierre, mon ami, I must have my horse back. I miss eet terribly."

"But Sasson," replies Pierre, "I cannot do zat. I bought a cart for thees horse to pull, and ze cart cost me five dolaire."

"Ah, but I will geev you twenty dolaire for both zee horse and zee cart," says Sasson. Pierre does a quick calculation—a five-dollar profit on a 15-dollar investment in one week—that's over a 1700 percent annualized rate of return! So he says, "Done, mon ami!"

Pierre and Sasson keep trading the horse, cart, and other minor additions back and forth until they no longer have enough cash to finance each successive trade. So, they get the local banker involved. The banker, looking at their creditworthiness and the historic appreciation of the horse's value, loans money first to Pierre and then to Sasson, with the price of the horse escalating on each trade. After each transaction, the banker gets paid back in full, plus interest, and both Pierre's and Sasson's cash flow is increasing geometrically.

Well, this goes on and on, until after several years, Pierre buys the horse for $1,500. Then a Yankee (an MBA from Harvard), gets wind of the price appreciation of the horse and, after making some sophisticated rate of return projections, makes a special trip to Louisiana and buys the horse from Pierre for $2,700.

When Sasson finds out about the sale, he is furious, and charges over to Pierre's farm yelling, "Pierre! Idiot! How could you sell zat horse for twenty-seven-hundred dolaire! We were making a great living on zat horse!"

In a nutshell, this story demonstrates the essence of the business cycle. Pierre, Sasson, and the banker were unwittingly propagating an illusion, creating paper money to bid up the price of the same horse. No new wealth was created, but plenty of money was, and everyone was enjoying their apparent prosperity. But, ultimately, the Harvard MBA was left holding the nag, and the bubble of apparent prosperity burst.

Booms and busts are the result of attempts to lower rates by means of credit expansion. To fully understand the meaning of this and, therefore, the cause of the business cycle, it is necessary to understand exactly what money and credit are and how they work in a complex market economy.

MONEY: THE MEDIUM OF INDIRECT EXCHANGE

Imagine a relatively complex, but small, localized market existing before the advent of money. Suppose, for example, that a farmer wanted to trade his surplus corn for a plow produced by the blacksmith. The blacksmith has a plow in inventory, but he doesn't need corn; he needs lumber with which to build wheels for a wagon to haul pig iron and coal. The lumber merchant needs neither a plow nor corn, but an additional laborer to deliver materials already promised to other customers in trade. The local millwright has back orders for cornmeal and also has a strapping son with time on his hands, but needs neither a plow nor lumber. In this scenario, the supply of goods and services exists, the demand for them exists, but their marketability is a difficult and cumbersome problem.

Introduce a universally desirable commodity, such as gold, and the problems of all can be facilitated in the process of *indirect exchange*. Indirect exchange is a process of interpersonal exchange utilizing a medium of exchange in one or a series of intermediate steps in the act of trading one economic value for another. The farmer gives gold coins to the blacksmith in exchange for the plow. The blacksmith trades all or some of the coins for lumber to build the wheels for his wagon. The lumber merchant hires the millwright's son, paying him in gold. The millwright's son hears through the lumber merchant that the farmer has corn on the market and, after telling his father about it, rents the blacksmith's wagon, drives out to the farm, and buys the farmer's corn for gold. By using gold as a medium of exchange, the process of interpersonal exchange goes full circle, everyone ends up with the product they wanted, and all have profited by trading their surpluses or available services for the more desirable surpluses of others. Gold, a value in itself, facilitated the exchange, but it had nothing to do with production.

Multiply the complexity of this simplified example to a modern-day market economy, and it is obvious that without a commonly used and acceptable medium of exchange, the trade process would be impossible. A commonly used medium of exchange, no matter what form it takes, is called *money*.[2] To quote von Mises:

Money is a medium of exchange. It is the most marketable good which people acquire because they want to offer it in later acts of interpersonal exchange. Money is the thing which serves as the generally accepted and commonly used medium of exchange. This is its only function. All the other functions which people ascribe to money are merely particular aspects of its primary sole function, that of a medium of exchange."[3]

The key to money's economic value in the marketplace is that it allows individuals to *extend the time period* between trading their products and acquiring the products and services of others. People acquire money because they cannot immediately satisfy their wants by trading products (including services) for other products directly. They choose instead to hold money in anticipation of being able to satisfy their desires at some later point by using it in indirect exchange.

This may sound elementary, even trivial. But understanding the role of money is vital to understanding the business cycle. Notice that von Mises calls money "the most marketable good." Implicit in this description is that money is an economic value; it fulfills a perceived need, is recognized by the market as such, and is attainable. To be the "most marketable" economic value, money must be universally desirable, as well as having other obvious properties such as durability, portability, and divisibility. It must also be scarce.

Like any other economic value, money's worth is determined by the market through the law of supply and demand. As in any other exchange, we pay a "price" to obtain money in trade, but one which cannot be expressed in monetary terms. The value of goods and services is measured in monetary terms, the value of money is a matter of a person's perception and judgment of its potential purchasing power. Both measures of value can only be determined in the market, which is governed by supply and demand.

The relationship of the supply of and the demand for money—what von Mises calls "the money relation"—is determined not on a macro scale, but rather by the cumulative sum of each person's unique context and evaluations as expressed in the market. Believe it or not, this simple fact has been a point of contention among economic theorists since the study of economics began. In fact, many economists have inferred that the "money relation" doesn't even exist.

Classical economists like John Stuart Mill and David Hume believed, for example, that money is "neutral," meaning that money doesn't have economic value in the same sense as other goods and services, that it has no driving force of its own. An outgrowth of this belief was the tenet that the general "price level" of goods and services rises and falls proportionally with the increase or decrease of the quantity of money in circulation. This may sound sensible, but it is far too oversimplified and, in fact, belies the very nature of economic activity.

The error of the classicists was in their imaginary construction of a *static* economy in "equilibrium." An economy is composed of many markets, and each market is composed of individuals or groups engaged in the process of evaluation and interpersonal exchange, which is a *constant, dynamic process*. The sole purpose of money is to facilitate trade under uncertain and changing conditions. Moreover, money is an instrument of change in itself. As von Mises puts it:

> Every change in the economic data sets [money] in motion and makes it the driving force of new changes. Every shift in the mutual relation of the exchange ratios between the various nonmonetary goods not only brings about changes in production and . . . distribution, but also provokes changes in the money relation and thus further changes.[4]

Viewed in this way, it is obviously impossible for a change in the money supply to affect the prices of all goods and services at the same time and to the same extent. Everything else being equal, the only sure outcome of a change in the money supply is that it will change the distribution of wealth; some will become richer, and others poorer.[5]

Assume, for example, that in our small, localized economy, the farmer suddenly receives a grant of "paper money" from a federal subsidy program. At first, nothing changes in the small economic system except for the paper money the farmer holds. But now, instead of trading his corn for gold, the farmer can go and buy the plow directly, without trading any of his product. Then, he can trade normally for other economic goods. The blacksmith, in turn, can use the paper the farmer gives him to buy the lumber he needs for his wagon. But as the process of trade continues, it will become apparent to the economic community that commodities are more easily obtained, and prices will begin to rise.

There is an initial stimulative effect on economic activity, but only because not everyone knows of the increased paper the farmer holds. Had the other producers known, they would have raised their prices to the farmer immediately. Their ignorance gives the farmer a greater claim to the goods and services on the market, and he becomes enriched at the expense of others because prices cannot rise simultaneously with an increase in the money supply.

Keynes understood that money is anything but neutral, but he took money's driving force way too far, while ignoring the inflationary effects of printing money. He believed that money could be used as the engine of further production. In his terms, incremental investment, and therefore incremental economic growth, is determined in aggregate by the marginal propensity to consume, in Keynesian terms, but to increase production, you have to shift the marginal propensity to consume by increasing consumer demand, as measured by dollars of disposable income. By increasing dollars of disposable income, you cause people, in aggregate, to spend more, thus increasing business profits and their incentive to expand production.

Like Hume and Mill, Keynes posed economic theory in the context of a static economy in which cause and effect relationships occur automatically, in an "aggregate." In my opinion, this is a huge error.

In reality, money represents a claim on unconsumed economic values (goods and services) to be acquired at some later time—nothing more. If you could freeze the economy at a given point in time, there would be a fixed amount of goods and services available, all cash holdings would belong to someone, and prices would be fixed according to perceptions of supply and demand. If, in the next instant, you were to unfreeze the economy and add to the quantity of cash that some people hold, the entire price structure would be disrupted. Because of the sudden imbalance, the recipients of the added cash would have a greater claim to the limited number of goods and services available. In exercising those claims, some people would be enriched at the expense of others.

This is exactly what happens on a massive scale with government "stimulative" monetary and fiscal policies that expand the money supply. Some businesses see increased revenues in the early stages of the increase, before prices begin to rise. And indeed, those businesses are likely to expand their production to meet their perception of increased demand. But as they are expanding production, which takes time, prices are tending to readjust to higher levels; as a result, their future revenues will be less than anticipated, and they will end up cutting back on production in the future. Unless, that is, government continuously keeps adding to the disposable income of consumers, which is impossible for government to do in real terms. The only thing government can actually do is increase the amount of cash that people hold (or take less of it away). If government does that, it is only a matter of time before the market starts factoring rising prices into its calculations, which will then eliminate the stimulative effects.

A one-shot monetary stimulation, such as a temporary tax cut, is nearly a zero-sum game, depending on the changes that occur in the money relation. New production can only come from invested savings. Suddenly increasing the cash holdings of some consumers is not a magic source of new savings. It may result in some new production, which may result in enough new saving to pay for some of the new investments, but the only certain outcome is an arbitrary redistribution of real wealth.

Individuals hold money only because they believe their wants will be better satisfied by waiting for some time period, whether it be seconds, days, or years. Each person's perspective of what the future will bring is different, each person's wants are different, each person's reasons for holding a specific cash balance are different. In other words, the amount of money (cash) individuals choose to hold depends on their interest in consuming or investing now versus later.

THE CONCEPT OF ORIGINARY INTEREST

If everyone believed the world was going to end in a week, production would come to a complete stop. Religious people who believe in an afterlife would attempt to prepare themselves for everlasting life. Nonbelievers might become believers, or go on some sort of hedonistic binge. Who knows what all the people would do? The point is, all economic evaluation occurs in the context of provisioning for the future. Without that prospect, there would be no economic activity.

Every individual's evaluation of existing goods and services involves a discounting process of the present versus the future. Thus, interest in consuming today versus tomorrow, or the next day, or 20 years from today is established.

The concept of interest is normally associated with credit, the cost of borrowing money. But in the truest economic sense, interest is responsible for—not a price for—the extension of credit. It is not a number, but a subjective ratio of what von Mises describes as "the value assigned to want satisfaction in the immediate future and the value assigned to want satisfaction in remote periods of the future."[6]

von Mises calls this "originary interest" because it is the basis for all forms of economic interest, including interest *rates*. In his words:

> Interest is neither the impetus to saving nor the reward or the compensation granted for abstaining from immediate consumption. It is the ratio in the mutual valuation of present goods as against future goods. . .[7]

Originary interest is the outgrowth of millions of individual evaluations in the market and is therefore constantly changing. And yet, supply-and-demand conditions in the market tend to seek the predominant rate of originary interest at any given point in time. The amount that people save rises with decreasing originary interest and falls with increasing originary interest. Thus, ideally, originary interest directs the investment activities of entrepreneurs independently of the market rate of interest. It manifests itself in the market in terms of the rate of growth or decline of capital goods—those designed for future production. Capital accumulation is not necessarily directly tied to the prevailing levels of interest rates, as will be discussed later in this chapter.

But the world is not ideal. It is impossible to accurately quantify originary interest, which is by its nature subjective and constantly changing. Instead, entrepreneurial decisions must be made on the basis of the prevailing market rate of interest, which, for now and for the foreseeable future, is subject to the control and influence of government. And making future plans on the basis of interest rates subject to governmental control can be a dangerous business.

CREDIT AND THE GROSS MARKET RATE OF INTEREST

Literally, credit means faith, confidence, or trust. In the economic sense, no matter what form it takes, credit is nothing more than the loaning of money (claims against unconsumed goods and services) in return for a promise to pay out of future production. As a first prerequisite, for one person to extend credit to another, the lender must have chosen to hold cash rather than spend it on goods presently available. In other words, the originary interest of the lender must be relatively low. Thus, originary interest is the driving force behind all credit transactions.

It is the driving force, but not the determining force. The determining force is the *gross market rate of interest*. The gross market rate of interest—the prevailing level of interest rates—has three components: (1) net (or real) interest, (2) an entrepreneurial component, and (3) a price premium component.[8, 9]

Originary interest reflects itself in interest rates as a net, underlying rate set according to the lender's discounting of the value of future goods against present goods. In general terms, the supply of money available for lending depends on the general level of interest in consuming now versus provisioning for future compensation through capital accumulation. If originary interest is high, there will be little money available for lending, and the net (nominal) interest level will be high, or irrespective of nominal rates, the amount of lending that occurs will be relatively small. Conversely, if originary interest is low, money for lending will be more plentiful, and the net interest level will be low. In other words, net interest rates, or the amount of lending occurring, always tend to reflect the level of originary interest.

Net interest alone, however, does not determine the market rate of interest. All creditors are, to some extent, entrepreneurs. By lending money, they enable the borrower to spend expected future proceeds, whether for consumption or investment. At the same time, however, creditors claim a share in the future proceeds, effectively becoming a partner in the debtor's future production. Since every entrepreneurial venture involves some degree of risk, lenders will naturally ask for a risk premium to be attached to the net interest rate, depending on the level of risk. This risk premium constitutes the entrepreneurial component of the gross market rate of interest, and it may vary, to some extent, on each loan.

The prime premium component is designed to discount changes in the money relation (the supply of and demand for money) that determines purchasing power. Changes in purchasing power can be either cash-induced (resulting from changes in the money supply), or goods-induced (resulting from changes in the numbers and types of goods and services available), or both; and all have effects on the money relation. But in our modern-day setting, most significant changes in the money relation are cash-induced; that is, created by changes in government monetary and fiscal policy.

At best, the price premium component is an estimate of the effects of future changes in the money relation that can deaden the repercussions of cash-induced changes for the money relation. But as the debt-ridden savings and loans (S&L's) so aptly demonstrate, the loan market usually reacts to, rather than correctly anticipates, the future purchasing power of money. As von Mises puts it, "The price premium always lags behind the changes in purchasing power because what generates it is not the change in the supply of money (in the broader sense), but the—necessarily later-occurring—effects of these changes upon the price structure."[10] In fact, as I will demonstrate shortly, the very reason recessions occur is largely the lagged nature of the price premium component; that is, the inability of both lenders and entrepreneurs to accurately anticipate the effects of cash-induced changes in the money relation.

THE NATURE OF THE BUSINESS CYCLE

With all this information in mind, we can now look at the business cycle in relation to von Mises' statement that booms and busts are caused by "attempts, repeated again and again, to lower the gross market rate of interest by means of credit expansion."

By the very nature of our banking system, credit expansion begins with an increase in free reserves held by member banks. Because ours is a fractional reserve system, every dollar of new reserves may be translated into at least $10 of new money that can potentially be created in the form of new loans.[11] Increased reserves can come from only one source, increased money holdings by individuals and businesses, whether in the form of demand or time deposits.

Assuming that, on average, people don't change their cash savings habits, increased reserves come from payments on performing loans and influxes of cash into the system that occur when the Federal Reserve Board buys government securities in open market operations. In the context of evaluating the cause of the business cycle, the latter is the important item of consideration.

The Fed has two principal tools of monetary policy: the control of short-term interest rates, and the ability to alter reserve holdings through open market operations. Prior to a recession bottom, the accepted policy is to make reserves plentiful and to lower short-term rates. Both moves are designed to stimulate banks to lend more, which in turn will stimulate business expansion. But the inevitable result of this form of credit expansion is a boom that will lead to a bust. The length of the boom and the severity of the bust depend on the nature and extent of the credit expansion, as well as the fiscal policy that government imposes on its citizens during the process.

For now, consider the effects of a credit expansion induced by the central bank independently of fiscal policy. At the bottom of a business cycle, on the eve of a credit expansion, the market has put all production processes it deems profitable into operation. According to the market, money is being placed in its best use; while factories that are closed, oil wells that are shut down, coal that is left unmined, and so forth, cannot be economically brought into production. The marginal capital investment remains untouched, waiting for new capital savings to be produced and employed before it can come to fruit. Any further capital expansion is possible only if additional capital, made available through capital savings, can be brought into production.

The government-induced credit expansion, however, makes it appear that the capital savings already exist and are available to bring the marginal investment to fruition. Money, remember, is a claim on unconsumed goods. Since the increased money stock is placed in the system as additional bank reserves, the gross market rate of interest is lowered (both with lower nominal rates and increased money supply), and banks normally become willing to lend more. Since entrepreneurs cannot distinguish between existing money and newly created money, they interpret their newfound ability to obtain a loan as the ability to claim unconsumed capital and put it to productive use.

But actually, the amount of unconsumed goods, including capital goods, remains unchanged. All that has changed is the money relation, which changes the entrepreneurs' perception of the supply of capital goods available. Eventually, a bidding war ensues for the limited amount of capital available, and the prices of capital goods begin to rise. These price changes, however, occur neither instantaneously or uniformly.

For the purposes of argument, assume that all the new loans resulting from the credit expansion are made to businesses, which would be the ideal goal of the central bankers. Production is expanded. Unemployed workers are brought into the work force. The nation is better off, right?

Wrong! The business expansion is brought about merely by the appearance that new capital is available. Actually, however, existing capital has been diverted from what would have been its former use to a different use. The capital that would have been used for production aimed at sustaining consumption at pre-expansion levels is employed for other purposes. By diverting capital to other uses, the waiting time for the production of replacement goods, consumer goods, and new goods has necessarily been extended. At the same time, the demand for consumer goods has risen due to increased employment in the labor sector.[12] Consequently, not only do producer prices rise, but consumer prices rise, again, not simultaneously or uniformly.

Businesses, however, take heart in the rising prices, reading them as increased demand and a reason to further expand production. They then invest more, which puts even greater pressure on producers' prices, including wages, which once again puts upward pressure on consumer prices. The boom progresses only as long as banks keep feeding the capital-availability illusion with more and more loans, driving the classic inflationary spiral.

How fast and when prices rise as well as which economic sectors are affected most or least and to what extent—all this depends on a number of factors. First and foremost, technological innovation can dampen the effects of rising prices by lowering the costs of production. Second, where and to whom lending institutions make new loans are critical factors. For example, between 1927 and 1929, there was a huge credit expansion, but producer and consumer prices rose very little. Instead, loans were made to stock investors, feeding the speculative frenzy that drove up the equities market. More recently, from 1982 through 1987, both stock prices and real estate prices soared, while the rate of growth of the CPI was on the decline. And third, government fiscal policy (taxation, borrowing, and spending) can either dampen or accelerate the whole process.

In most cases, however, the cycle of price increases follows a similar pattern:

- Producer prices rise first, but because of the immediate nature of increased consumer demand, consumer prices soon begin to rise more rapidly.
- Entrepreneurs, deluded by illusory profits, interpret the rising prices as increased demand, and they return to the lending institutions for more loans to expand production.
- Creditors, seeing the increased demand for loans combined with rising prices, add a price premium component to market interest rates, and nominal interest rates rise.
- However, because of the decline of originary interest, the gross market rate of interest, regardless of nominal levels, is still falling.
- Consequently, more loans are made.

- Once again, there is a cash-induced change in the money relation.
- Once again, the waiting period for additional goods is extended while consumer demand remains the same or increases.
- Once again, consumer prices tend to rise.

The cycle continues, and on each cycle, the price premium component is insufficient to compensate for the effects of rising prices. If it were sufficient, then the credit expansion would come to a halt. This, in essence, is the source of our modern-day business expansions.

The limiting factor on the extent and duration of a business expansion brought about by a credit expansion is originary interest. Once producers and consumers begin to realize that their purchasing power is dropping and that projected future income will be insufficient to compensate for the decline, originary interest begins to rise; that is, a flight to real values begins, with a preference to economic arenas (stocks, real estate, gold, or whatever) that promise the best inflation hedge. The added demand for the limited supply of consumer goods continues to drive prices up at an accelerated pace.

The breakdown finally occurs when banks become frightened and quit extending credit, or when the central bank removes reserves from the system and effectively slows or stops the credit expansion. At this point, numerous expansion ventures have been undertaken that depend on a continuing supply of credit at market rates set artificially below what an unhampered loan market would allow (e.g., savings and loans and real estate). Business plans and calculations based on the illusion of capital availability cannot be pushed forward. Distressed firms, desperate for cash, throw their inventories on the market. Producers' prices drop, usually suddenly. Factories are closed, workers are laid off. Construction projects are abandoned, leaving behind the skeletons of misallocated resources, now so prevalent in many American cities.

While many firms desperately need additional cash to survive, lenders, now all too aware of the prospect of failure, push the entrepreneurial component of interest rates to excessive heights, and loans become next to impossible to procure. At this point, the entire economy is ripe for panic, which can be triggered by virtually any further bad news. Markets crash, production slows, fortunes are lost virtually overnight, more workers are laid off, demand declines . . . a bust occurs.

The bust is absolutely unavoidable. As von Mises writes:

The essence of the credit-expansion boom is not overinvestment, but investment in wrong lines, i.e., malinvestment. [Entrepreneurs] embark upon an expansion of investment on a scale for which the capital goods do not suffice. Their projects are unrealizable on account of the insufficient supply of capital goods. They must fail sooner or later.[13]

But while many businesses fail, others survive the bust; and in fact, when all is said and done, technological innovation may have actually resulted in a general increase, on average, in the wealth of the nation. Nevertheless, when viewed in the sober light of the adjustment period, countless projects must be abandoned as totally hopeless; and it becomes apparent that real wealth, in terms of economic values, has been consumed (e.g., the S&L crises).

THE FUTILITY OF GOVERNMENT INTERVENTION DURING RECESSIONS

Recessions are the unavoidable outcome of boom periods. As a result of the credit expansion, resources have been misallocated, the money relation has changed, interest rates have been altered, and the psychological makeup of the market is different, probably very confused. Recession is a necessary period of readjustment of economic resources to the prevailing market data after the boom period, assuming, government leaves things alone long enough for them to adjust.

Typically, during recessions, there is an outcry for government to "do something" to bring the economy out of recession. But government is powerless to alter the economic reality that an adjustment period is necessary. The only thing it can do is to eliminate fiscal policy that confiscates capital and redirects it to areas where the market would not. This means cutting both taxes and spending. Practically, however, this almost never happens.

The other alternative is to engage in another round of credit expansion. Historically, this has been the preferred choice. It has also been, I believe, the source of virtually every major economic disaster in history.

We have a recent example to examine. In 1991 and 1992, the federal government tried to stimulate the U.S. economy into another round of credit-driven expansion. Tried—and failed. The Federal Reserve Board attempted to lower the gross market rate of interest by increasing reserve deposits (through purchases of securities in Open Market Operations), while simultaneously lowering the discount rate an unprecedented number of times. The loan market, however, refused to budge because fiscal policy restrained economic growth, or, as I have just explained, the entrepreneurial component of the gross market rate of interest was so high that lending institutions remained unwilling to loan at virtually any nominal rate.

As an aside, I find this an encouraging development. It especially encourages me that the bond market has relentlessly kept yields above 7.5 percent regardless of short rates. It tells me that the markets are getting wise to the effects of inflationary expansionism. But on the downside, I watched the stock market soar in December 1991 after a surprise cut of the discount rate by a full point to 3.5 percent, the largest single percentage cut in history. It continued to creep up until October 1992 under the expectation that a new period of growth was imminent, especially with interest rates at historical lows.

And that, as I see it, is the problem. Labeling any nominal interest rate "low" or "high" without considering the economic conditions within which the nominal rate exists is a false premise. The important relationship to consider is always whether nominal rates reflect the true level of originary interest, and that is necessarily a judgment call.

If a government-induced credit expansion artificially lowers the gross market rate of interest (and therefore originary interest), there will be a boom, and conversely. And the key indicator is the rate of growth of the money supply.

CONCLUSION

There you have it, a necessarily short and somewhat abstract synopsis of my view of the business cycle. To sum it up, I believe the underlying cause of the business cycle is government efforts to reduce the gross market rate of interest through credit expansion. When this happens, entrepreneurs think that more capital goods exist than actually do exist. Basing their calculations and projections on illusory data, they engage in many ventures that are doomed from the outset. But the enormous innovative capacity of the men and women in the marketplace often dampens the effects, allowing net new real wealth to be produced during each cycle.

Nevertheless, nothing that human beings do with the money and credit markets can alter the fact that new production must be preceded by increased capital saving. Credit cannot create new wealth to a nation. Confidence cannot create new wealth. Increased aggregate demand cannot create new wealth. Increased consumption, other things equal, will decrease the potential for the production of new wealth. Only capital savings arising from production can lead to the generation of new wealth.

The business cycle is a vicious circle, an endless bait-and-switch game planned and implemented by government "experts." Their intentions are usually good, but the results are always the same. As long as central banking systems exist, as long as government attempts to regulate business growth or decline by manipulating the gross market rate of interest, there will be booms and busts, with continuous increases in prices. Fortunately, as we will see in the coming chapters, you can use knowledge outlined in this chapter to understand the game, ride the tide of false premises, and reap more profits in the future from these Soros opportunities.

4
Political Influences on the Business Cycle

To accurately forecast the future of business activity, and therefore, price movements in the financial markets, you must be able to identify and integrate the effects of both monetary and fiscal policy on the business cycle. In Chapter 3, we looked at some of the effects of monetary policy. We observed that a monetary policy designed to encourage the extension of credit will tend to generate a business expansion, but only at the expense of an unavoidable recession. Easy monetary policy tends to induce business expansion, but monetary policy alone does not determine the business cycle. The other factor is government's fiscal policy: taxes, spending, and borrowing. In this chapter, I want to demonstrate the effects of government economic policies—starting with what I see as its underlying purpose. After all, if economics is the study of the "means applied to the attainment of ends chosen," the ends chosen by our government leadership are crucial elements of the equation.

When I look at the actions and proclamations of our elected officials, I see an underlying philosophy: that economic activity should result in a tendency toward income equality. "Fairness" is the rallying point behind new tax proposals. Without challenge or apology, our elected representatives seek to establish government-imposed economic egalitarianism at the expense of liberty.

As measured by the tone and content of modern congressional rhetoric, the accepted current purpose of government economic management seems clear: to redistribute wealth according to a standard of "fairness" without totally suppressing the entrepreneur's willingness to produce. I totally disagree with this viewpoint and could probably write a whole book on the reasons why. But my purpose here isn't to refute prevailing thinking. Rather, it is to demonstrate the consequences of current thinking in terms of market forecasting.

THE EFFECTS OF TAXATION ON THE LONG-TERM TREND

Taxes are here to stay, there is no doubt about that. But what form they take, to whom or what they apply, and how large they are will dramatically affect the long-term performance of the economy and, therefore, the financial markets.

von Mises summed up the dangers of taxation and explains the critical reason taxes matter:

> If the methods of taxation . . . bring about capital consumption or restrict the accumulation of new capital, the capital required for *marginal employments* [author's emphasis] is lacking and an expansion of investment which would have been effected in the absence of these taxes is prevented.[1]

As this statement implies, not all taxes necessarily restrict business activity and growth. It is arguable that using taxes to pay for the services rendered by government, at least some of which are necessary, is tantamount to an economic exchange, similar to any other trade. To the extent that the level of taxation does not exceed the level needed to guarantee the smooth functioning of a government providing necessary services, the outlays will repay themselves. Unfortunately, however, the supply of, demand for, and cost of government services are set not by market forces, but by political fiat. When that fiat is driven by the Robin Hood principle, taxes and spending are bound to run out of control, as they are now. And, by definition, excessive taxes cause a forced redistribution of wealth, aberrations in the exchange ratios of the goods and services available in the market, distortions in the money relation, and a tendency toward capital consumption.

Analysts who look at the economy in terms of aggregates argue that taxes are either "neutral," meaning they have no net effect on consumption, or stimulative, meaning they actually tend to bring about new production. Clinging to the Keynesian premise that production is driven by the marginal propensity to consume, they point out that every dollar taken out of one person's pocket ends up in another person's pocket. Moreover, since the poorer segment of the population is apt to increase consumption with increased income, taxing the rich, who have a greater propensity to save, and giving the money to the poor through social programs will increase consumption, which will increase aggregate demand, which will stimulate businesses to produce more. As Keynes put it:

> If fiscal policy is used as a deliberate instrument for the more equal distribution of income, its effect in increasing the propensity to consume is, of course, all the greater.[2]

The fatal flaw in this thinking is that if an increase in consumption is not preceded by an increase in production, *capital is consumed.* If the next effect of a tax is indeed to increase the demand for consumer goods by placing more dollars into the hands of lower-income groups, the increased demand must necessarily arise due to a decrease in consumption of wealthier individuals. What actually happens, however, is that perhaps the consumption habits of the wealthy change, but their "propensity" to save always drops, and those are savings that would have otherwise been used for capital expansion.

In the very best case, the outcome of "Robin Hood" taxes is a diversion and diffusion of the means of production to other economic sectors, and in addition, slower, less efficient economic growth than would have occurred without them. In the worst case, they lead to direct capital consumption and a net reduction in the wealth of the nation. Let's examine the best case first.

Assume that government imposes a "prosperity tax" on the income of each person who makes over $50,000 per year. The tax is to be directly distributed (skipping the bureaucrats in the middle) to those who make less than $15,000 per year. The purpose of the tax is twofold: (1) to increase income equality, and (2) to increase the aggregate propensity to consume, and presumably, therefore, the level of production (this is exactly what Bill Clinton's policy is based on). Now assume the tax is successful on both fronts. The income leveling effect of the tax is obvious. But for the redistribution to cause a net increase in consumer demand, there *absolutely must be* a net decline in the savings rate of higher income individuals.

Prior to the distribution, there was a limited supply of capital producing a limited supply of consumer goods. After the redistribution, the same limited supply of capital and consumer goods exists and there is less savings available to serve as replacement capital and for capital expansion. Simultaneously, there has been an increase in consumer demand, putting upward pressure on prices.

Businesspeople, responding to the increase in demand, expand production to meet the demand. But the waiting time required to satisfy the new, higher levels of consumer demand is necessarily lengthened, so prices must rise. For businesspeople to expand their production, they must employ capital; meaning, the demand for the limited supply of capital goods will rise as well. Assuming no change in the money supply, the increased demand for capital goods, combined with the now lower amount of capital supply, will cause producers' prices to rise as well, but most likely not as fast as consumers' prices, where the increased demand occurs sooner.

With increased revenues gained from more sales at higher retail prices, certain businesses will increase both the real and apparent capital at their disposal for investment, a benefit that is partially offset by rising producers' prices. On the other hand, the businesses that would have benefited from the additional capital supply potentially available without the income redistribution lose out. Initially, there is a net increase in production due to increased demand, but because the amount of capital available for investment has been reduced, the increase is necessarily smaller and more expensive than it would have been without the tax. Add to this the government's inherently inefficient "middleman's" cut, and even more growth potential is lost. The long and the short of it is, anytime you divert capital savings toward consumer spending, some growth potential (both today and for the future) is lost. That's the best case.

A more realistic case would be that the tax not only redirects capital savings toward consumption by lower income groups, but also that the marginal propensity to consume among higher income groups drops. The activities of businesses are not uniform. Some businesses are designed to satisfy the wants of high-income individuals, and some are designed to satisfy the wants of low-income individuals. When resources are redistributed to the low-income groups, the businesses that serve high-income

groups will suffer, resulting in layoffs of workers (often low-income people), plant closings, bankruptcies, nonperforming loans, and so forth. Not
only will existing capital be consumed, but future capital, tapped in the
form of nonperforming loans, will be consumed. This will be offset to
some extent by gains and expansion enjoyed by the businesses serving
low-income groups, but by the very nature of the process, the gains cannot
offset the losses equally.

Once again, the reason is the arbitrary and sudden disruption of the
supply-demand relationship. For those high-end businesses that fail, the
investment of time and capital resources is lost, to some extent forever.
Some capital goods are, by their nature, inconvertible. At the same time
that those capital goods lie idle, plummeting in price, the demand for
capital goods for the low-end businesses will rise and their prices will
increase. There is no tit for tat. While some capital is consumed or remains unemployed, the limited supply of capital required for other business expansion will increase in price.

To meet the added demand brought on by the redistribution of wealth,
businesses serving low-income groups must make capital investments. As
a result, the waiting period required to meet the new, higher demand for
low-end consumer goods lengthens. Prices for those consumer products
rise, as do the prices for producers' goods in that arena. In final effect,
net capital is consumed; that is, there is a general impoverishment of the
economy, and the nation.

A good example of a tax that resulted in the net consumption of capital
is the 10 percent tax on "luxury" items. The reasoning behind this tax
was totally altruistic. "Anyone who can afford to buy a plane or a yacht
can certainly afford to pay 10 percent more for it," said the advocates of
the tax, and it passed. Guess what? They were wrong. Ten percent made
a lot of difference. The pleasure boat industry collapsed. So did sales of
small planes. So did sales of small refrigerators, built mainly for pleasure
boats. Thousands of blue-collar workers were laid off. Production facili-
ties still sit largely idle even though the tax is being rescinded.

The moral of this story is fairly obvious: If the market could have justified a price hike of 10 percent, prices would have already been 10 percent higher. Any price hike imposed by new taxation will necessarily
prevent the marginal purchase, which will necessarily drive the marginal
producer out of business. That's exactly what happened.

CAPITAL GAINS TAXES

In my view, the capital gains tax can have nothing but negative economic effects. To make matters worse, at a 28 percent effective rate (not including state taxes), the United States currently has one of the highest capital gains taxes in the world. Ignoring the fact that it is not adjusted for inflation, which is equal to theft, a capital gains tax is just that, a direct tax on the very foundation of new investment: *gains*—newly produced wealth earned by investing money in business ventures, or, as in my case (I hope), money that changes hands due to the bad investments of others.

The current capital gains tax consumes equity of the United States by redirecting 28-plus percent of capital gains toward consumption-oriented government spending. Capital gains taxes are eating up the capital savings that could otherwise be reinvested to produce economic growth. As the capital gains tax rate goes up, the quantity of new investment goes down. I can demonstrate this directly.

When investors are deciding where to place their money, they must choose among many alternatives: direct investing in private businesses, stocks, bonds, various funds, limited partnerships, and so forth. In evaluating the alternatives, for each option, they look at the potential reward and risk involved, and compare the two. Then, based on relative risk-to-reward ratios, they choose what they perceive to be the most attractive alternative. Each individual person determines risk/reward differently, but in general, if two or more alternatives offer the same potential return, the vast majority of investors will put their money into the investment they perceive as having the lowest risk. And in general, the higher the risk involved, the higher must be the potential return to attract new investment.

In many cases, potential investments fall into an uncertain, gray area in investors' minds: They are *marginal* investments. These are newly proposed or existing enterprises offering returns moderately higher than low-risk alternatives such as tax-free municipal bonds, but not enough higher to readily attract new capital for start up or growth investment. For example, a company that has delivered an average, annual before-tax return of 25 percent to its stockholders over a five-year period will have no trouble raising new capital to finance its business. But a new venture, promising a 10 percent or even a 15 percent before-tax average annual return to new stockholders, will certainly have trouble when you consider the effects of the capital gains tax. Each incremental increase in the capital gains tax results in a corresponding, and probably proportional, increase in the numbers of investments that become marginal in investors' minds and therefore attract less investment capital than they otherwise could.

Consider, for example, the likelihood of a new venture promising a 10 percent earnings growth rate being capitalized as a new stock issue at different capital gains tax rates. View this venture's prospect in the light of the investment alternatives shown in Table 4.1 and ask yourself, from the standpoint of an "average" investor with $10,000, at what point you might invest in the new venture.

It might seem apparent that average investors would put their money in the high-growth stock. Not so. There are plenty of investors who understand that a 40 PE stock could easily fall 25 percent or more in the face of even one bad earnings report. In the current economic environment, at a net 33 percent capital gains tax rate, my guess is most investors would select a mix consisting of the median growth stock and the bond fund.

The point is, why would anyone invest money in a new venture promising just 2.17 percent in marginal returns over the virtually risk-free muni-bond fund yield? The new venture involves significant risk—an investor could lose everything! But at a 15 percent capital gains tax rate, the marginal potential return above muni-bonds rises to 4.69 percent, probably enough to lure more investors to participate. At a 0 percent capital gains rate, the potential return is nearly double the muni-bond yield, surely enough to attract some of the more risk-oriented investors.

To demonstrate how directly and dramatically capital gains taxes ruin the prospects for marginal new enterprises, consider the following hypothetical entrepreneurial venture. Joe Smith owns a highly successful interstate trucking company and has a dream. He wants to become the McDonald's of highway truck stops, serving low-priced, but high-quality, food for truckers and other highway travelers. His basic plan is to build on inexpensive land along heavily traveled interstate highways. He does his homework, and decides that it is feasible to start by building 100 units. Then, over a 10- to 15-year period, he hopes to expand the business to 1,000 units.

After doing detailed cost estimates, Joe determines it will cost $500,000 to start up each unit; he needs $50 million to go into business. Joe's private banker will loan him $25 million against his trucking business. Joe needs more capital to make the venture worthwhile, so he

Table 4.1 Investment Alternatives Comparison Analysis at Different Capital Gains Rates

Basis:
1. $10,000 initial investment.
2. Goal is to double initial investment value.
3. Corporate earnings growth is compounded (minus dividends).

Investment Descriptions:

1. *New Venture.* A new company projecting 10 percent earning growth offering common stock shares at a projected 10 PE.
2. *High-Growth Stock.* Common stock in an existing company with a five-year record of 25 percent continuous earnings growth paying no dividend.
3. *Median-Growth Stock.* Common stock in an established S&P 500 company with an earnings growth record of 15 percent paying a 3.3 percent annual dividend.
4. *Muni-Bond Fund.* A municipal bond fund currently yielding 7 percent making yearly yield payments.

Investment Type	Earnings Growth Rate	PE	Years Required for Initial Investment to Double	After-Tax Avg. Annual Gain before Dividends	After-Tax Avg. Annual Return before Dividends	After-Tax Avg. Annual Return after Dividends
1. New venture	10% (projected)	10 (proj.)	7.27	@ 33% $ 917.01 @ 15% $1,169.19 @ 0% $1,375.52	@ 33 9.17 @ 15 11.69 @ 0 13.76	N/A N/A N/A
2. High-growth stock	25% (historical)	40	2.93	@ 33% $2,275.34 @ 15% $2,901.02 @ 0% $3,412.97	@ 33 22.75 @ 15 29.01 @ 0 34.12	N/A N/A N/A
3. Median-growth stock	15% (historical)	15	4.85	@ 33% $1,374.57 @ 15% $1,752.58 @ 0% $2,061.86	@ 33 13.74 @ 15 17.53 @ 0 20.62	15.97% 20.33% 23.62%
4. Tax-free muni-bond fund	7% (uncompounded)	N/A	10.31	@ $ 700.00	@ 0 7.00	

decides to incorporate "Joe's Truck Stops" and contacts an investment banker to underwrite his new stock issue. He is certain investors will eagerly participate in what he knows will be a "sure thing."

He develops a detailed proposal for the investment banker, including well-researched cash flow projections. The bottom line is average unit sales volume of at least $500,000 and a 15 percent net operating profit. As the operation expands to more and more units, he estimates that economies of scale could increase his profit margin to 20 percent. He plans to own half the company himself and to offer another 2.5 million shares of common stock at $10 per share to raise the necessary additional capital. By pricing the stock at what should be a 6.67 PE, he feels certain the investment banker will see the new issue as a "growth" stock and readily underwrite it.

But to Joe's dismay, the investment banker starts shaking his head as soon as he sees the return projections. "Joe," he says, "you've got a great idea here, but we can't do it. The return just isn't good enough."

"Whattaya mean," says Joe, "a 15 percent return isn't half bad—it's almost double current bond yields!"

"Ahhh," sighs the banker, "a corporate return of 15 percent doesn't look bad, but you have to consider it from an investor's standpoint. You project a return of 15 percent. Assuming you reinvest that each year, your company's earnings should grow by 15 percent each year, and your stock value should do at least as well. But people buy stocks primarily for long-term gains due to value appreciation. Assuming your stock appreciates an average of 15 percent per year, the 33 percent capital gains tax will knock down your investors' after-tax return to 10 percent. They can get 7 percent right now in a tax-free, muni-bond fund, with virtually no risk. Combine these numbers with the fact that over 80 percent of new restaurant ventures fail, and look at what you're asking your investors to do. You're asking them to be willing to lose everything for marginal gains of just 3 percent per year. Sorry Joe, the risk/reward just isn't there."

Joe tries other bankers, but the answer is the same everywhere. Joe gives up, sells his trucking business for $25 million, puts the money into tax-free muni-bonds, buys a cabin in Colorado, and lives on the yield for the rest of his days. And for all the world knows, the next potential Ray Kroc of truck stops just went into early retirement.

No matter what the perceived prospects for the success of a newly proposed venture, if investors are to put their money at risk, their potential returns must be substantially higher than for other, lower risk alternatives. Exactly how much higher, no one knows—it is a subjective issue depending on the psychological makeup of each individual investor. But if the capital gains tax was 15 percent instead of 33 percent, the potential bottom line for investors in Joe's Truck Stops would increase to 12.75 percent per year, an 82 percent higher yield than that of the hypothetical bond fund. If the capital gains tax was 0 percent, then the potential yield would be 15 percent, a 114 percent higher yield. As the potential return increases, at some point, the business is no longer categorized as marginal in the investor's mind. Whether or not this particular hypothetical venture would appeal to investors is of no importance. The point is, the lower the capital gains tax rate, the easier it is to find investors for new ventures.

But, critics of a capital gains cut say, if we lower the capital gains tax, it will increase government deficits. Aside from the fact that this alleged problem could be solved by slashing government spending, it is wrong from a simple, pragmatic standpoint. For example, in the decade of the 1970s, federal government revenues totaled $3.275 trillion, whereas in the decade of the 1980s, the era of Reagan's massive tax cuts, total revenues rose a whopping 277 percent to $9.061 trillion. Unfortunately, government spending grew 302 percent in the 1980s to $10.823 trillion. Irresponsible spending is the problem creating deficits, not the lack of tax revenues.

Every year, perhaps hundreds of marginal new ventures are scratched because of the capital gains tax. As a result, untold thousands of jobs are not created and untold billions are lost in potential new tax revenues each year. For example, assume that capital gains taxes don't exist and consider the potential new tax revenues that would be generated by a successful Joe's Truck Stops venture.

Assume that Joe's start-up and cash flow projections are correct. He builds 100 units and achieves his goal of $500,000 in per unit sales in the first full year of operation. He operates at a 20 percent labor cost, and hires only hungry, unemployed people who will work hard for him. His food cost averages 30 percent. The average cost of real estate at each location is $100,000, and Joe puts $250,000 in improvements on each property, resulting in increased property taxes of $6,000 per year per unit. He buys $100,000 of new equipment for each unit, and spends another $50,000 per unit to pay the investment banker's fee, the attorney's fees, points for mortgage loans, permits, and other such fees. Making some very simple assumptions, more than $10 million in new tax revenues would be generated in the first year alone (see Table 4.2).

These are all *new tax revenues* generated as a result of producing new wealth. I have intentionally made the numbers very conservative by excluding any additional corporate income taxes that might be paid, the additional income taxes paid by formerly out-of-work construction workers, the decreased burden of the state and federal government as people go off the dole, and so forth. Furthermore, I haven't even mentioned the cascading beneficial effects from the creation of new jobs—lower restaurant prices due to increased competitiveness in the market, and so on down the line.

The simple fact is this: If the capital gains tax inhibits the growth of marginal ventures like Joe's Truck Stops, then to the extent that capital is

Table 4.2 Joe's Truck Stops
Simplified Estimation of New Tax Revenues Generated in First Year of Operation

Increased Property Taxes: 100 Units @ $6,000 per year		600,000
Increased Employee Payroll Taxes:		
(assumes formerly unemployed persons are hired)		
Gross payroll:	$10,000,000	
Income tax @ 20%	2,000,000	
Social Security @ 12%	1,200,000	
State & Local @ 5%	500,000	
Total Payroll Taxes	$ 3,700,000	3,700,000
Additional Taxes Paid by Recipients of Start-Up Expenses:		
(assumes an average of 15% of gross receipts		
paid in taxes of all forms)		
100 × $50,000 × 15%		750,000
Additional Taxes Paid by Equipment Wholesaler:		
(same assumption)		
100 × $100,000 × 15%		1,500,000
Additional Taxes Paid by Builders:		
(same assumption)		
100 × $250,000 × 15%		3,750,000
Total Estimated Increased Tax Income Generated		
in First Year of Operation		$10,300,000

diverted to consumption, potential new jobs, wealth, and tax revenues are lost completely. So which is better, a 33 percent capital gains tax that prevents millions of dollars of new wealth from being created each year, or a lower capital gains tax that encourages growth and produces new sources of tax revenues?

Even at 1,000 units, Joe's Truck Stops is a relatively small venture—a $500 million a year business. Nevertheless, assuming that Joe hires 20 people per location, he creates 20,000 new jobs and increases real GDP by millions of dollars per year. Multiply this by the hundreds or perhaps even thousands of new ventures never pursued due to the capital gains tax, and you are talking about the difference between an economy in recession, and an economy enjoying sustained growth. You are also talking about billions of dollars of lost opportunity in terms of government revenues.

Critics might say, "Your story has such a sad ending. Poor Joe. He owns $25 million in muni-bonds and the capital gains tax stopped him from making even more money. Your example is proof that a cut in the capital gains tax would only benefit the rich!"

This kind of thinking totally ignores the manifold economic benefits that each profitable new business venture creates. Assume, for example, that Joe opens a restaurant near Farmington, a hypothetical community suffering the economic plight of so many real rural areas. John and Mary live near Farmington and own a farm along Highway 81. Farm commodity prices have been dropping, and they have fallen three months behind on their mortgage payments to the First National Bank of Farmington. They need $800 more per month to survive, but jobs are nowhere to be found. George, their banker, has told them that soon he will have no choice but to foreclose on them and auction off their farm and equipment.

George the banker, meanwhile, is suffering from hypertension. The bank examiners have been breathing down his neck and are threatening to close him down if he can't increase his reserves against loan losses. If they force him to foreclose on John and Mary, that will be it. Property values have fallen so dramatically in the area that auctioning their property would only cover about two-thirds of the outstanding loan balance. The additional loss would take George's bank over the brink. Then the Fed would move in, foreclose on even more of his friends and neighbors, and effectively bankrupt the town of Farmington and the surrounding community.

Then one day, Mary is driving along the highway and sees a new building with a sign in front saying, "Joe's Truck Stop." Underneath the sign, the marquee reads, "Food Servers Needed." She goes in, applies for a job, and starts work the following week. She and her husband just make the monthly mortgage payment, and within three months, they are able to pay the entirety of their past-due balance.

George notices that not only John and Mary, but other bank customers as well, are starting to make note payments on a more timely basis. Twenty of the community's inhabitants have found new jobs at the nearby Joe's Truck Stop. A manager for Joe's was transferred into town and bought the Johnson's place that had been on the market for nine months. The town's only restaurant, which even in hard times makes a modest profit, has been doing a windfall lunch business for months, the result of the construction workers who have been building Joe's. Jack, who owns the John Deere store in town, reports that revenues are up and is suddenly making regular payments rather than asking for extensions on loans against his inventory. The school is enjoying more property tax revenue and rehired Frank Simmons to finish the masonry work on that new wing that was never completed. Sales are up at the local hardware store, where Betsy Smith, the woman who had been receiving unemployment checks for the past three months, now works. Joe's is depositing $5,000 to $15,000 a day in George's bank, and the average balance of his regular customers has risen as well. George just meets his loan loss reserve requirement, the bank examiners go away, and George's blood pressure drops into the normal range. Farmington will survive.

Is this how a capital gains tax cut results in benefits only to the rich? Without a capital gains tax, or with a lower capital gains rate, more potential ventures like Joe's Truck Stops would broach that "marginal" stigma in investors' eyes each year. As a result, more resources would be directed to the creation of new wealth—new goods and services—resulting in more new jobs creation and more competitive prices (assuming low inflation), resulting in more spending, resulting in more profits, resulting in more savings, resulting in more investment, and so on, and so on, and so on.

I could simply say that wealth begets wealth, a version of the so-called trickle-down theory of investment, which describes how tax benefits to the wealthy filter down to lower-income groups. But when you consider the full cascade of economic benefits derived from a lower capital gains tax, the "rich" investor only enjoys a small portion of the total benefits created by new and profitable business ventures. In the case of Joe's Truck Stops, Joe would certainly become substantially more wealthy, but his percentage of new income versus that delivered to the rest of the economy in terms of growth is a mere trickle. The theory is misnamed. It should be called "the trickle-up theory."

There is an even better counter to the argument that a lower capital gains tax will benefit only the rich. Compare the benefits that middle-class American homeowners derive from a 20 percent versus a 33 percent capital gains tax. Of 112 million taxpayers, 74 million own homes. If homes were to appreciate an average of 6 percent per year, as they did before the Tax Reform Act of 1986 (which established an effective 33 percent capital gains rate), a house would double in value in 12 years. Using the current median purchase price of a home—$158,000, and considering that the average homeowner sells every 12 years, the median additional appreciation enjoyed by the homeowner paying 20 percent instead of 33 percent is $20,540, an average tax savings of $1,711 per year. (True, you can avoid paying taxes on the sale of a home by buying another of greater value, but sooner or later, the piper must be paid. There is, however, a one-time $125,000 exclusion if you sell a home after you have reached the age of 55.) It should also be pointed out that, under current regulations, there is no capital loss deduction permitted for losses on a primary residence—another issue altogether.

Tell the average homeowner this and then ask which would be preferable: an income tax break to middle-class Americans of $200 per year for two years (to be offset by increased taxes on the wealthy, as of this writing), as many congressmen are proposing right now, or the prospect of building additional equity in a home to the tune of $1,700 per year. The answer is obvious.

It should also be obvious that the equity built by this kind of tax savings can be leveraged for new investments or expenditures. When homeowners build equity, they can get second mortgages to make improvements on their home, to buy cars, to put their children through school, and so forth. The capital gains tax is a direct drain on equity (accumulated capital) and therefore limits loans against it. When you realize that one-third of our nation's equity is subject to government appropriation through the capital gains tax, you can begin to imagine the massive scale of lost investment potential.

The capital gains tax is the most economically damaging of all the different types of taxes available to government. In general, the least damaging taxes are those that are relatively low and uniform, and are designed for only one purpose: to finance the expenditures of a severely limited government. By their very nature, taxes aimed at income equality will have a negative effect on economic growth. They result in capital consumption, which reduces capital savings, which slows down business expansion.

GOVERNMENT SPENDING AND DEFICIT SPENDING

To a point, government taxation and spending are arguably necessary economic costs that will repay themselves. For example, to provide for the national defense, both the military infrastructure and the military industry must be subsidized by other producers through some form of taxation. But, the military industry exists as a necessary parasite, like the bacteria in the human digestive system, on the productive capacity of the nation. It is dependent not on government, but on other industry for its survival. Such is not the case with most government-financed programs.

Unfortunately, many people look at government as an inexhaustible resource, as a potential panacea for any alleged woe that befalls any group or foreign country large enough or powerful enough to command political attention. Flooding along the New Jersey coastline? Federal aid to the rescue. $500 billion in bad S&L debt? Federal money to the rescue. Alarming illiteracy in the United States? More federal money to an already bloated education budget. Argentina's government is on the verge of bankruptcy? Government-guaranteed loans to the rescue. The people in the former Soviet Union are on the verge of starvation? U.S.-backed loans and underpriced wheat to the rescue.

Generous though we Americans may be, we are also naive. Our government (people) may have deep pockets, but they are empty—they are full of nothing but holes. Government has not balanced a budget since 1969, and over the past 40 years, the deficit has grown at a mean rate of 15.3 percent per year. Worse yet, there is no end in sight. The official

Office of Management and Budget forecasts, in spite of a $500 million "deficit-reduction" bill passed in October 1990, increased its five-year deficit projections in September 1991 from $62.3 billion to $1.087 trillion. But is this really a problem?

Some economists believe that government deficits, even at current levels, are not a major concern. With a deficit of only 5.9 percent of GDP, the government, they argue, is in better shape than most individuals.

Aside from the fact that the comparison should be to debt as a percentage of income, what these economists fail to note is that individuals and businesses *produce* in order to service debt. The government does not. When the government deficit-spends, it consumes future capital savings. Every time a newly issued government bond, note, or bill is sold, there is a proportional loss of potential investment capital that is redirected to pay for *already consumed* goods and services. The real evil of government deficit spending is that it cheats American entrepreneurs out of the opportunity to borrow growth capital. Deficit spending forces government to sell new issues of bills, notes, and bonds, all at competitive yields with virtually no risk attached to them.

Of course, investors will buy government debt, and they'll do it with money that would have otherwise been invested in new capital ventures. Using taxes such as the capital gains tax to finance deficit spending is a double whammy. Not only is the government cutting away at the roots of economic growth to pay its bills, it is eating the seed stock of future growth.

CONCLUSION

By the OMB's estimates, 1993 will see government spending reach 25 percent of GNP, 5.9 percent of which will be deficit financed. As we will see in the next chapter, these numbers are most likely understated. But assuming they are right, our government will have to maintain oppressively high levels of taxation to support projected levels of spending. At the same time, the Fed has lowered interest rates and pumped the banking system full of excess reserves. It is a monetary and fiscal policy mix unprecedented in my memory.

On the one hand, stimulative monetary policy will have a tendency to cause a business boom based on the illusion of abundant capital availability, as described in Chapter 3. Taxation and spending policy, on the other hand, are bound to dampen the effects of a credit-driven boom by snatching a large percentage of (primarily illusory) profits from those who enjoy the benefits of the expansion and redirecting capital resources toward consumption.

The most healthy possible outcome from this unusual policy mix will be slow growth with low to moderate inflation. And yet, as I write, the stock market is once again climbing past Dow 3200, a level that will only be justified if a boom expansion occurs in 1993. Evidently, the market is betting that President Clinton and Congress will increase spending and let the deficit go its own course. If the market is right, the outcome will be a meteoric rise in business activity, followed by price increases, followed by another long and protracted recession sometime within the next few years.

But is what we're seeing the onset of a Soros opportunity, or is it the last gasp of investors stubbornly refusing to believe that a false premise is about to be discredited? In the next chapter, I will attempt to answer that question by applying fundamental analysis to the current environment and the future of investments in the 1990s.

5

Applying Macrofundamental Analysis to Economic Forecasting: An Outlook for the 1990s

When you think about it, "macrofundamentals" are really just the consequences of government intervention in the market. Monetary and fiscal policy, various types of legislation (tax law, regulation, subsidies, tariffs, and price controls, etc.) and military actions all dramatically affect the future course of production and trade, and therefore price trends in the various financial markets.

Projecting the effects of government policy is mostly a matter of understanding the basic nature of the policy, making a few assumptions, and then logically applying the principles outlined in the preceding chapters to project the most probable outcomes. This gives you a "big picture" forecast of what to expect. But the strokes on this picture are so large and sweeping as to provide an image only from a very long-term point of view. Filling in the details needed for near-term viewing requires that you project forthcoming government policy changes, as well as factor in significant political, demographic, and cultural trends within the context of fundamental economic principles.

In this chapter, I hope to shed some light on how to use historical statistical analysis to project the future. Rather than telling you how I think it should be done, I will demonstrate how I do it, and time will be my judge.

THE BIG PICTURE: THE MONETARY AND FISCAL POLICY MIX

In projecting the current big picture, the critical factors to be considered are not monetary policy and fiscal policy considered separately, but rather the overall monetary and fiscal policy mix. For example, based solely on the current monetary policy of low interest rates and ample free reserves, I would be nothing but bullish for the coming few years, tempered by what I think I know about Alan Greenspan, which I will discuss later. Based on current fiscal policy alone—high taxes coupled with relatively lower spending—I would be very bearish. When you mix the two and consider the effects of both in operation at once, the result is not necessarily the sum of the parts, but it will bear some relationship to that sum.

Our current monetary policy can't help but have a stimulative effect. In early 1992, *The Wall Street Journal,* reported that corporations, moving to take advantage of low interest rates, were starting to sell massive new bond issues to finance their businesses. Throughout 1992, home mortgage rates were under pressure, with scattered reports of 30-year fixed-rate mortgages as low as 6.5 percent, which stimulated home buying to some degree, but to an even greater degree allowed many to refinance at lower rates, which increases disposable income.

As of December 1992, banks, still reluctant to lend after being burned so badly since 1989, were gradually starting to make loans involving the lowest risk; in the initial stages of the recovery, banks will make prudent, secured loans that are most likely to be performing.

I consider the reluctance of banks to lend right now a positive sign; it tells me the administrators in lending institutions have learned, at least on some level, the long-term consequences of business growth brought about by inflation of the money supply through credit expansion. The Fed has attempted to stimulate business activity by lowering nominal rates and filling the system with excess reserves. But banks aren't going for it.

The adjusted monetary base (the best indication of the underlying monetary potential for credit expansion) grew in calendar year 1991 by approximately 8.7 percent (adjusted Fed credit grew at 9.5 percent) while M2 grew only by 2.6 percent. Since every dollar of added bank reserves translates to 10 dollars or more of credit availability (which would translate to M2 growth), the slow growth of M2 tells me that the entrepreneurial component of interest rates is currently very high, regardless of nominal rates. My personal banker (from a money-center bank) probably summed it up the best when he said in January 1992, "If the discount rate were at zero, we still wouldn't make any unsecured loans; and my superiors have made it clear to me that any loan I approve that turns out to be nonperforming will mean my job."

This is a typical attitude from lending institutions at recession bottoms. But in this case, the attitude has prevailed for over a year, and that reluctance will continue. I think bankers, as a rule, are better educated about the consequences of credit expansion and inflation than ever before. They fear inflation and will remain reluctant to make fixed, long-term loans at any nominal rate, except on assets they can package and resell to the government, such as mortgages. Over time, as their caution pays off in terms of building a reserve base founded on a good inventory of performing loans, the entrepreneurial component will drop slightly, and business expansion will start to accelerate.

In 1992, another significant factor affected the willingness and ability of banks to lend. The Bassel Accords required that banks establish a capital-to-asset ratio of 8 percent by the end of 1992. Some banks that have survived established their base largely by rebuilding the capital foundation with performing loans. This would be an extremely positive step toward laying the foundation for sustained economic growth if it were universally the case. But the purpose of the Accords was merely to save the FDIC from default. Consequently, banks are allowed to hold and leverage government securities as an equivalent to capital, creating a flight to Treasury debt.

For this and other reasons (when interest rates turn up), the positive effects of a relatively easy monetary policy and prudent lending policies are (and will be) offset to a significant degree by fiscal policy. The single most important stimulating factor will be massive levels of government spending under the Democratic administration and, in particular, government deficit spending.

DEFICIT SPENDING: IF NOTHING CHANGES, NOTHING CHANGES

In keeping with the whole concept of this book, here is an actual example of how to use historical data to predict future consequences that you can use for profit. Let me outline how I analyzed the 1990 "deficit reduction" compromise.

As I watched the 1990 "deficit reduction" bill turn into a deficit accelerator, I started asking myself a few questions: How long can such huge expenditures and deficits go on? How deeply can the government mortgage our future before investors seriously begin to doubt the merit of holding U.S. government securities?

As a trader, I look at trends. Traders have a simple observation about trends: "If nothing changes, nothing changes!" In the case of the deficit, this means that until Congress and the president change fiscal policy at a fundamental level, you have to assume that the trend of deficit spending will continue. More specifically, it will continue until financial realities override the political benefits of deficit spending—until deficit spending is simply no longer feasible.

But will that happen? I'm not optimistic. Government might reduce spending, especially in light of worldwide military developments, but at best, spending will be cut only marginally; the rate of growth of the deficit may be reduced, but the deficit won't be reduced in real terms. Based on the past, the likelihood is that the increased tax revenues and cuts in spending will be overridden by even more spending in other areas. Let's take a look at the historical facts and see what we can deduce about the future.

First, some background. According to the Family Research Council, in 1950, the federal government took 2 percent of the average family's income in taxes and not only balanced the budget, but operated at a surplus of $17.2 billion (as reported by the OMB's records of National Income Accounts). Today, the average family forwards at least 24 percent of its income to the U.S. Treasury coffers, and not only is Congress not balancing the budget, but it doesn't even have the resolve to consistently *reduce the rate of growth of deficits,* as mandated by the Gramm-Rudman amendment. To put our status in perspective, the 1991 budget deficit of $269.5 billion was significantly greater than the current market value (as measured by the outstanding common stock share value on 1/1/92) of

IBM, General Motors, Mobil Oil, Coca-Cola, Johnson & Johnson, Du Pont, and Sears combined.

As to the practical issue of how we got into this predicament, the answer is virtually self-evident: The government has continued to mortgage future production by spending more than it brings in. The worst part of it is, no matter how much more revenue (taxes) the government takes in, it continues to increase spending at a rate that outstrips the rate of growth of revenues. Table 5.1 illustrates this sad and alarming trend.

These increases cannot be attributed to increased prices or cost of living. Since September 1946, the CPI has increased 6.6 times, from 20.4 to 135.9 (1982–1984 = 100). In the same 44-year period, government revenues increased 24.6 times from $43.3 billion to $1.06 trillion per year. Spending over the same period increased 39.8 times from $33.1 billion to $1.32 trillion per year.

In looking at the trend of deficit spending at the federal level, history points an ominous finger at the future. You can arrive at government budgetary estimates for the 1990s in several ways. You *could* make the mistake of believing government projections such as the estimates that the S&L crisis, which we now know will ultimately cost taxpayers over $500 billion, would cost only about $125 billion. Or, you can use the only objective reference possible—historical statistical trends. That's what I do. Unless I see strong evidence of a fundamental change in the

Table 5.1   Decade Breakdown of Federal Revenues (Tax Income), Expenditures, and Their Rates of Growth

Decade	Total Revenues (Billions)	Rate of Growth (%)	Spending (Billions)	Rate of Growth (%)	Mean[a] Deficits (% of taxes)
1950s	739.1	—	749.1	—	0.2
1960s	1,367.4	185	1,393.5	188	2.4
1970s	3,275.4	239	3,589.5	276	10.6
1980s[b]	9,060.9	277	10,823.5	302	20.5

[a]The mean is the average of deficits over the decade. The figures are expressed as a percentage of taxes, not GNP.

[b]During the 1980s, gross federal debt increased more than the sum of the added yearly deficits due to "off budget" debt increases.

Source: Office of Management and Budget Records of National Income Account Figures.

trend of government policy making, I look at the historical trend and assume that it will continue. So, consider the following historical facts.

As shown in the Table 5.1, deficits, measured as a percentage of tax revenues, have increased steadily from 0.2 percent in the decade of the 1950s to 20.5 percent in the decade of the 1980s. As of January 1, 1992, mean deficits as a percentage of taxes are 23.3 percent in the 1990s. If you look at the yearly breakdown, shown in Table 5.2, the median increase in government revenues (taxes) since 1947, is 6.7 percent per year, whereas the median increase in spending is 8.1 percent per year.

Assuming government will continue to increase spending at the 44-year median rate of 8.1 percent per year with revenues increasing at the median rate of 6.7 percent, for the five years ending in 1995, our elected representatives on Capitol Hill will have spent $9.2 trillion in the 1990s, while adding at least $1.9 trillion to the national debt.

It is hard to put this in human terms because no individual or institution other than government has the ability to deficit finance itself by fiat. If you tried to operate at a deficit over the coming decade as our government is going to do, you would be unable to borrow money and would go bankrupt. These numbers don't factor in what happens to government revenues and expenditures in recession years. If you look at Figure 5.1,

Table 5.2 Annual Federal Government Fiscal-Year-to-Fiscal-Year Percentage Changes in Revenues (Taxes), Expenditures, and Deficits

Year	Revenues	Spending	Deficits[a] < Surplus >
1947	4.2	−9.6	< 33.7 >
1948[b]	−5.1	−32.1	< 7.7 >
1949[b]	−11.9	5.8	10.9
1950	54.1	−2.6	< 29.8 >
1951	14.5	67.5	2.7
1952	5.5	8.5	5.4
1953[b]	−6.3	5.2	17.9
1954[b]	0.1	−12.5	2.9
1955	14.9	2.0	< 8.4 >
1956	6.7	7.4	< 7.9 >
1957[b]	−1.1	9.1	1.6
1958[b]	4.4	14.9	11.8
1959	8.7	−1.1	1.6
1960[b]	4.7	4.2	1.2

Table 5.2   (Continued)

Year	Revenues	Spending	Deficits[a] < Surplus >
1961	8.1	9.1	2.2
1962	6.4	8.1	3.6
1963	7.1	3.6	0.0
1964	0.4	1.0	0.1
1965	8.7	10.7	2.6
1966	14.7	16.2	4.0
1967	7.0	11.3	8.2
1968	18.9	9.7	0.0
1969	6.5	4.3	< 2.2 >
1970[b]	−3.4	9.2	10.5
1971	7.4	7.5	11.1
1972	15.3	14.5	9.9
1973	14.0	4.5	6.6
1974[b]	9.4	17.2	7.8
1975[b]	5.5	18.2	20.8
1976	11.0	6.8	16.2
1977	13.3	10.0	12.8
1978	18.3	9.4	4.3
1979	10.8	12.0	5.5
1980[b]	12.0	18.6	11.6
1981[b]	9.5	12.8	15.0
1982[b]	−1.3	13.2	32.0
1983	6.6	1.0	25.1
1984	9.9	10.0	25.2
1985	8.4	9.3	26.4
1986	6.0	2.4	22.1
1987	10.0	5.6	17.2
1988	6.1	4.7	16.0
1989	5.8	4.5	14.2
1990	4.1	9.4	43.7
1991[b]	2.2	5.7	20.9

[a]As a percentage of tax revenues.
[b]Recession years, according to the National Bureau of Economic Research.

Statistics	Revenues	Spending	Deficits
Median	7.1	8.1	6.7
Mean	7.9	8.4	15.3

Notes:
1. The median is the number that occurs in the middle of the distribution of numbers when put in high-low order.
2. The mean is the average of all the numbers.

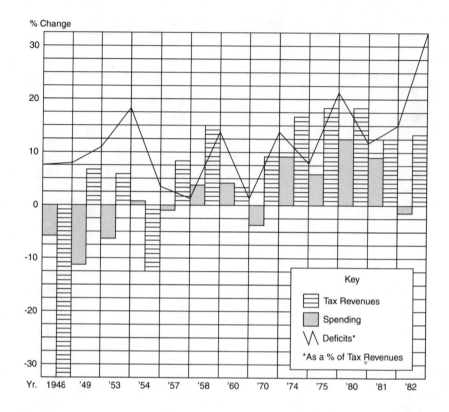

FIGURE 5.1 Government income (taxes), expenditures, and deficits in recession years.

you will note that, since 1955, during recession years, revenues drop while government spending increases when compared with the previous year.

If you look at recession periods from peak to trough, as measured by the National Bureau of Economic Research, then the mean decrease in government revenues in recession years is 7.8 percent from the previous year, while the mean increase in government spending is 17.5 percent.

Obviously, revenues decrease in recession years because taxpayers make less income and therefore pay less taxes. At the same time, government expenditures increase both because of the increased demand for government social welfare dollars (which our politicians have historically supplied) and government's Keynesian economic policy of increasing spending in an attempt to bolster economic activity.

With all these facts and more in mind, I have projected our government's budgetary future using four conservative methods:

1. *Mean Deficits.* According to the National Income Account budget numbers, in the decade of the 1980s, mean deficits expanded 5.7 times over that of the 1970s. The corresponding numbers for the 1970s and the 1960s are 12.0 and 13.8, respectively. If you assume growth of mean deficits of only 3 times in the 1990s, a very conservative number, then the average deficit in the 1990s will be $537 billion per year.

2. *Average Rates of Growth of Revenues and Spending per Decade.* If you assume that the rate of growth of revenues and spending will be the average of the decades of the 1960s, 1970s, and 1980s combined, then revenues will increase by 234 percent to $21.2 trillion and spending will increase by 255 percent to $27.6 trillion for the decade of the 1990s. This will mean average annual deficits of $640 billion per year.

3. *Median Rates of Growth of Revenues and Spending.* If you assume that revenues will grow at the 44-year median level of 6.7 percent, while spending increases at the median level of 8.1 percent, then the deficit in 1999 will be $672 billion and the average deficit for the decade will be $416 billion per year. By the way, this method of projection predicted a 1991 budget deficit of $251.6 billion and a $288 billion for 1992 (below current official estimates).

4. *Median Deficit as a Percentage of Taxes.* If you assume that government revenues increase at the median rate of 6.7 percent per year, and if you assume that deficits as a percentage of taxes stay at the median level reached in the 1980s of 20.4 percent, then the average yearly deficit for the 1990s will be $371 billion per year.

Taking the average of all four methods gives an *average annual estimated budget deficit for the 1990s of $474 billion per year.*

Are these numbers realistic? Just look at the assumptions. In each case, based on historical trends, the numbers are highly conservative. I didn't use current rates of growth, I used rates that were dampened by the relative fiscal responsibility of the 1950s and part of the 1960s. To answer in another way, if in 1979, when the entire budget was in the $500 billion range and people were worried about a $25 billion to $30 billion deficit, someone had projected a $1.32 trillion budget and a $266 billion deficit in 1991, the forecaster would have been dismissed as a quack. And yet, the statistical caveat was there, warning of the continuing trend of higher rates of both spending and deficit spending. In other words, yes, I think the average deficit projection I came up with is very realistic, unless something changes.

By another analysis, the upper limit of deficit spending might be reached as early as the year 2000, I arrived at that by analyzing another historical trend. A linear regression analysis of the ratio of government receipts to interest expenses from 1961 to 1989 is a very good fit, as shown in Table 5.3. Assuming this trend continues, then by the year 2000, the ratio will have dropped to 1.93, and will go negative in 2005. Assuming government revenues increase at the 44-year median rates of 6.7 percent, then by the year 2000, revenues will reach $1.972 trillion. Now, let's consider the structure that such a budget might have.

For fiscal 1990, budget projections (which were understated) were as shown in Table 5.3.

Assuming that Social Security, Income Security, and Medicare are "untouchables" in terms of percentage of revenues, and assuming that the percentage of receipts (1.1 trillion) to interest (134.0 billion) is 16.5%, then the fiscal year 2000 expenditures in an *unbalanced* budget would have to look like the figures in Table 5.4.

Note what has occurred in these projections. Interest on the national debt has risen to a point where 37.5 percent of the budget must be allotted to it, and 22.36 percent less of the budget is allotted to defense and other programs. In other words, if current trends continue, then by the

Table 5.3   Fiscal 1990 Budget Projections

Item	Expenditures (Billions of $)	% of Expenditures
Social security	$248.6	19.89%
Income security	148.2	11.85
Medicare	97.0	7.76
Interest	184.0	14.72
Defense	300.0	24.00
Others	272.2	21.78
Total	$1,250.0	100.00%

Note that the last two items—defense and "other" expenditures—total 45.78 percent of total expenditures.

Table 5.4   Potential Budget Structure in the Year 2000

Item	Expenditures (Billions of $)	% of Expenditures
Social security	$ 539.6	19.80%
Income security	322.9	11.85
Medicare	211.5	7.76
Interest	1021.8	37.50
Defense and others	629.2	23.09
Total	$2,725.0	100.00%

year 2000, paying the interest on our national debt will require Congress to drastically cut long-established programs, while still operating at a huge deficit. This would be a political "no-win" situation, and something would have to change.

It will probably change long before that. As I write, there is growing interest in eliminating the 30-year U.S. government bond as a means of reducing the burden of interest payments on the budget as well as upward pressure on long rates. This would force government to finance its debt with bills and notes, with at least two important consequences.

First, the interest burden would indeed drop, but not by much. Germany operates without 30-year bonds, and as of 1992, the yields on their 10-year notes were at least 1.5 basis points higher than U.S. long-term bonds. In addition, any savings gained will most likely be offset by additional spending. Congress has a tendency to spend to the limits of its purse and then some. If the legislators act typically, interest payments to government bondholders will drop, while the government spends more *real* GNP. In other words, income will drop while the government spends more, which, as discussed in Chapter 4, will tend to slow economic growth. Even worse, it will postpone the federal government's day of fiscal reckoning. Also, note that long-term interest rates for mortgages would not drop. Instead, they would be pegged to another type of long-term bond such as AAA corporate bonds.

Viewed in terms of Table 5.2, low interest rates and elimination of long-term debt allow the government to shift the ratio of receipts to interest payments back up, only to continue the downtrend once again. Lowering the rate of government interest payments on its debt merely prolongs the period of time the government can afford to borrow. And the longer the government is allowed to deficit-spend, the greater will be the burden on the productive capacity of the nation.

Second, government demand in the bill and note market will expand dramatically, depriving business of investment funds in this market, with predictable consequences. Corporations would have the opportunity to move in aggressively on the long-term market as an alternative. But all this means is that government will effectively tax corporations by forcing them to pay higher long-term interest rates than they otherwise would have. Again, slower economic growth is a consequence.

No matter how the government chooses to finance it, the overall effect of continued reckless spending will be merely to offset the expansionary effects of monetary policy (which I don't expect to remain expansionary) because it will lead to inflation and a decline in the dollar, as I'll explain in the next chapter.

CONCLUSION

Reckless spending, as I've described it, can continue to the extent that debt service is affordable, which from history points to just under 30 percent. The interest expense/tax revenue ratios of Latin American countries that hyperinflated (i.e., Mexico in 1982 with 27% and Brazil in 1984 with 29%), can serve as a guide to how long this can continue. According to Table 5.4, you will never see interest expense at 37 percent, because there must be a change before that date.

6

The History and Future of the Dollar

The history of the dollar is important because the dollar is the world's reserve currency. A position such as this bears great responsibility because it allows foreign banks to hold billions of U.S. dollars as *reserve* assets against loans in their own currencies. (Switzerland is an exception. Interestingly, the Swiss treat U.S. government bonds as they would a high-grade corporate bond.)

In the 1980s, as deficits soared, investments in the United States held up because growth and interest rates were maintained high enough to attract foreign capital. In 1989, real interest rates were high enough that almost one-fifth of total U.S. government debt was owned by foreign investors. By July 1992, however, as the Fed cut the discount rate to 3 percent, real rates fell to zero. We are now paying the price of the 1980s debt with a secular decline in the value of the dollar (see Table 6.1).

The dollar is a commodity held by five major market participants: (1) capital investors who move money into world markets to participate in the growth of that country (i.e., people who buy stocks, bonds, real estate, and other tangible assets); (2) arbitrage traders, who buy any currency they assume to be stable or appreciating, taking into account the effects of interest rates; (3) businesses that transact exports and imports on an international basis; (4) tourists who constantly buy and sell currencies to travel; and (5) central banks.

Table 6.1   History of the Federal Reserve Dollar Index

Discount Rate	Years	Dollar Index	Change (%)	CPI
6 - 4 - 4¾	1/1913–2/1919	8.26–8.76	6.1	9.9–16.2
4¾ - 7	2/1919–12/1920	8.76–24.65	181.4	19.4
7 - 4	12/1920–4/1922	24.65–16.39	−33.5	16.7
4 - 4	4/1922–7/1926	16.39–40.60	147.7	17.5
4 - 3½	7/1926–1/1927	40.60–30.19	−25.6	17.5
3½ - 6	1/1927–8/1931	30.19–30.39	0.7	15.1
6 - 1½	8/1931–12/1932	30.39–33.21	9.3	13.1
1½ - 1	12/1932–7/1936	33.21–20.16	−39.3	13.9
1 - ½	7/1936–5/1940	20.16–51.75	156.7	14.0
½ - ½	5/1940–12/1940	51.75–46.23	−10.7	14.1
½ - ½	12/1940–12/1945	46.23–47.92	3.7	18.2
½ - 1	12/1945–6/1946	47.92–71.86	50.0	21.5
1 - 1	6/1946–12/1947	71.86–71.22	−0.9	23.4
1 - 1	12/1947–2/1948	71.22–92.49	29.9	23.5
1 - 1¼	2/1948–8/1949	92.49–92.37	−0.1	23.8
1¼ - 1½	8/1949–6/1950	92.37–114.53	24.0	23.8
1½ - 3	6/1950–7/1957	114.53–109.97	−4.0	28.3
1¾ - 6	7/1957–9/1969	109.97–123.82	12.6	37.1
6 - 4½	9/1969–7/1973	123.82–92.71	−25.1	44.3
4½ - 8 - 5¼	7/1973–6/1976	92.71–107.05	15.5	56.8
5¼ - 14	6/1976–7/1980	107.05–84.65	−20.9	82.7
14 - 7½	7/1980–2/1985	84.65–158.43	87.2	106.0
7½ - 5½	2/1985–12/1987	158.43–88.70	−44.0	115.4
6 - 7	12/1987–6/1989	88.70–106.52	20.1	124.0
7 - 6	6/1989–2/1991	106.52–80.60	−24.3	134.8
6 - 5½	2/1992–7/1991	80.60–98.23	21.9	136.2
5½ - 3	7/1991–9/1992	98.23–78.43	−20.2	140.9
3 -	9/1992–	78.43–		

Column 1 lists the discount rate changes during the period listed.

Column 3 lists the Federal Reserve dollar index, which weighs the dollar against a basket of Western nation currencies.

Column 4 lists the percentage change in the dollar index during the period listed.

Column 5 shows the CPI number for the final month of the period listed (1982–1984 = 100).

If a country is going into a recession, it typically will tighten credit by raising rates and selling government securities. This in general causes the currency to go down in value, since the capital players will be selling assets and pulling money out of that country. The reverse is also true when a country goes into a recovery or expansion.

Presently, the United States has lowered rates with mixed results. Stocks and bonds have risen, but the economy has done poorly on a relative basis. There are many reasons for this, most of which I cover elsewhere in this book. What is important to understand is that the dollar can be influenced by many factors but will primarily be motivated by the capital players.

When real U.S. interest rates are lower than those in Japan, Germany, and the rest of the European Community, foreign investments in U.S. treasuries slow dramatically. Since this was the case from 1990 through 1992, the slack has been picked up by domestic investment in government debt, especially by the banks. As a result, loans to business in the domestic private sector have dropped, and the value of the dollar relative to foreign currencies has fallen.

Although this should help the export business, it is very disturbing from a fundamental standpoint because it will raise domestic prices. How long will the dollar remain a world reserve currency when its value relative to the Fed's basket of other currencies has plunged some 50.5 percent in just six years? The Deutsche mark appreciated over 150 percent in price versus the dollar between February 1985 and September 1992, and the yen 154 percent between November 1982 and April 1993.

This brings me to another example of how you must never accept what you are told by others but must prove the truth for yourself. Over and over, we hear how cheap oil is for the U.S. consumer as opposed to the cost for consumers in Germany and Japan, our strongest economic rivals. This argument is used to rationalize raising gas taxes. This is a gross distortion.

What is the truth in this case (see Figure 6.1)? Crude oil traded around $30 a barrel from 1980 to late 1985. Oil is priced in U.S. dollars, which is one reason the dollar is the world's reserve currency. In Germany and Japan, a depreciating dollar lowers the price of their most precious consumer commodity. The price of crude oil has dropped from a contract price of $32 a barrel to approximately $20 between 1982 to 1993. In the same time period, the mark has appreciated in price from a low of 28.81 to a high of 71.96, or from 3.47 marks to the dollar to 1.39 marks to the

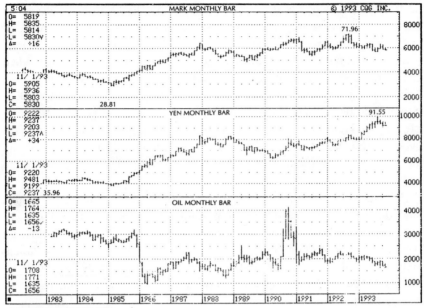

© Copyright 1993 CQG INC.

FIGURE 6.1   Comparing changing values of Deutche mark, Japanese yen, and crude oil.

dollar. This is a 60 percent increase in the purchasing power of dollar-valued commodities. For Germany, oil was about 111 marks a barrel in 1985, and was lower than 28 marks a barrel in September 1992. In other words, oil at $20 a barrel is really oil at $8 in Germany. In Japan, it's slightly lower—or $7.80 a barrel.

How long will foreign investors continue to buy U.S. government securities, the yields of which are lowered by a decline in the underlying currency's value throughout the world? How long will political pressures and agreements among the G-7 be sufficient to convince foreign central banks to hold huge balances of dollars? Keep in mind the current state of the U.S. budget deficits and the national debt. If the trend continues, something will have to give. And, what will have to give is what little strength the dollar has left. Also keep in mind that if you are an Arab prince, you have lost a great deal of potential revenue since 1986 by pricing oil in dollars. I believe that someday OPEC will price oil in proportionate monetary units, such as 25 percent gold, 25 percent U.S. dollar, 25 percent mark, and 25 percent yen. If (when) this occurs, the dollar will crash.

This problem will be exacerbated if the Fed continues to maintain nominal rates substantially below those of key foreign central banks. Capital, including domestic capital, will quite naturally flow to higher yielding, appreciating or stable-currency foreign markets, diffusing the expansion of the U.S. capital base. Interest rates substantially below the world market will give the appearance of an ample supply of U.S. capital to invest abroad, and we will end up financing expansion in Mexico, the developing European Community, and the Eastern Bloc rather than industry on our own soil.

In the "best" case, foreign central banks may embark on a credit expansion while the United States does not. This would bring the dollar back to a strong position once inflation of foreign currencies began to take hold and would give the United States a more dominant position in terms of world purchasing power. But this effect, too, would take time. All currencies depreciate in value, but at different rates (see Table 6.2).

The discussion of the business cycle in Chapter 3 makes it evident that credit expansion causes damage to the extent that resources are misallocated. The chances for misallocation grow with the complexity of the existing industrial base in the country where the credit expansion takes place. In post-World War II, for example, the United States financed the reconstruction of Europe with the Marshall Plan, which was nothing more than credit expansion on a massive scale. By the late 1940s, U.S. government debt was more than 100 percent of gross national product. And yet, the negative consequences were minimized because so much real wealth was created both at home and abroad. In effect, the United States diffused its massive capital base to the rest of the world and still managed to expand domestically.

There are both parallels and differences between now and then. On the one hand, you have countries in the Eastern Bloc loaded with resources, but without the capital required to bring them into production—very similar to the situation in Europe after World War II. But on the other hand, you don't have the huge and expanding industrial base of the United States to finance it. What is happening, as we keep American capital cheap in terms of low interest rates but high taxes and impossible regulations relative to other countries, is that American capital

Table 6.2 Currency Performance
38 Years: 1950–1988[a]

| | CPI | | 1988 Value | 38-Year Decline in Value |
	1950	1988	(1950 = 100)	Purchasing Power (%)
1. German mark	32.0	101	32	−68
2. Swiss franc	31.0	104	30	−70
3. U.S. dollar	22.0	110	20	−80
4. Canadian dollar	20.0	113	17	−83
5. Japanese yen	14.0	102	13	−87
6. French franc	10.0	109	9	−91
7. Dutch guilder	11.0	120	9	−91
8. British pound	9.5	113	8	−92
9. Australian dollar	11.0	127	8	−92
10. Italian lira	7.2	117	6	−94

20 Years: 1968–1988[a]

| | CPI | | 1988 Value | 20-Year Decline in Value |
	1968	1988	(1968 = 100)	Purchasing Power (%)
1. German mark	48.0	101	48	−52
2. Swiss franc	47.0	104	45	−55
3. Japanese yen	32.0	102	31	−69
4. Dutch gilder	36.0	120	30	−70
5. U.S. dollar	32.0	110	29	−71
6. Canadian dollar	29.0	113	25	−75
7. French franc	22.0	109	20	−80
8. British pound	17.5	113	15	−85
9. Australian dollar	16.7	127	13	−87
10. Italian lira	13.0	117	11	−89

10 Years: 1978–1988[a]

is draining into China, the underdeveloped Eastern Bloc, Latin America, and other European countries. After all, this is now a global economy where capital can move almost anywhere quickly.

As this happens, returns will flow back into the United States, but only over time. There will be a significant lag time before investments in developing countries produce surplus capital that will return to the United States for reinvestment here. Meantime, capital expansion on U.S. soil, where existing efficiencies in the market could place the capital into

Table 6.2   *(Continued)*

	CPI		1988 Value	10-Year Decline in Value
	1978	1988	(1978 = 100)	Purchasing Power (%)
1. Japanese yen	78.0	102	76	−24
2. German mark	75.0	101	74	−26
3. Swiss franc	75.0	104	72	−28
4. Dutch guilder	73.0	120	61	−39
5. U.S. dollar	60.0	110	54	−46
6. Canadian dollar	57.0	113	50	−50
7. British pound	53.0	113	47	−53
8. French franc	50.0	109	46	−54
9. Australian dollar	56.0	127	44	−56
10. Italian lira	37.0	117	32	−68

5 Years: 1983–1988[a]

	CPI		1988 Value	5-Year Decline in Value
	1983	1988	(1983 = 100)	Purchasing Power (%)
1. Dutch guilder	95.0	100	95	− 5
2. Japanese yen	95.8	101.4	94	− 6
3. German mark	95.6	101.2	94	− 6
4. Swiss franc	94.0	104	90	−10
5. U.S. dollar	93.0	110	84	−16
6. Canadian dollar	92.0	113	81	−19
7. French franc	88.0	109	80	−20
8. British pound	90.0	113	79	−21
9. Australian dollar	90.0	127	71	−29
10. Italian lira	83.0	117	71	−29

[a]From IMF rebased consumer price indexes (CPI).

Source: Daniel Poole, Chief Economist, Van Eck Funds.

productive use more quickly, will not occur as rapidly as it can elsewhere with more competitive costs (i.e., cheaper labor, fewer environmental and other regulations, and lower capital gains taxes). In short, interest rates held below the world market rate may not induce the business expansion (the main Keynesian strategy) on U.S. soil that it is designed to produce.

From every dimension, under current policy, I expect to see slow growth within the coming year and probably for several years thereafter if the Fed maintains its discipline and Congress fails to establish fiscal responsibility. The only alternative would be a massive credit expansion, which I don't see as likely under the current Fed administration.

POLITICAL TRENDS: PRESENT AND FUTURE

From 1989 to 1991, we have witnessed the so-called triumph of democracy. Totalitarian dictatorships have fallen like an elaborate domino setup. Historians will evaluate the causes, but I think the fundamental reason is economic: the Marxist impotency of nations under totalitarian rule. The rebellion occurred because regimes who preached about the evils of the "materialistic" West reduced their people to an absolutely materialistic state in which they spent virtually every hour in an attempt at subsistence survival, all the while listening to their leaders proclaim "from those according to their ability, to those according to their need." By contrast, they saw the West as miraculously prosperous and naturally wanted to be free to better themselves under free market, capitalist structures.

Yet, in the West, while the Eastern Bloc toppled, young people resigned themselves to the possibility that, for the first time in history, they would not be able to meet or exceed the standard of living of their parents. In that sense, the West, especially the United States, has been in a state of decline. The reason? Government policies that tend to raise the market price of goods and services diminish the wealth of consumers.

This trend cannot continue. Just as people finally threw out the leaders who kept them in poverty in the Eastern Bloc, Americans are going to throw out the men and women who are spending away their standard of living. Americans will rebel if government continues to tax at such high levels. In fact, they are beginning to rebel now.

Politicians are becoming aware of this, and they will act to protect themselves. The problem is, will politicians institute fundamental, long-term reform, or will they resort to credit expansion—the short-term solution—to solve their problems?

Without the influence of the banking community, led by politicians like Alan Greenspan, there is no doubt in my mind that Congress and the President would choose credit expansion. This strategy has been moving forward, and under Clinton is being escalated as the sole answer to attaining "growth." Currently, it is being done by lowering interest rates, but the real inflation will begin when the Fed expands its balance sheet by 20 percent per year versus the current 10 percent; to see this coming, always watch "adjusted Fed credit." Greenspan is by no means outspoken, but he understands and believes the premises of Austrian School economics. For proof, read his chapter on gold in Ayn Rand's book *Capitalism: The Unknown Ideal.* To allow a credit expansion and the ensuing inflation to take hold would be a fundamental moral compromise for him. I hope he has the courage to stay committed to low inflation. If he does, then we will not see high economic growth due to credit expansion in the next few years.

Clinton's policies will result in increased deficits and slow growth. We will not see any real cuts in government spending. That will come only after American taxpayers "can't take it anymore" and start throwing long-established Congressional leaders out of office. The trend (I hope) will probably be apparent by the 1994 congressional election.

What about the immediate future? I believe that the financial markets will most likely continue to act on the expectation of rapid growth, which will not come. The stock market continues to be bid up on expectations for this growth—in the form of inflation. When growth arrives, however, the Fed will eventually have to tighten since that expansion will be credit driven, not real. Then the market will mirror what happened in Japan from 1989 to 1992. During all this, business activity will slow down to a crawl. After the next major downleg, the market most likely will change its character in the coming few years, adjusting to new rules as it becomes apparent that old rules no longer apply; particularly, as it becomes apparent that low interest rates alone no longer guarantee business expansion.

In lieu of a massive credit expansion, or a greater than 20 percent increase in the Fed balance sheet (which I consider unlikely), strong forces are at work that will tend to keep real interest rates low in the foreseeable future. First, the United States is aging demographically. More and more importance will be placed on provisioning for the future, which means that originary interest will tend to be low. Thus, the real, or net, component of the gross market rate of interest will tend to be relatively low. In addition, assuming annual CPI increases are controlled in the 3- to 5-percent range, the price premium component will remain low. It is the entrepreneurial component that will vary the most with demand for capital.

The demand for capital will be high, both from government spending and the private sector. Relatively speaking, lending institutions will be in the enviable position of being able to evaluate and choose only the best alternatives. This positive factor could be significantly offset if the U.S. government continues its trend of guaranteeing loans that the free market will not, particularly in the emerging markets in China and the Eastern Bloc.

The way I see it, if any attempts at inflationary expansion are made, the bond market and dollar will crash, and that would be the beginning of a new consensus on real change. There is a critical point here that I feel very strongly about. History shows that since 1896, the average annual inflation rate under 40 years of Democratic rule was 6.8 percent. This is because the Democratic philosophy always calls for Keynesian socialism (inflation). Compare this with 56 years of Republican administrations, under which there was an average annual inflation rate of 2.5 percent. When inflation returns, and our Democratic leadership tries to sweep it under the rug as temporary, the United States will undergo chaos. Bonds and the dollar will begin to free-fall. Since the financial markets rule Washington, they will be forced to act. What will they do? Will they rescue bonds or the dollar? Which is more important? In my opinion, legislatures will invent U.S. government *Whoppers,* and bondholders will be sacrificed to save the dollar.

What's a Whopper? When New York City was going bankrupt in the early 1970s, the answer to the problem was to create a special bond called a *Big Mac.* It had special privileges over the preexisting bonds. In my view, the same idea will be applied, and I recommend they call the new bonds Whoppers since the marketing for New York City worked so well. When the Whoppers are issued, the market values of the existing bonds will immediately plummet.

Thus, today's bondholders lose out to the Whopper, but the dollar is saved. The world would crash if the dollar were officially devalued to any great extent, because of its reserve status. For verification, just look at the 1987 crash, which took place because Germany would not yield to James Baker's suggestion that the Germans' inflate. Notice that the S&P 500, Nikkei Index, and dollar all made lows in December 1987 when Germany and Japan agreed to stimulate their economies. This time, they are already stimulating.

Without inflation (stimulation), we then would see another sustained and prolonged recession, probably within a 3- to 5-year time frame. But I think the banking system, managed by relative youngsters since 1980, has been hurt too badly for the old school to prevail. This generation of bankers and other lenders are unlikely to be caught in the same con game twice; the pain is too recent, and the most powerful motivating force in the world is the desire to avoid pain (in this case, losses). The suffering will come from those who live off the government dole, and that includes many businesses. The real way out of this is to cut taxes and really reduce government spending over time (but beginning immediately).

CONCLUSION

The best case scenario for the economy in the 1990s, and therefore the dollar, stems from betting on the integrity of the Fed's administrators as well as the American people forcing fiscal responsibility on their elected officials. In the best case, we will see slow growth accompanied by restrained monetary policy (purchases of government bills and bonds by the Fed) and a political trend toward fiscal restraint, while lowering taxes. In this case, the United States will recapitalize its industrial base and take off into a period of more rapid, sustained growth toward the middle of the decade.

In the worst case, the Fed, pushed by our "leaders" in Washington will succumb to the short-term expedient of credit expansion. In this case, we will most likely see rapid but inflationary growth in the near term with higher stock market values and a marginally higher dollar, followed by a prolonged recession near the middle of the decade, with new all-time lows in the dollar.

PART TWO
TECHNICAL ANALYSIS

7

Volatility, Opportunity, and Growth of Gross National Product

In 1985, while the Dow Jones Industrials average was making all-time highs, many traders (other than stock pickers and takeover experts) were having difficulty making money. Some called it "the toughest market to trade in recent memory." I ended with only a 9.58 percent return on the year, and I wanted to understand the source of my frustration.

At the time, I was mainly day trading and taking intermediate-term (weeks to months) positions in the index futures and index options. In other words, for the most part, I was trading the averages and not specific stocks—I was a market player. My sense of the situation was that there wasn't enough volatility to create a good market player's environment.

So I started asking myself some questions: How can I characterize volatility? What is the source of volatility on the stock averages? How can I project this kind of difficult market environment and know in advance to emphasize stock selection rather than the movement of the averages?

The purpose of my inquiry was twofold. First, I knew the market was less volatile than normal, so I wanted to characterize the difference. I wanted to examine market history and see if I could somehow characterize "normal" market behavior in terms of volatility. Second, I thought the information might help me trade better in the future.

In this chapter, I will present the results of my study (originally done in 1985 and now updated), describe how I approached the problem, and relate the conclusions of the study to my expectations of the future.

TRADING OPPORTUNITY AND MARKET VOLATILITY

In developing the study, the first question to answer was: What is "normal" trading opportunity in a given calendar year? In terms of my trading strategy at the time, I considered a 2 percent move occurring within a one-month period a worthwhile opportunity. So, I went all the way back to 1897 and determined the number of months in each year where a 2 percent move occurred, with the results shown in Table 7.1. Thus, I found that the median number of such opportunities was 7 per year, while the mean, or average, was 8.7 per year. In other words, in a historically median year, the trading opportunity arises approximately every 1½ months.

Table 7.1   Trading Opportunities per Year
Dow Jones Industrials

Basis: A trading opportunity is a price movement greater than or equal to a 2 percent absolute change (positive or negative) occurring within a calendar month.

Year	Number of Opportunities	Year	Number of Opportunities
1897	11	1945	7
1898	8	1946	9
1899	11	1947	5
1900	10	1948	8
1901	7	1949	7
1902	5	1950	6
1903	7	1951	8
1904	9	1952	7
1905	10	1953	3
1906	9	1954	10
1907	8	1955	5
1908	10	1956	9
1909	8	1957	10

Table 7.1   *(Continued)*

Year	Number of Opportunities	Year	Number of Opportunities
1910	7	1958	9
1911	6	1959	7
1912	8	1960	9
1913	9	1961	8
1914	6	1962	7
1915	11	1963	7
1916	8	1964	2
1917	9	1965	6
1918	6	1966	6
1919	9	1967	8
1920	9	1968	5
1921	9	1969	8
1922	9	1970	9
1923	7	1971	8
1924	9	1972	4
1925	9	1973	9
1926	8	1974	6
1927	10	1975	9
1928	8	1976	6
1929	11	1977	5
1930	9	1978	7
1931	11	1979	7
1932	12	1980	7
1933	10	1981	6
1934	6	1982	6
1935	6	1983	5
1936	8	1984	5
1937	9	1985	5
1938	8	1986	7
1939	11	1987	10
1940	7	1988	7
1941	7	1989	7
1942	9	1990	7
1943	8	1991	7
1944	3	1992	5
		1993	5 (11/1/93)

A summary of these results shows:

Number of Opportunities/Year	Number of Years Occurred
2	1 (in 1964)
3	2
4	1
5	9
6	12
7	20
8	16
9	20
10	8
11	6
12	1 (in 1932)

Next, I looked at volatility. I computed the absolute average monthly changes for each year in the history of the Dow Jones Industrials average, as shown in Table 7.2. Then, using this as a measure of market volatility,

Table 7.2   Dow Jones Industrials Market Trading Volatility

Basis: Volatility is compared by computing the average monthly absolute percentage change (positive or negative).

Year	Total Monthly Cum. Change (%)	Avg. Monthly Change (%)	Year	Total Monthly Cum. Change (%)	Avg. Monthly Change (%)
1897	67.3	5.6	1945	38.4	3.2
1898	65.1	5.4	1946	51.2	4.3
1899	68.2	5.7	1947	23.4	2.0
1900	62.9	5.2	1948	46.9	3.9
1901	42.0	3.5	1949	30.5	2.5
1902	22.0	1.8	1950	30.9	2.6
1903	61.4	5.1	1951	37.8	3.2
1904	63.0	5.3	1952	32.8	2.7
1905	50.5	4.2	1953	23.9	2.0
1906	45.9	3.8	1954	48.9	4.1
1907	64.2	5.4	1955	26.6	2.2
1908	61.5	5.1	1956	45.0	3.8
1909	32.1	2.7	1957	35.9	3.0
1910	40.7	3.4	1958	34.0	2.8
1911	29.9	2.5	1959	29.6	2.5

Table 7.2   *(Continued)*

Year	Total Monthly Cum. Change (%)	Avg. Monthly Change (%)	Year	Total Monthly Cum. Change (%)	Avg. Monthly Change (%)
1912	34.4	2.9	1960	39.1	3.3
1913	37.8	3.2	1961	26.4	2.2
1914	25.9	3.2	1962	53.5	4.5
1915	90.7	7.6	1963	32.1	2.7
1916	48.5	4.0	1964	15.8	1.3
1917	47.1	3.9	1965	28.8	2.4
1918	32.7	2.7	1966	33.7	2.8
1919	64.3	5.4	1967	39.1	3.3
1920	67.5	5.6	1968	34.3	2.9
1921	48.5	4.0	1969	41.6	3.5
1922	38.1	3.2	1970	49.6	4.1
1923	46.1	3.8	1971	40.1	3.3
1924	50.7	4.2	1972	23.7	2.0
1925	44.9	3.7	1973	46.6	3.9
1926	38.9	3.2	1974	51.4	4.3
1927	54.1	4.5	1975	57.1	4.8
1928	60.5	5.0	1976	37.8	3.2
1929	94.3	7.6	1977	27.3	2.3
1930	77.8	6.5	1978	44.8	3.7
1931	149.0	12.4	1979	37.9	3.2
1932	159.6	13.3	1980	44.3	3.7
1933	137.9	11.5	1981	30.0	2.5
1934	47.9	4.0	1982	42.0	3.5
1935	41.3	3.4	1983	31.2	2.6
1936	40.3	3.4	1984	34.2	2.9
1937	64.7	5.4	1985	32.6	2.7
1938	91.9	7.6	1986	53.8	4.5
1939	72.6	6.0	1987	76.4	6.4
1940	44.8	3.7	1988	33.5	2.8
1941	39.3	3.3	1989	42.1	3.5
1942	37.7	3.2	1990	45.8	3.8
1943	41.1	3.4	1991	41.9	3.5
1944	20.8	1.7	1992	21.8	1.8
		Beginning of November 1993		17.4	1.7

Note: The Total Monthly Cumulative Change is computed by calculating the percentage change from the end of a month to the end of the next month (whether the change is positive or negative does not matter in this case) and adding the monthly changes from the 12-month period. Average Monthly Change is computed by dividing the Total Monthly Cumulative Change by 12. This average change is what I refer to as *volatility*.

I compared trading opportunities with market volatility, as shown in Table 7.3. Although the correlation isn't perfect, there is obviously a historical tendency for trading opportunity to be commensurate with market volatility.

The volatility effect is summarized as:

Percent Change	Number of Years Occurred	
0.0% − 2%	7	1.3% Low
2.1% − 3%	22	
3.1% − 4%	36	
4.1% − 5%	11	
5.1% − 6%	12	
6.1% +	8	13.3% High

This may seem like an exercise in proving the self-evident, but it isn't. First of all, it supplies information that may prevent overtrading in a dull market. For example, if, compared with historically typical markets, the market is dull and can see the fundamental reasons why, then trading the index and futures options becomes a sell strength/buy weakness game instead of a buy-and-let-your-profits-run strategy. Also, selling straddles instead of buying them becomes the appropriate method of trading. Second, these observations can help ground you in dull years such that you can shift your speculation and investment focus away from market trading and toward stock picking. Obviously, the most volatile markets are down years. In this case, market trading can be most profitable. Further, this path of inquiry led me to one more step, identifying the source of market volatility: the rate of change of GNP growth. Thus, if you can logically project GNP growth by some means, you should be able to anticipate market volatility with greater precision.

Table 7.3   Trading Opportunities Compared with Market Volatility

Opportunities	1–3	4–6	7–9	10–12
Volatility %	0–1.5	1.6–3.0	3.1–4.5	4.6+
Occurrences	4	21	57	14
Correlation	75%	76.2%	63.2%	71.4%

GROSS NATIONAL PRODUCT VOLATILITY VERSUS MARKET VOLATILITY

In a book published in 1969, Gordon Holmes deftly demonstrated, "The slope of a given [stock] price trend almost always precedes the correspondent or equivalent earnings trend slope in time. The amount of time displacement is about three months."[1] In other words, stock price changes proportionally discount the rate of change of earnings growth, positive or negative. Few analysts would disagree with this premise.

I had known this fact for years, but it wasn't until 1985 that I realized if, as a rule, stock price volatility is related to earnings growth volatility, then volatility in the market averages should be related to GNP volatility. So I decided to do a study to test the statistical correlation between GNP volatility and stock price volatility.

First, it was necessary to establish some method of measuring GNP volatility. As summarized in Table 7.4, I chose to characterize volatility with a four-quarter moving average of quarterly percentage changes in GNP. The algorithm was as follows:

1. Compute quarterly percentage changes in real GNP.
2. Calculate the absolute value of the quarter-to-quarter change.
3. Compute a four-quarter moving total of the computed absolute value.
4. Divide the four-quarter moving total by 4 to arrive at the four-quarter moving average of quarter-to-quarter percentage changes.

The first thing I noticed when I completed the initial study in 1985 was that it appeared to confirm my hypothesis as to why it was such a lackluster market. As measured by the average monthly change in GNP, 1985 was, at the time, the third least volatile since 1963. But as I examined the numbers further, I could establish no simple *definitive statistical relationship* between GNP volatility and stock market volatility. It did not appear that the market consistently discounted changes in the rate of change of GNP growth.

I think there are several reasons no correlation could be found. First, the Dow Industrials represents only a sector of business activity. Second, I used real GNP numbers, but the Dow discounts the effects of inflation into the averages. Third, the market puts more weight on interest rate

Table 7.4   Gross National Product Volatility

Date	GNP Change (%)	Absolute Difference (%)	4-Quarter Moving Total (%)	Average Quarterly Change (%)
6/47	+1.87			
9/47	+1.83	0.04		
12/47	+4.41	2.58		
3/48	+2.63	1.78		
6/48	+3.00	0.37	4.77	1.19
9/48	+2.72	0.28	5.01	1.25
12/48	+0.53	2.19	4.62	1.16
3/49	−2.03	2.56	5.40	1.35
6/49	−1.34	0.69	5.72	1.43
9/49	+0.74	2.08	7.52	1.88
12/49	−0.81	1.55	6.88	1.72
3/50	+4.21	5.02	9.34	2.34
6/50	+3.55	0.66	9.31	2.33
9/50	+6.39	2.84	10.07	2.52
12/50	+3.90	2.49	11.01	2.75
3/51	+4.60	0.70	6.69	1.67
6/51	+2.47	2.13	8.16	2.04
9/51	+2.04	0.43	5.75	1.44
12/51	+1.25	0.79	4.05	1.01
3/52	+0.80	0.45	3.80	0.95
6/52	+0.06	0.74	2.41	0.60
9/52	+1.67	1.61	3.59	0.90
12/52	+3.51	1.84	4.64	1.16
3/53	+1.69	1.82	6.04	1.50
6/53	+0.90	0.79	6.06	1.52
9/53	−0.27	1.17	5.62	1.41
12/53	−1.44	1.17	4.95	1.24
3/54	−0.17	1.27	4.40	1.10
6/54	−0.06	0.11	3.72	0.93
9/54	+1.21	1.27	3.82	0.96
12/54	+2.43	1.22	3.87	0.97
3/55	+3.35	0.92	3.52	0.88
6/55	+2.06	1.29	4.70	1.18
9/55	+2.17	0.11	3.54	0.89
12/55	+1.53	0.64	2.96	0.74
3/56	+0.44	1.09	3.13	0.78
6/56	+1.36	0.92	2.76	0.69
9/56	+1.22	0.14	2.79	0.70
12/56	+2.03	0.81	2.96	0.74

Table 7.4   (Continued)

Date	GNP Change (%)	Absolute Difference (%)	4-Quarter Moving Total (%)	Average Quarterly Change (%)
3/57	+1.87	0.16	2.03	0.51
6/57	+0.48	1.39	2.50	0.63
9/57	+1.61	1.13	3.49	0.87
12/57	−1.20	2.81	5.49	1.37
3/58	−1.62	0.42	5.75	1.44
6/58	+0.89	2.51	6.87	1.72
9/58	+3.00	2.11	7.85	1.96
12/58	+2.89	0.11	5.15	1.29
3/59	+2.14	0.75	5.48	1.37
6/59	+2.85	0.71	3.68	0.92
9/59	−0.33	3.18	4.75	1.19
12/59	+1.23	1.56	6.20	1.55
3/60	+2.40	1.17	6.62	1.66
6/60	−0.12	2.52	8.43	2.11
9/60	+0.34	0.46	5.71	1.43
12/60	−0.63	0.97	5.12	1.28
3/61	+0.67	1.30	5.25	1.31
6/61	+2.16	1.49	4.22	1.06
9/61	+1.73	0.43	4.19	1.05
12/61	+2.73	1.00	4.22	1.06
3/62	+2.14	0.59	3.51	0.88
6/62	+1.53	0.61	2.63	0.66
9/62	+1.10	0.43	2.63	0.66
12/62	+0.95	0.15	1.78	0.45
3/63	+1.34	0.39	1.58	0.40
6/63	+1.49	0.15	1.12	0.28
9/63	+1.88	0.39	1.08	0.27
12/63	+1.76	0.12	1.05	0.26
3/64	+2.11	0.35	1.01	0.25
6/64	+1.39	0.72	1.58	0.40
9/64	+1.39	0.00	1.19	0.30
12/64	+0.93	0.46	1.53	0.38
3/65	+3.08	2.15	3.33	0.83
6/65	+1.93	1.15	3.76	0.94
9/65	+2.16	0.23	3.99	1.00
12/65	+2.99	0.83	4.36	1.09
3/66	+2.97	0.02	2.23	0.56
6/66	+1.56	1.41	2.49	0.62
9/66	+1.41	0.15	2.41	0.60

Table 7.4   *(Continued)*

Date	GNP Change (%)	Absolute Difference (%)	4-Quarter Moving Total (%)	Average Quarterly Change (%)
12/66	+1.88	0.47	2.05	0.51
3/67	+0.75	1.13	3.16	0.79
6/67	+1.01	0.26	2.01	0.50
9/67	+2.17	1.16	3.02	0.76
12/67	+2.18	0.01	2.56	0.64
3/68	+2.17	0.01	1.44	0.36
6/68	+3.09	0.92	2.10	0.53
9/68	+2.04	1.05	1.99	0.50
12/68	+1.74	0.30	2.28	0.57
3/69	+2.32	0.58	2.85	0.71
6/69	+1.76	0.56	2.49	0.62
9/69	+1.91	0.15	1.59	0.40
12/69	+0.70	1.21	2.50	0.63
3/70	+1.04	0.34	2.26	0.57
6/70	+1.47	0.43	2.13	0.53
9/70	+1.75	0.28	2.26	0.57
12/70	+0.54	1.21	2.26	0.57
3/71	+3.99	3.45	5.37	1.34
6/71	+1.87	2.12	7.06	1.77
9/71	+1.66	0.21	6.99	1.75
12/71	+1.77	0.11	5.89	1.47
3/72	+3.31	1.54	3.98	1.00
6/72	+2.56	0.75	2.61	0.65
9/72	+2.08	0.48	2.88	0.72
12/72	+3.13	1.05	3.82	0.96
3/73	+4.05	0.92	3.20	0.80
6/76	+1.88	2.17	4.62	1.16
9/73	+2.30	0.42	4.56	1.14
12/73	+2.92	0.62	4.13	1.03
3/74	+0.80	2.12	5.33	1.33
6/74	+2.60	1.80	4.96	1.24
9/74	+1.95	0.65	5.19	1.30
12/74	+1.53	0.42	4.99	1.25
3/75	+0.41	1.12	3.99	1.00
6/75	+2.49	2.08	4.27	1.07
9/75	+4.07	1.58	5.20	1.63
12/75	+2.74	1.33	6.11	1.53
3/76	+3.10	0.36	5.35	1.34
6/76	+1.59	1.51	4.78	1.20

Table 7.4   *(Continued)*

Date	GNP Change (%)	Absolute Difference (%)	4-Quarter Moving Total (%)	Average Quarterly Change (%)
9/76	+1.79	0.20	3.40	0.85
12/76	+2.52	0.73	2.80	0.70
3/77	+3.51	0.99	3.43	0.86
6/77	+3.29	0.22	2.14	0.54
9/77	+3.13	0.16	2.10	0.53
12/77	+1.77	1.36	2.73	0.68
3/78	+2.15	0.38	2.12	0.53
6/78	+5.31	3.16	5.06	1.27
9/78	+2.94	2.37	7.27	1.82
12/78	+3.59	0.65	6.56	1.64
3/79	+2.36	1.23	7.41	1.85
6/79	+1.82	0.54	4.79	1.20
9/79	+3.23	1.41	3.83	0.96
12/79	+1.96	1.27	4.45	1.11
3/80	+2.80	0.84	4.06	1.02
6/80	+0.23	2.57	6.09	1.52
9/80	+2.34	2.11	6.79	1.70
12/80	+3.67	1.33	6.85	1.71
3/81	+5.11	1.44	7.45	1.86
6/81	+1.47	3.64	8.52	2.13
9/81	+3.13	1.66	8.07	2.02
12/81	+0.62	2.51	9.25	2.31
3/82	−0.06	0.68	8.49	2.12
6/82	+1.16	1.22	6.07	1.52
9/82	+0.62	0.54	4.95	1.24
12/82	+0.96	0.34	2.78	0.70
3/83	+2.06	1.10	3.20	0.80
6/83	+2.94	0.88	2.86	0.72
9/83	+2.45	0.49	2.81	0.70
12/83	+2.54	0.09	2.56	0.64
3/84	+3.53	0.99	2.45	0.61
6/84	+2.59	0.94	2.51	0.63
9/84	+1.37	1.22	3.24	0.81
12/84	+1.73	0.36	3.51	0.88
3/85	+1.38	0.35	2.87	0.72
6/85	+1.10	0.28	2.21	0.55
9/85	+1.63	0.53	1.52	0.38

changes, and even if interest rate changes do not affect economic activity in a major way (1991–1992, for example), the market assumes they will!

CONCLUSION

Performing these statistical studies is somewhat like panning for gold but with a much higher success rate. Sometimes you end up with a real find, and sometimes you come up empty. But even when you come up empty, you almost always learn something from it.

For example, even though I really couldn't establish a significant relationship between GNP volatility and stock market volatility, I was led on a continuing path of inquiry that culminated in a significant study that I performed later in 1985. I knew intuitively, as most traders do, that the market discounts future economic activity. But I wanted to make my case and prove it. In the next chapter, I'll present the updated results of a study that proves the stock market leads the economy.

8

The Stock Market as Economic Forecaster: The Lessons of History

---

"How is the economy?" That simple question is asked daily by investors, businesspeople, consumers, and politicians. They would like to be able to understand what is happening now, and what is likely to happen tomorrow.

The most common approach to understanding and forecasting the economy is analyzing the multitude of business indexes and other indicators that reflect recent developments. Tens of thousands of people—statisticians, economists, computer specialists—work to compile the statistics, sort them out, and decipher what they mean. Yet, despite all the resources committed to predicting the economy, there is widespread dissatisfaction with the results. With good reason: All the efforts of all those people can tell us only what *has* happened, not what *will* happen. As Irving Kristol pointed out in *The Wall Street Journal* on January 9, 1986:

> All efforts to bring greater quantitative precision to this science [economics] are an expense of talent in a waste of statistics. . . . There is not a single quantitative correlation in economics that has more than a fleeting plausibility. All economic forecasts, however, are derived from such correlations, piously entered into a computer and wedded to still other correlations. These

correlations are merely summaries of temporary trends. So it is inevitable that economic forecasting is a species of informed guesswork.[1]

Surprisingly enough, we already have available to us a forecasting tool that is both easy and remarkably accurate: the stock market itself. In this chapter, I will summarize the results of my studies of nearly 100 years of market data. I believe this study proves, without a doubt, that the stock market forecasts future business activity—that movements in the market today are echoed by similar movements in the general economy tomorrow.

TWO FORECASTING METHODS

Basically, the traditional method of economic forecasting has been to study recent data, look for a trend, and assume the trend will continue for some time. That is essentially the method used by a committee of the National Bureau of Economic Research (NBER) charged with classifying business cycles.

The NBER, a nonprofit organization founded in 1920, is devoted to objective quantitative analysis of the American economy. Among other things, it analyzes business cycles and classifies the dates of their peaks and troughs. To make this classification, a special committee of seven or eight businesspeople and economists, with infinite access to business statistics, meet to review and discuss the data. Approximately six months to a year *after* a peak or trough occurs, the committee agrees on a month when the turn occurred. This academic view is interesting to historians but is of little practical value to anyone else. Indeed it dated the March 1990–July 1991 recession after it was already over.

Another approach for forecasting economic changes—using the predictive value of the stock market itself—was originally suggested by Robert Rhea in his 1938 book *Dow Theory Applied to Business and Banking.*[2] He compared market changes (measured by Dow Industrials and Rails) with business activity (measured by Barron's Monthly Index of the Physical Volume of Industrial Production) from 1896 to 1938. In this 42-year period, Dow Theory confirmation dates showed that the market moved ahead of business with remarkable consistency. Specifically, he noted that "through ten bull markets Dow's Theory gave its bull confirmations when 80.6 percent of the advances in the Industrials were yet to occur; 72.6 percent for Rails, and 74.3 percent for Business. The Theory similarly anticipated 69.7 percent, 65.9 percent, and 79.9 percent of the respective declines of Industrials, Rails, and Business in bear periods."

In 1985, I updated his study using the Industrial Production Index.[3] For bull markets, the updated numbers were 70.1 percent for Industrials, 69.3 percent for Transports, and 74.6 percent for Business. For bear markets, the corresponding numbers were 57.9 percent, 53.3 percent, and 61.76 percent. These numbers alone should make it clear that the stock market truly has forecasting ability.

HIGHLIGHTS OF THE STUDY

I set out to determine the correlation between the changes in the stock market with the changes in the overall economy. To do so with any statistical integrity required the use of consistent and objective reference points for both elements. The two I used are the most widely accepted: For the general economy, I used the classifications of business by the National Bureau of Economic Research; for the market, I used the confirmation dates of Dow Theory.

Here is a sample of what I found:

- The stock market tops and bottoms occur several months ahead of economic recoveries and recession (the median lead time is 5.3 months).
- Bull and bear markets, determined by Dow Theory confirmation dates, occur several weeks ahead of recoveries and recessions (the median lead time is 1.1 month).
- Economic recoveries (measured by NBER) and bull markets (measured by a rigorous interpretation of Dow Theory) correspond closely: median duration of 2 years and three months (NBER) compared with 2 years and 2 months (Dow Theory). The same is true of recessions: both measures show a median duration of 1 year and 1 month.

But the most valuable finding is this: If we look at all the major movements in the economy since 1897, when Charles Dow created the averages, or for the past 95 years, and compare the actual date when the economy turned, as determined by NBER, with the date when the stock market changed, as determined by Dow Theory confirmation dates, we find that, with a few exceptions, the two dates align exactly. There is one crucial distinction: the NBER determination is made after the fact; the stock market signal comes in advance.

The benefits of being able to predict the future course of the economy are obvious: Anyone who knows that can profit by it, or perhaps get elected, which most of the time means the same thing. Businesspeople can act decisively to raise or lower inventories, expand or contract manufacturing, start or postpone business projects, dictate a spending or saving policy. Politicians, recognizing that a failing economy would make reelection difficult, could act decisively to implement government policies that would bolster the economy.

DEFINING THE TERMS

Before I demonstrate how I performed this analysis, a few definitions are in order:

Trends: There are three trends in the stock averages and in any market: the short-term trend, lasting from days to weeks; the intermediate-term trend, lasting from weeks to months; and the long-term trend, lasting from months to years. All three trends are active all the time and may be moving in opposing directions.

Bull Market: A long-term (months to years) upward price movement characterized by a series of higher intermediate (weeks to months) highs interrupted by a series of higher intermediate lows.

Bear Market: A long-term downtrend characterized by lower intermediate lows interrupted by lower intermediate highs.

Primary Swing: An intermediate (weeks to months) price movement moving in the same direction as the long-term movement. For example, an intermediate uptrend in a bull market is called a bull market primary upswing.

Secondary Reaction (Correction): An important intermediate-term price movement moving in the contrary direction to the long-term (bull or bear) market, usually retracing between 33 and 67 percent of the previous primary price movement. Corrections are frequently erroneously assumed to represent a change in the long-term trend, especially when either one or the other of the averages breaks above or below previous intermediate highs or lows in bear or bull markets, respectively. Dow Theory, however, requires that both averages break previous highs or lows to confirm a primary change of trend. There is only one example in history when a false confirmation signal was given (December 1991), which came before the 1 percent cut in the discount rate.

Dow Theory Confirmation Date: The date on which the second of the Dow Industrials or Transportation averages breaks below a previous intermediate low in a bull market, or a previous intermediate high in a bear market. This confirms, by definition, that a bear or bull market has begun, respectively.

A NEAR CENTURY OF DATA

Using these definitions and almost one hundred years' worth of market data, I performed a statistical study of the market's forecasting value by evaluating several relationships. The results are depicted in a series of tables.

First, the data: Table 8.1 is a summary of business peaks and troughs, using NBER classifications of business cycles. Unfortunately, because of the nature of the classification process, the numbers are reported only to the nearest month. For interpolation purposes, I assumed the exact peak or trough occurred in the middle of the month.

Tables 8.2 (bull markets) and 8.3 (bear markets) are summaries of market cycles as measured by Dow Theory. To fully understand the numbers shown in Table 8.2, it is necessary to understand that in Dow Theory, a "top" or "bottom" occurs on the date when *both* the Industrials and Transportation averages have made a high that fails to carry forward. One average may make its high before the other, but the market doesn't "top" until the second average fails to make its high creating a divergence. Then when both move above or below their previous important (intermediate) high or low points together you have a confirmation.

Table 8.1   Summary of NBER Classifications of Business Cycle Peaks and Troughs, 1897 to 1991

Trough		Peak		Duration (Months)	
Month	Year	Month	Year	Recession	Recovery
December	1854	June	1857		29
December	1858	October	1860	18	22
June	1861	April	1865	8	46
December	1867	June	1869	32	18
December	1870	October	1873	17	34
March	1879	March	1882	63	36
May	1885	March	1887	38	22
April	1888	July	1890	13	26
May	1891	January	1893	10	19
June	1894	December	1895	17	18
June	1897	June	1899	18	24
December	1900	September	1902	18	21
August	1904	May	1907	23	23
June	1908	January	1910	13	19
January	1912	January	1913	24	12
December	1914	August	1918	23	44
March	1919	January	1920	7	10
July	1921	May	1923	18	22
July	1924	October	1926	14	27
November	1927	August	1929	13	21
March	1933	May	1937	43	50
June	1938	February	1945	13	80
October	1945	November	1948	20	37
October	1949	July	1953	11	45
May	1954	August	1957	10	39
April	1958	April	1960	8	24
February	1961	December	1969	10	106
November	1970	November	1973	11	36
March	1975	January	1980	16	58
July	1980	July	1981	6	12
November	1982	July	1990	16	92

For example, in Dow Theory terms, let us examine the bull market that began on 6/15/84 with the Industrial's low of 1086.30. The Transports had already bottomed at 457.82 on 5/29/84. From there, in the second longest bull market in history, the Dow appreciated to a top of 2791.41 on 10/9/89, while the Transports topped at 1532.01 on 9/5/89. In other words, the previous bear market "bottomed" on 6/15/84, and the bull market "topped" on 10/9/89.

The ensuing bear market began on 10/9/89 and lasted until the Industrials and the Transports both made important bear market lows (Dow: 2365.10 on 10/11/90; Transports: 821.93 on 10/17/90). In the interim, however, the Industrials broke their previous high of 2791.41, climbing to 2999.75 on 7/16/90. But because the Transports did not confirm with a corresponding new high (a divergence) to break the previous high of 1220.84, Dow Theory did not classify the rise in the Industrials as a bull market primary swing, but rather as a secondary correction in a bear market. Table 8.4 illustrates how market movements are classified and should help clarify the method.

To be clear about bull and bear tops and bottoms, it is important to note that it is not at all unusual for one average to precede the other in reaching a top or a bottom. In terms of the Dow Industrials and Transports, of the 26 bottoms and 25 tops in history:

- The second average topped within 1 month of the first average 27 times.
- The second average topped between 1 and 2 months after the first average 15 times.
- The second average topped between 2 and 3 months after the first one 8 times.
- The second average topped after 3 months only 1 time.

My first analytical step was to compare the two sets of dates: market tops and bottoms to NBER recoveries and recessions. The purpose of the comparison was to look for correlations between the timing of changes and also the extent, or duration. I also looked at the relationship between Dow Theory confirmation dates and NBER peaks and troughs; in particular, I was interested in measuring the lead time provided by Dow Theory.

The results of this analysis are shown in Tables 8.5 and 8.6. Specifically, Table 8.6 shows how far in advance in market signals a change in

Table 8.2   Bull Market Classifications since 1896

		Dow Industrials				
No.	Start	End	Bottom[a]	Top	% Gain	Calendar Days
1	8/10/96	4/04/99	29.64	76.04	156.5	967
2	6/23/00	9/19/02	53.68	67.77	26.2	818
3	11/09/03	1/19/06	42.15	103.00	144.4	802
4	11/15/07	11/19/09	53.00	100.53	89.7	735
5	7/26/10	9/30/12	73.62	94.13	27.9	797
6	12/24/14	11/21/16	53.17	110.15	107.2	698
7	12/19/17	11/03/19	65.95	119.62	81.4	684
8	8/24/21	10/14/22	63.90	103.42	61.9	416
9	7/31/23	9/03/29	86.91	381.17	338.6	2226
10	7/08/32	3/10/37	41.22	194.40	371.6	1706
11	3/31/38	11/12/38	98.95	158.41	60.1	226
12	4/08/39	9/12/39	121.44	155.92	28.4	157
13	4/28/42	5/29/46	92.92	212.50	128.7	1492
14	5/17/47	6/15/48	163.21	193.16	18.4	395
15	6/13/49	1/05/53	161.60	293.79	81.8	1302
16	9/14/53	4/06/56	255.49	521.05	103.9	935
17	10/22/57	8/03/59	419.79	678.10	61.5	650
18	10/25/60	12/31/61	566.05	734.91	29.8	432
19	6/26/62	2/09/66	535.76	995.15	85.7	1324
20	10/07/66	12/03/68	744.32	985.21	32.4	788
21	5/26/70	5/26/72	631.16	971.25	53.9	731
22	10/04/74	9/21/76	584.56	1014.79	73.6	718
23	2/28/78	4/27/81	742.12	1024.05	38.0	1154
24	8/12/82	11/29/83	776.92	1287.20	65.7	477
25	6/15/84	10/09/89	1086.90	2791.41	156.8	1955
26	10/11/90		2365.10			

[a]All quoted prices are daily closes on the day of the high or low.
[b]Average % gain is the average gain of the Industrials and Transportation averages.

Dow Transports (Rails)						Avg. % Gain[b]	Avg. % Gain Low-High Order
Start	End	Bottom	Top	% Gain	Days		
8/10/96	4/03/99	39.04	87.04	123.0	966	139.8	22.9
6/23/00	9/09/02	72.99	129.36	77.2	808	51.7	27.0
9/28/03	1/22/06	88.80	138.36	55.8	847	100.1	38.1
11/21/07	8/14/09	81.41	134.46	65.2	632	77.5	38.6
7/26/10	10/05/12	105.59	124.35	17.8	802	22.9	42.0
12/24/14	10/04/16	87.40	112.28	28.5	650	67.8	49.0
12/19/17	10/06/19	70.75	82.48	16.6	656	49.0	51.7
6/20/21	9/11/22	65.52	93.99	43.5	448	52.7	52.7
8/04/23	9/03/29	76.78	189.11	146.3	2222	242.5	67.8
7/08/32	3/17/37	13.23	64.46	387.2	1713	379.4	70.4
3/31/38	1/04/39	19.00	34.33	80.7	279	70.4	71.5
4/08/39	9/27/39	24.14	35.90	48.7	172	38.6	77.5
6/02/42	6/13/46	23.31	68.31	193.1	1472	160.9	78.6
5/19/47	7/14/48	41.16	64.95	57.8	422	38.1	81.3
6/13/49	12/22/52	41.03	112.53	174.3	1288	128.1	87.7
9/14/53	5/09/56	90.56	181.23	100.1	968	102.0	95.1
12/24/57	7/08/59	95.67	173.56	881.4	561	71.5	100.1
9/29/60	10/11/61	123.37	152.92	24.0	377	27.0	102.0
6/25/62	12/15/66	115.89	271.72	134.5	1331	110.1	110.1
10/07/66	12/02/68	184.34	279.48	51.6	787	42.0	128.1
7/07/70	4/07/72	116.69	275.71	136.3	640	95.1	139.8
10/03/74	7/14/76	125.93	231.27	83.6	650	78.6	160.9
3/09/78	4/16/81	199.31	447.38	124.5	1134	81.3	242.5
8/12/82	11/22/83	292.12	612.57	109.7	467	87.7	245.7
5/29/84	9/05/89	457.82	1532.01	334.6	1891	245.7	379.4
10/17/90			821.93				

Table 8.3   Bear Market Classifications since 1896

		Dow Industrials				
No.	Start	End	Bottom	Top	% Decline	Calendar Days
1	4/04/99	6/23/00	76.04	53.68	29.4	445
2	9/19/02	11/09/03	67.77	42.15	37.8	416
3	1/19/06	11/15/07	103.00	53.00	48.5	665
4	11/19/09	7/26/10	100.53	73.62	26.8	249
5	9/30/12	12/24/14	94.13	53.17	43.5	815
6	11/21/16	12/19/17	110.15	65.95	40.1	393
7	11/03/19	8/24/21	119.62	63.90	46.6	660
8	10/14/22	7/31/23	103.42	86.91	16.0	290
9	9/03/29	7/08/32	381.17	41.22	89.2	1039
10	3/10/37	3/31/38	194.40	98.95	49.1	386
11	11/12/38	4/08/39	158.41	121.44	23.3	147
12	9/12/39	4/28/42	155.92	92.92	40.4	959
13	5/29/46	5/17/47	212.50	163.21	23.2	353
14	6/15/48	6/13/49	193.16	161.60	16.3	363
15	1/05/53	9/14/53	293.79	255.49	13.0	252
16	4/06/56	10/22/57	521.05	419.79	19.4	564
17	8/03/59	10/25/60	678.10	566.05	16.5	449
18	12/31/61	6/26/62	734.91	535.76	27.1	195
19	2/09/66	10/07/66	995.15	744.32	25.2	240
20	12/03/68	5/26/70	985.21	631.16	35.9	539
21	5/26/72	10/04/74	971.25	584.56	39.8	861
22	9/21/76	2/28/78	1014.79	742.12	26.9	525
23	4/27/81	8/12/82	1024.05	776.92	24.1	472
24	11/29/83	6/15/84	1287.20	1086.90	15.6	238
25	10/09/89	10/11/90	2791.41	2365.10	15.3	367

Dow Transports (Rails)							Avg. % Decline
				%		Avg. %	Low-High
Start	End	Bottom	Top	Decline	Days	Decline	Order
4/03/99	6/23/00	87.04	72.99	16.1	446	16.1	16.3
9/09/02	9/28/03	129.36	88.80	31.4	384	31.4	17.2
1/22/06	11/21/07	138.36	81.41	41.2	668	41.2	20.4
8/14/09	7/26/10	134.46	105.59	21.5	346	21.4	20.5
10/05/12	12/24/14	124.35	87.40	29.7	810	29.7	22.7
10/04/16	12/19/17	112.28	70.75	37.0	441	37.0	22.8
10/06/19	6/20/21	82.48	65.52	20.6	623	20.6	24.1
9/11/22	8/04/23	93.99	76.78	18.3	327	18.3	25.7
9/03/29	7/08/32	189.11	13.23	93.0	1039	93.0	26.5
3/17/37	3/31/38	64.46	19.00	70.5	379	70.5	26.6
1/04/39	4/08/39	34.33	24.14	29.7	94	29.7	28.7
9/27/39	6/02/42	35.90	23.31	35.1	979	35.1	29.4
6/13/46	5/19/47	68.31	41.16	39.7	340	39.7	30.8
7/14/48	6/13/49	64.95	41.03	36.8	334	36.8	31.4
12/22/52	9/14/53	112.53	90.56	19.5	266	19.5	33.3
5/09/56	12/24/57	181.23	95.67	47.2	594	47.2	33.6
7/08/59	9/29/60	173.56	123.37	28.9	449	28.9	34.6
10/11/61	6/25/62	152.92	115.89	24.2	257	24.2	36.6
12/15/66	10/07/66	271.72	184.34	32.2	234	32.2	37.8
12/02/68	7/07/70	279.48	116.69	58.2	582	58.2	38.6
4/07/72	10/03/74	275.71	125.93	54.3	909	54.3	44.9
7/14/76	3/09/78	231.27	99.31	13.8	603	13.8	47.1
4/16/81	8/12/82	447.38	292.12	34.7	483	34.7	47.1
11/22/83	5/29/84	612.57	457.82	25.3	189	25.3	59.8
9/05/89	10/17/90	1532.01	821.93	46.3	407	46.3	91.1

Table 8.4   Price Movement Classifications[a]

Market No./Type	Date	Dow Price	Date	Trans. Price
25 Bear				
Advance	10/09/89	2791.41	09/05/89	1532.01
Decline	11/06/89	2582.17	11/07/89	1188.30
Advance	01/02/90	2810.15	12/05/89	1220.84
Confirmation	01/25/90	2561.04	01/04/90	1187.77
Decline	01/30/90	2543.24	01/30/90	1031.83
Advance	07/16/90	2999.75	06/06/90	1212.77
Decline	10/11/90	2365.10	10/17/90	821.93
26 Bull				
Decline	10/11/90	2365.10	10/17/90	821.93
Advance	12/26/90	2637.13	12/21/90	923.91
Decline	01/09/91	2543.24	01/07/90	894.30
Confirmation	01/18/91	2646.78	01/17/91	979.55

[a] Example of classification of intermediate moves.

the general economy, in two different measures: market tops and bottoms, and Dow Theory confirmation dates. What this table shows is that, in comparable cases, the market is always ahead; noncomparable cases are discussed later in this chapter.

The next step was to begin to measure the forecasting ability of market movements in concrete terms. I went back in history and determined how much business activity could have been captured by someone making buy/sell decisions according to Dow Theory confirmation dates. I used the same Barron's Index that Robert Rhea used up until 1938, and thereafter used the Industrial Production Index. Table 8.7 shows the hypothetical results of buying the index on bull market confirmation dates and selling on bear market confirmation dates: Without any human intervention, acting on those dates captured 61.8 percent of gains and 40.5 percent of declines.

Then, having determined with certainty that the stock market is an excellent business forecaster, I decided to look at investment potential. The results are summarized in Table 8.8. It may surprise you to know that any money manager in the world could build a computer model that would virtually guarantee a 14 percent annual return over the long term, based solely on buying and selling on the basis of Dow Theory confirmation dates.

EXCEPTIONS AND ANOMALIES

Since the beginning of the Dow Industrials Average in 1896, there have been 13 cases where market changes did not correlate directly to recessions and recoveries in the general economy. In each case, the disparities are easily explained by such unexpected developments as world wars and governmental intervention in the markets. These discrepancies are summarized in Tables 8.9 and 8.10.

A review of the historical data in these tables shows that, since 1896, the NBER has classified 21 complete business cycles while Dow Theory has classified 26 complete stock market cycles. More specifically, the NBER classified 4 recessions that were not accompanied by an associated bear market in stocks; there have been 8 bear markets classified by Dow Theory not associated with an NBER-classified recession; and there has been 1 bull market in stocks not associated with an NBER-classified recovery. Let me explain the reasons for each of these in turn. I'll discuss the 4 cases of NBER recessions first.

The first NBER recession not coupled to a bear market in stocks occurred from August 1918 to March 1919. As you probably realize, this was the post-World War I period. Robert Rhea discussed accompanying stock market developments as follows:

> A bear market developed in stocks late in 1916, anticipating the abrupt decline in business that was to occur in 1917, but before the latter year ended the averages turned up again in anticipation of the final industrial expansion that preceded the armistice.
>
> With the ending of the World War and the resulting immediate cancellation of orders for war materials, business collapsed. In this instance the decline in business occurred prior to the peak of stock prices, which was not reached until 1919, and in 1921 the low point in business preceded the end of the bear market in stocks.[4]

War always throws the markets out of whack, especially the discounting aspect of market behavior. By their nature, wars bring uncertainty

Table 8.5   Lead Times for Peaks, Troughs, and Confirmation Dates

Market Bottoms and Tops		Dow Theory Confirmation Dates	
Bottom	Top	Bottom	Top
8/10/96	4/04/99	6/28/97	12/16/99
6/23/00	9/19/02	10/20/00	06/01/03
11/09/03	1/22/06	7/12/04	04/26/06
11/21/07	11/19/09	4/24/08	05/03/10
7/26/10	10/05/12	10/10/10	01/14/13
12/24/14	11/21/16	4/09/15	08/28/17
12/19/17	11/03/19	5/13/18	02/03/20
8/24/21	10/14/22	2/06/22	06/20/23
8/04/23		12/07/23	
	9/03/29		10/23/29
7/08/32	3/17/37	5/24/33	09/07/37
3/31/38	01/04/39	6/23/38	03/31/39
4/08/39	09/27/39	7/17/39	05/13/40
6/02/42	06/13/26	9/24/42	08/27/46
5/19/47	07/14/48	5/14/48	11/09/48
6/13/49	01/05/53	9/29/49	04/02/53
9/14/53	05/09/56	1/19/54	10/01/56
12/24/57	8/03/59	5/02/58	03/03/60
10/25/60	12/31/61	12/28/60	04/26/62
6/26/62	2/09/66	11/09/62	05/05/66
10/07/66	12/03/68	01/11/67	02/25/69
7/07/70	5/26/72	08/24/70	05/14/73
10/04/74	9/21/76	01/27/75	10/24/77
3/09/78	4/27/81	04/14/78	07/02/81
8/12/82	11/29/83	10/07/82	01/25/84
6/15/84	10/09/89	08/01/84	10/15/87
10/17/90			

NBER Bottoms and Tops		Lead Times			
		Bottoms	Tops	Confirmation Dates	
Bottoms	Tops	Bottoms	Tops	Bottoms	Tops
6/97	6/99	9.2	2.4	−0.4	−6.0
12/00	9/02	5.7	−0.1	1.9	−8.5
8/04	5/07	9.2	15.5	1.1	12.6
6/08	1/10	6.8	1.9	1.7	−3.6
1/12	1/13	17.6	3.3	15.2	0.0
12/14	8/18	−0.3	20.8	3.8	−0.4
3/19	1/20	15.1[a]	2.4	10.1[a]	−0.6
7/21	5/23	−1.3	7.0	−6.7	−1.2
7/24	10/26	10.3	N/A	7.3	N/A
11/27	8/29	N/A	−1.6	N/A	−2.3
3/33	5/37	8.2	1.9	−2.3	−3.7
6/38		2.5	N/A	−0.3	N/A
		N/A	N/A	N/A	N/A
	2/45	N/A	−15.8[a]	N/A	−30.4[a]
11/45	11/48	−21.1[a]	4.1	−19.0[a]	0.2
11/49	7/53	5.1	6.7	1.5	3.4
5/54	8/57	8.0	15.2	3.9	10.4
4/58	4/60	3.3	8.4	−0.6	1.4
		3.6	N/A	1.6	N/A
		N/A	N/A	N/A	N/A
2/61	12/69	N/A	12.4	N/A	9.6
11/70	11/73	4.3	17.6	2.6	6.0
3/75	1/80	5.3	38.8[a]	1.6	25.7[a]
7/80	7/81	28.2[a]	3.6	27.0[a]	0.4
11/82		3.1	N/A	1.3	N/A
		N/A	N/A	N/A	N/A
	7/90	N/A	N/A	N/A	N/A

[a]These cases are not comparable due to extraordinary events explained in the text.

Table 8.6   Market Lead Times over the Business Cycle

Lead Times of Stock Market Tops and Bottoms over Comparable NBER Business Cycle Highs and Lows (Months)		Lead Times of Dow Theory Confirmation Dates over Comparable NBER Business Cycle Trend Changes (Months)	
Chronological Order	High/Low Order	Chronological Order	High/Low Order
9.2	17.6	−0.4	15.2
2.4	17.6	−6.0	12.6
5.7	15.8	1.9	10.4
−0.1	15.5	−8.5	9.6
9.2	15.2	1.1	7.3
15.5	12.4	12.6	6.0
6.8	10.3	1.7	3.9
1.9	9.2	−3.6	3.4
17.6	9.2	15.2	2.6
3.3	8.4	0.0	1.9
−0.3	8.2	−3.8	1.7
2.4	8.0	−0.4	1.6
−1.3	7.0	−0.6	1.6
7.0	6.8	−6.7	1.5
10.3	6.7	−1.2	1.4
−1.6	5.7	7.3	1.3
8.2	5.3 ˝ Median	−2.3	1.1 ˝ Median
1.9	5.1	−2.3	0.4
2.5	4.3	−3.7	0.2
15.8	4.1	−0.3	0.0
4.1	3.6	0.2	−0.3
5.1	3.6	1.5	−0.4
6.7	3.3	3.4	−0.4
8.0	3.3	3.9	−0.6
15.2	3.1	10.4	−0.6
3.3	2.5	−0.6	−1.2
8.4	2.4	1.4	−2.3
3.6	2.4	1.6	−2.3
12.4	1.9	9.6	−3.6
4.3	1.9	2.6	−3.7
17.6	−0.1	6.0	−3.8
5.3	−0.3	1.6	−6.0
3.6	−1.3	0.4	−6.7
3.1	−1.6	1.3	−8.5

into the market. Not only does government spending on armaments and war supplies dislocate capital from private uses, creating a short-term boom for some industries, but the duration of the government's purchases is never known. Moreover, it is virtually impossible to predict when a major war will end. It's not over 'til it's over, so to speak. So it is impossible for the market to discount coming events with accuracy.

The second NBER recession not accompanied by a bear market was, in fact, anticipated by the market. According to the NBER, there was a recession lasting from October 1926 until November 1927. During this period, the Barron's business index dropped 9.5 percent. In Dow Theory terms, although there was not confirmed bear market associated with this recession, but there were two market corrections during this period, the first from February to March in 1926, and the second from August through October. The second correction brought stock prices down an average of 9.7 percent. It is arguable that these corrections were a portent of the business recession to come, which was relatively minor in nature. In addition, this was in the midst of a period of rampant stock speculation with massive public involvement, in which banks made loans on the basis of stock equity (on paper) to finance further purchases of stocks, thus dampening the discounting effect of the stock market. Thereby, Dow Theory deemed the sell-off a correction and the NBER called it a recession.

The third recession occurred from February 1945 to October 1945 as the economy adjusted to more peacelike endeavors at the end of World War II. I believe that one of the reasons the stock market does not discount forthcoming recessions after victorious wars is that the market is confident that a recapitalization of industry for peacetime activities is imminent. In spite of the inevitability of postwar recession, investors buy and hold stocks, confident that things will finally return to normal. This is analogous to the psychology of market participants at bear market bottoms, when the market seems immune to any further bad news. Perhaps, after a war, investors are so used to calamity that a recession seems dim by comparison.

There are other reasons wars cause distortions in stock market activity. Here is a typical scenario. When war breaks out, the stock market usually enters a bear market for fear of the unknown consequences of the war. Foreign holders of American equity usually lead the way by selling stocks to finance the war effort or to raise cash as a panic hedge. Soon thereafter, however, investors realize that a boom due to war-related

Table 8.7 Percentage of Business Captured by Buying and Selling Business Index on Dow Theory Confirmation Dates

	Gains and Declines between Business Index Peaks and Troughs				Gains and Declines between Dow Theory Confirmation Dates		
Date	High/Low	Gain	Decline	Confirm. Date	Price	Gain	Decline
10/96 low[a]	77.0[a]			BI 6/28/97	83.0		
10/99 high	104.0	27.0		Br 12/16/99	103.0	20.0	
11/00 low	88.0		16.0	BI 10/20/00	90.0		13.0
7/03 high	106.2	18.2		Br 6/01/03	105.5	15.5	
7/04 low	91.4		14.8	BI 7/12/04	91.4		14.0
5/07 high	112.9	21.5		Br 4/26/06	103.4	11.6	
3/08 low	81.0		31.9	BI 4/24/08	83.3		20.4
3/10 high	107.8	26.8		Br 5/03/10	100.9	17.6	
10/10 low	97.2		10.6	BI 10/10/10	97.2		3.7
1/13 high	106.0	8.8		Br 1/14/13	106.0	8.8	
11/14 low	82.1		23.9	BI 4/09/15	89.5		16.5
5/17 high	124.9	42.8		Br 8/28/17	118.6	29.1	
				BI 5/13/18	120.1		-1.5
				Br 2/03/20	109.9	-10.2	
3/21 low[b]	6.2[b]		49.9	BI 2/06/22	7.49		22.2
5/23 high	10.3	4.1		Br 6/20/23	10.13	2.64	
8/24 low	8.3		2.0	BI 12/07/23	9.65		0.48
7/29 high	13.0	4.7		Br 10/23/29	12.08	2.43	
3/33 low	6.2		6.8	BI 5/24/33	8.65		3.43
4/37 high	13.7	7.5		Br 9/07/37	13.41	4.76	
5/38 low	9.2		4.5	BI 6/23/38	9.76		3.65
				Br 3/31/39	11.70	1.94	
				BI 7/17/39	12.01		-0.31
				Br 5/13/40	13.69	7.66	
8/44 high	27.4	18.2		BI 9/24/42	21.40		-7.73

	[a]						
2/46 low	17.7			Br 8/27/46	21.00	−0.40	
7/48 high	24.6	6.9	9.7	Bl 5/14/48	23.48	−0.23	−2.48
10/49 low	21.6		3.0	Br 11/19/48	23.25		1.04
				Bl 9/29/49	22.21	9.80	
7/53 high	32.4	10.8	3.1	Br 4/02/53	32.01		2.34
4/54 low	29.3			Bl 1/19/54	29.67	5.93	
3/57 high	36.3	7.0		Br 10/01/56	35.60		4.18
4/58 low	31.4		4.9	Bl 5/02/58	31.42	7.71	
1/60 high	39.6	8.2		Br 3/03/60	39.13		0.20
12/60 low	36.2			Bl 12/28/60	38.93	2.37	
			3.4	Br 4/26/62	41.30		−0.76
				Bl 11/09/62	42.06	13.54	
10/69 high	64.1	27.9		Br 5/05/66	55.60		−2.40
10/70 low	59.6		4.5	Bl 11/1/67	58.00	4.96	
11/73 high	75.2	15.6		Br 2/25/69	62.96		1.34
5/75 low	64.5		10.7	Bl 8/24/70	61.62	11.56	
3/80 high	86.2	21.7		Br 5/14/73	73.18		6.65
				Bl 1/27/75	66.53	12.87	
7/80 low	81.2		5.0	Br 10/24/77	79.40		−1.53
7/81 high	87.1	5.9		Bl 4/14/78	80.93		
12/82 low	79.3		7.8	Br 7/02/81	80.13	−0.80	
				Bl 10/07/82	80.23		−0.10
				Br 1/25/84	90.65	10.42	
				Bl 8/01/84	93.90		−3.25
9/90 high	110.6	31.3		Br 1/25/90	102.20	8.30	
4/91 low	105.1		5.5	Bl 1/10/91	106.90		−4.70
Totals	320.2		218.0	Totals	197.86		88.35

[a]Barron's Business Index.
[b]Industrial Production Index (1987 = 100).
Percentage of advances captured—61.8%.
Percentage of declines captured—40.5%.

Points gained buying and holding—127.21.
Points gained buying and selling with Dow Theory—286.21.
Dow Theory percentage improvement—125.0%.

Table 8.8 Percentage of Stock Market Advances and Declines Captured by Buying and Selling Business Index on Dow Theory Confirmation Dates

	Gains and Declines between Dow Industrials Peaks and Troughs					Gains and Declines between Dow Theory Confirmation Dates			
Date	High/Low	Gain	Decline	Confirm. Date	Price	Gain	% Return	Decline	% Return
8/10/96	29.64			BI 6/28/97	44.61				
4/04/99	76.04	46.4		Br 12/16/99	63.84	19.23	43.11		
6/23/00	53.68		22.36	BI 10/20/00	59.44			4.40	6.89
9/19/02	67.77	14.09		Br 6/01/03	59.59	00.15	0.25		
11/09/03	42.15		25.62	BI 7/12/04	51.37			8.22	13.79
1/19/06	103.00	60.85		Br 4/26/06	92.44	41.07	79.94		
11/15/07	53.00		50.00	Br 4/24/08	70.01			22.43	24.26
11/19/09	100.53	47.53		Br 5/03/10	84.72	14.17	20.23		
7/26/10	73.62		26.91	BI 10/10/10	81.91			2.81	3.32
9/30/12	94.13	20.51		Br 1/14/13	84.96	3.05	3.72		
12/24/14	53.17		40.96	BI 4/09/15	65.02			19.94	23.47
11/21/16	110.15	56.98		Br 8/28/17	86.12	21.10	32.45		
12/19/17	65.95		44.20	BI 5/13/18	82.16			3.96	4.60
11/03/19	119.62	53.67		Br 2/03/20	99.96	17.80	21.66		
8/24/21	63.90		55.72	BI 2/06/22	83.70			16.26	16.27
10/14/22	103.42	39.52		Br 6/20/23	90.81	7.11	8.49		
7/31/23	86.91		16.51	BI 12/07/23	93.80			-2.99	-3.29
9/03/29	381.47	294.56		Br 10/23/29	305.85	212.05	226.07		
7/08/32	41.22		340.25	BI 5/24/33	84.29			221.56	72.44
3/10/27	194.60	153.38		Br 9/07/37	164.39	80.10	95.03		
3/31/38	98.95		95.75	BI 6/23/38	127.40			36.99	22.50
11/12/38	158.41	59.46		Br 3/31/39	131.84	4.44	3.49		
4/08/39	121.44		36.97	BI 7/17/39	142.58			-10.74	-8.15
9/12/39	155.92	34.48		Br 5/13/40	137.63	-4.95	-3.47		
4/28/42	92.92		63.00	BI 9/24/42	109.11			28.52	20.72
5/29/46	212.50	119.58		Br 8/27/46	191.04	81.93	75.09		

Dow Theory buy/hold turning points (left section):

Date	DJIA	Advance	Decline
5/17/47	163.21		49.29
6/15/48	193.16	29.95	31.56
6/13/49	161.60	132.19	38.30
1/05/53	293.79		
9/14/53	255.49	265.56	101.26
4/06/56	521.05	258.31	112.05
10/22/57	419.79		
8/03/59	678.10	168.86	199.15
10/25/60	566.05		
12/31/61	734.91	459.39	250.83
6/26/62	535.76		
2/09/66	995.15	240.89	354.05
10/07/66	744.32		
12/03/68	985.21	340.09	386.69
5/26/70	631.16		
5/26/72	971.25	430.23	272.67
10/04/74	584.56		
9/21/76	1014.79	281.93	247.13
2/28/78	742.12		
4/27/81	1024.05	510.28	200.30
8/12/82	776.92		
11/29/83	1287.20	1704.51	426.31
6/15/84	1086.90		
10/09/89	2791.41		
??/??/91	2365.10		
Totals		**5823.20**	**3487.84**

Dow Theory signals (right section):

Signal	DJIA				
BI 5/14/48	188.60				
Br 11/19/48	173.94	−14.66	−7.77	2.44	1.28
BI 9/29/49	182.43				
Br 4/02/53	280.03	97.60	53.50	−8.49	−4.88
BI 1/19/54	228.27				
Br 10/01/56	468.70	240.43	105.32	51.76	18.48
BI 5/02/58	459.56				
Br 3/03/60	612.05	152.99	33.29	9.14	1.95
BI 12/28/60	615.75				
Br 4/26/62	678.68	62.93	10.22	−3.70	−0.60
BI 11/09/62	616.13				
Br. 5/05/66	899.77	283.64	46.04	62.55	9.22
BI 11/1/67	822.49				
Br 2/25/69	899.80	77.31	9.40	77.28	9.40
BI 8/24/70	759.58				
Br 5/14/73	909.69	150.11	19.76	140.22	18.46
BI 1/27/75	692.66				
Br 10/24/77	802.32	109.66	15.83	217.03	23.86
BI 4/14/78	795.13				
Br 7/02/81	959.19	164.06	20.63	7.19	0.90
BI 10/07/82	965.97				
Br 1/25/84	1231.89	265.92	27.53	−6.78	−0.71
BI 8/01/84	1134.61				
Br 10/15/87	2355.09	1220.48	107.57	97.28	7.90
BI 3/??/88	?????				
Br 1/25/90	2561.04	???	???	???	???
BI 1/10/91	??????				
Totals		**3307.72**	**1047.38**	**997.28**	**282.08**

Percentage of advances captured—56.08%.
Percentage of declines captured—28.59%.
Points gained buying and holding—????
Points gained buying and selling with Dow Theory—4305.00.
Dow Theory percentage improvement—????

Dow Theory average annual return—14.22%.
Dow Theory average annual compounded ROR—11.30%.
Period—93.51 years.

Table 8.9   NBER Recessions Not Associated with Dow Theory Bear Market

NBER Recession		
Dates	% Downturn in Business Index	Explanation of Differences
8/18–3/19	25.9	World War I related. Market performance distorted by massive government spending.	Major associated news: 6/28/14–12/14 War begins. Stock Market closed from July until December 1914. 9/16 Basic income tax raised to 2%; highest surtax raised to 13%. 4/17 U.S. enters war. 12/17 Government takes control of railroads. Excess profits tax enacted. 1/19 Postwar inflationary boom begins.
10/26–11/27	9.5	Dow Theory correctly anticipates a business downturn, but market averages enter a prolonged correction as opposed to an official bear market.
2/45–10/45	29.1	World War II related. Major associated news: 4/12/45 FDR dies; Truman becomes president. 5/6/45 Germany surrenders. 8/6/45 Atom bomb dropped on Hiroshima. 8/14/45 Japan surrenders. 12/31/45 World War II excess profits tax enacted.
1/80–7/80	5.8	President Carter institutes credit controls. Dow Theory correctly anticipates business drop but with two corrections instead of a bear market (from October to November in 1979, and from February to March in 1980).

Table 8.10 Dow Theory Bear and Bull Markets Not Associated with NBER Recession or Recovery

Dow Theory Bull or Bear Markets Not Associated with NBER CYCLE (Numbers refer to Tables 8.2 and 8.3)	Probable Reasons for Discrepancies
Bear Market 6 10/16–12/17	Market anticipates negative consequences of 1916 income tax increase, but economic indicators watched by NBER are stimulated by WWI spending.
Bear Market 11 11/38–4/39	Market sells off due to fear and uncertainty when Germany annexes Czechoslovakia. Shortest bear market in history.
Bull Market 12 4/39–9/39	Market recovers in anticipation of stabilization in Europe. Shortest bull market on record ends with outbreak of World War II.
Bear Market 12 9/39–4/42	Bear market begins when Germany invades Poland in September 1939. Market is uncertain and fearful. FDR declares national emergency as England and France declare war on Germany. Uncertainty continues as Germany blitzes French border on 5/19/40 and takes Dunkirk. Japan attacks Pearl Harbor on 12/7/41 and United States declares war on following day. In September 1941, FDR signs the biggest tax bill in American history. Market bottoms in April 1942 when Bataan surrenders.
Bear Market 13 5/46–5/47	Fed tightens credit due to postwar inflation.
Bear Market 18 12/61–6/62	First U.S. troops arrive in Vietnam on 12/11/61. Fed starts tightening credit. U.S. Steel announces price increases on 4/11/62, and President Kennedy confronts them publicly.
Bear Market 19 2/66–10/66	Fed tightens credit and market responds, anticipating a recession. But before the recession begins, Fed reverses its tight policy and loosens again.
Bear Market 22 9/76–2/78	Bear market begins in response to new tax laws passed in September 1976. Jimmy Carter elected in November. In December, market sells off dramatically as OPEC announces two-tier price increases. Anticipated recession doesn't occur because Fed policy monetizes oil price increases.

Note: Prior to 1949, most discrepancies between Dow theory and NBER classifications were war related. Since then, most bear markets not associated with NBER recession were caused by government intervention in the markets, especially the Fed's fine-tuning policies, which effectively cheated the market of its ability to forecast future business activity. Dow Theory responds more rapidly to changes in Fed policy because of the 6- to 12-month time lag between changes in policy and measurable economic consequences.

activity will drive up earnings, and a new bull market ensues. When the war ends, all war-related economic activity virtually comes to a halt. But because most wars are financed through credit expansion (inflation), and because government emergency programs are still in place to guarantee further inflation, a monetary boom continues. Thus, speculative ventures such as stock investments continue to rise while indexes of business activity fall off.

The fourth recession occurred from January 1980 to July 1980 in response to Jimmy Carter's imposition of credit controls to stop inflation. During this period, the Industrial Production Index dropped 5.8 percent. Once again, the market anticipated the drop with two corrections: one lasting from October to November in 1979, and the other lasting from February to March in 1980. In the latter correction, stock prices dropped an average of 19.7 percent.

On the flip side of the coin, there are eight cases in which bear markets anticipated a recession that didn't occur, and one case in which a bull market anticipated a recovery that did not occur. In virtually every case, these events were not caused by the market's failure to correctly anticipate business trends, but rather by war-related events or by sudden or unexpected changes in government monetary and fiscal policy that were impossible to anticipate.

The first case was the bear market of October 1916 to December 1917. In addition to the fears and uncertainties associated with the war, the market reacted negatively when in September 1916 the income tax was raised to 2 percent with the highest surtax being raised to 12 percent. Although this negatively affected stocks, business thrived due to government expenditures on the war effort.

The second case was the shortest bear market on record, from November 1938 until April 1939. Again this was war-related. Hitler was in power in Germany, and threatening neighboring borders. When Neville Chamberlain came back with his compromise, perhaps the market knew best that Germany was to invade Czechoslovakia in March of 1939.

This is perhaps the best place to discuss the only bonafide case of a bull market that did not correctly anticipate a forthcoming recovery. When Neville Chamberlain came back from Germany with his compromise, effectively handing over the Sudetenland to Hitler, the world seemed to return to stability for a while. The result was the shortest bull market on record, lasting from April 1939 to September 1939. But for obvious reasons, the hopeful atmosphere was short-lived.

The third case was a longer bear market, from September 1939 until April 1942. This was, again, a period of war-related uncertainty. During this period, not only did Hitler annex Czechoslovakia, but Franklin Roosevelt declared a national emergency, France and Britain declared war on Europe, and the world was introduced to a new form of fighting—the blitzkrieg. The market did not recover until the U.S. war effort was well underway and the bulk of the uncertainty preceding U.S. involvement had ended.

Not surprisingly, there was a period of inflation after World War II. In response, the Fed, just beginning to get a feel for Keynesian-oriented "fine tuning," tightened credit to fight inflation. This started the education of the market to the power of the fed. The result was a bear market in stocks lasting from July 1946 to July 1947. But while credit was being contracted, business had not yet slackened. The slowdown would not come until November 1948. In addition, one could easily argue that the market did, in fact, forecast the coming recession—it was just a little early.

After this point, most distortions of market forecasting were due to non-war-related government intervention in the form of monetary or fiscal policy changes. The first to occur was the bear market lasting from December 1961 to June 1962. This bear market was most likely precipitated when the first troops were sent to Vietnam in December of 1961, but other factors were involved as well. The Fed began tightening credit, in 1961 in a minor way but there was also an atmosphere, under Kennedy, to "get the fat cats." When U.S. Steel announced price increases in April 1962, Kennedy intervened, launching a public campaign against them. This set off the era of new antitrust legislation that probably is the single biggest reason U.S. Steel declined to a second-rate global steel manufacturer. After the mini-crash the Fed changed its mind and *eased* and no recession occurred.

The stock market entered another bear market in February 1966 that lasted until October 1966. It was responding to the Fed's tightening of credit and was projecting a recession. In this case, I have little doubt that a recession was forthcoming, *but before it took hold, the Fed changed its mind and loosened again.* The Fed did not permit a recession, and instead opted for future inflation. The inevitable result was the 1969–1970 recession.

The next incidence occurred in the bear market that lasted from September 1976 to February 1978. This one is both extraordinary and a perfect example of government mismanagement of the economy. The initial stimulus of the stock market sell-off was the passage of new tax laws in September designed to offset government's growing deficit problem. Then, Jimmy Carter was elected, and the real trouble began. OPEC announced two-tier oil price increases and sent the market into a tumble. In response, Carter asked for austerity measures and windfall profits taxes directed at the oil companies, and became an advocate of oil price controls. The Fed, in turn, turned on the spigots and monetized rising oil prices with a massive credit expansion that would eventually lead to near-runaway inflation. It was the Fed's lax policy that stopped the economy from going into recession, or, more accurately, stalled the recession until 1981–1982.

The next bear market, lasting from November 1983 to June 1984, was directly related to Fed activity. In anticipation of Fed tightening, most major market indexes topped in June 1983. The Fed tightened in May 1983, and the markets entered a bear market in earnest, fully expecting a recession. Then, on July 24, 1984, Volcker announced in a public hearing before the Senate that the Fed's current policy was "inappropriate." Most major indexes bottomed that day, having had no expectation of a change in Fed policy and another change of mind.

CONCLUSION

Nearly 100 years of market data show us unequivocally that the stock market is an accurate predictor of business trends. The weight of historical evidence is undeniable: The stock market highs and lows consistently mirror ups and downs in the general economy, *in advance.* If we look at the market in general, we get a lead time of nearly six months. If we take the more conservative approach and use Dow Theory confirmation dates as the reference point, we still have a lead time of more than one month.

In summary, the stock market led business 91.2 percent of the comparable cases, and assuming a one-month lag as coincident, it accurately led 97.1 percent of the time. Using confirmation dates, Dow Theory confirmed a change of trend while business was still in an uptrend in 64.7 percent of the samples and within two months of the peak in 82.4 percent of the samples. Most important of all, since 1949, the market (as measured by Dow Theory) has led or coincided with turns in the economy 100 percent of the time.

The only factor that can diminish the accuracy of this forecasting tool is the unexpected actions of people in power. This may take the form of war, or a *sudden change* in monetary and fiscal policy. But in each case, the only force strong enough to shake the power of the market as forecaster is misapplied political power. But even at that, the market sees the fed tightening and sells off until the fed changes its mind. It is a whimsical decision process based on politics. If the fed continues its policy the economy will go into recession, if it stops quickly the economy starts up again. The market merely follows the fed in tandem or anticipates the Feds future policy changes.

9
The Technical Basis of Risk-Reward Analysis

"Risk" and "reward" are two of the most commonly used words on Wall Street, and yet, they are probably the most ill-defined terms in the business. They represent concepts that few ever bother to spend time refining because "everyone knows what they mean." Risk is generally associated with losing money, and reward is generally associated with making money. While these associations are accurate, they don't provide nearly enough information to use as the basis for risk-reward analysis. Just as an atomic physicist would be lost without a detailed understanding of the nature of atoms, so a market professional will flounder without a well-defined concept of risk and reward.

Suppose, for example, that you are trying to manage a long portfolio of stocks. As a starting point, the first question is not which stocks to own, but whether and to what extent to be long. To answer this question, you must not only have a grasp of the direction of the broader market trend (up or down), but you must also have some indication of the *likelihood that the current trend will continue.* Furthermore, if it does continue, you need some indication, some measure, of *how much the market is likely to move in its current direction before reversing.* Restated, you must know the potential risk, and the potential reward, of being long.

Obviously, words such as "likelihood" and "potential" mean you are dealing in odds rather than in absolute terms. Nevertheless, if you can objectively and consistently define the odds of success versus the odds of failure—if you can determine the ratio of probabilities of the market going up X percent versus going down Y percent within a given time period, you have established a concrete context within which to make intelligent investment decisions. Within that context, you can then refine your portfolio decisions by applying both technical and fundamental analysis to determine the risk-reward of individual stock selections.

Up to this point, we have examined fundamental concepts to promote understanding the market in broad, conceptual terms. Although invaluable for establishing an analytical framework, conceptual analysis does little to help you determine risk and reward. If you can establish a way to quantify risk and reward, then it is possible not only to apply numbers to risk-reward analysis, but also to define entry and exit points that are independent of your thinking process. In other words, you can establish inviolable rules that stop you from rationalizing yourself into losses.

Defining concrete entry and exit points is not an arbitrary process. First, you must understand the fundamental condition of the economy. Next, you must understand the current condition of the market within the context of the economy. Then, using statistical and technical methods derived from Dow Theory, you can characterize market movements and establish an objective frame of reference for risk-reward analysis. That is what I will discuss in this chapter.

A TOOL FOR MEASURING RISK AND REWARD

In 1974, I was trading individual stocks and stock options on a short-term to intermediate-term basis. I was doing well, but I missed the October lows, losing thousands of dollars of income potential. In analyzing why I had missed so much of the move, I started asking myself some questions: What exactly is a trend? How high or low does it usually go? How long does it usually last?

At that point in my career, I had read about Dow Theory and was applying some Dow principles to trading, but I had not yet systematized my knowledge. After refreshing my knowledge by rereading everything I could find by William Peter Hamilton and Robert Rhea, I realized that Rhea's definition of the three types of trends could be used to develop a method of characterizing market movements:

Dow's Three Movements: There are three movements of the averages, all of which may be in progress at one and the same time. The first, and most important, is the primary trend: the broad upward or downward movements known as bull or bear markets, which may be of several years' duration. The second, and most deceptive movement, is the secondary reaction: an important decline in a primary bull market or a rally in a primary bear market. These reactions usually last from three weeks to as many months. The third, and usually unimportant, movement is the daily fluctuation.[1]

Using these definitions as a basis, Rhea applied other Dow Theory principles to go back in history and classify each bull market, bear market, bull market primary swing, bull market correction, bear market primary swing, and bear market corrections, both for the Dow Industrials and Rails (Transportations). His classifications included both the *extent* of each move—the percentage increase or decrease from the previous important intermediate high or low—and the *duration*—the number of calendar days from peak to trough. Basically, his analysis ended there. He didn't bother to classify "the daily fluctuation" because he considered it to be of minor importance, nor did he apply the statistical data he developed to market analysis except in broad, conceptual terms.

In reviewing Rhea's work, it struck me that if I went back in history and updated his work, I might have a very useful tool for technical market analysis. So, adding some of my own refinements to the classification process, I went back and classified every market movement in history. After completing the study, which took some time, I then compiled the numbers in both numerical and chronological order to look for any significant relationships. When I looked at the results, I was truly astounded.

What I found was concrete evidence that market movements have statistically significant frequency distributions, in terms of both extent and duration. In other words, market movements have a life expectancy, just like people. In a flash of insight, I realized that if insurance companies could make money by setting premium rates according to statistical life expectancy profiles, I should be able to judge the odds of success in any given market trade according to market extent and duration frequency profiles.

There is, of course, one major difference between the kinds of numbers insurance companies use and the numbers I derived. Insurance companies make money by having a large number of customers and betting, as morbid as it sounds, that the vast majority of them will die within the statistically normal range. When you "bet" on a market movement, however, it is tantamount to insuring one person. Therefore, before setting your "premium" on the market, so to speak, you must carefully consider the market's overall "health" using macrofundamental analysis, technical analysis, and so forth.

What market life-expectancy profiles tell you is the essential age of the market. For example, at this writing (February 1992), stocks are in a bull market primary swing—an intermediate-term (weeks-to-months) uptrend in a bull market. Instead of using just the Dow Industrials and Transports, as Rhea did, I characterize market movements by averaging 18 major indexes. Currently, these indexes have appreciated an average of 18.6 percent over an average period of 74.4 days. In terms of the life expectancy distributions, 53.5 percent of all bull market primary swings have been greater in extent, and 67.3 percent have lasted longer. Stated another way, the market is approaching median levels both in terms of extent and duration. From a statistical standpoint alone, there is on average a 40 percent chance that the market's "life" will end imminently. Therefore, if you used this as your sole criterion, you should be long no more than 60 percent of portfolio maximums in stocks.

Although this is not enough information on which to base such a cut-and-dried decision, it is enough to establish a concrete frame of reference within which to analyze the risk of market involvement. Returning to the life insurance analogy, being long right now, the market is roughly equivalent to the prospect of writing an insurance policy on a man in his early 60s. Naturally, before writing a policy and setting a premium rate, you would want to take a close look at the health of a man in that age bracket. Similarly, you would want to examine the nature of the current market movement carefully before establishing if or to what degree you should be long.

You can also use the statistics to examine the risk inherent in individual market segments in more detail. For example, although the current market has appreciated the average extent over the average duration stated earlier, the OTC market has skewed the average toward the upside, making it look "older." If you view the current move in the OTC industrials separately, for example, you would find it has appreciated 41.7 percent over a period of 215 days. Only 14.2 percent of all similar moves in history have been greater in extent, and only 26.5 percent have lasted longer. If you are trading in the OTC industrials, therefore, you're not dealing with a man in his early 60s, but a man in his 80s. Close examination of other current factors lead to the conclusion that not only are the OTCs an old man, but one who needs major surgery. Consequently, I am short selected OTC stocks, awaiting a correction in that market.

On the other hand, if you filter out the OTC stocks, the likelihood that the rest of the market will continue its uptrend is increased. The Dow Industrials, for example, have currently appreciated 14.4 percent over a period of 60 days. In terms of history, 69.9 percent of all similar moves on the Dow have been greater in extent, and 77 percent have lasted longer. This indicates that in terms of age alone, there is a moderately low risk that the uptrend in the Dow will die imminently. In fact, as I write, the Dow is making new highs while the NASDAQ Industrials are selling off.

This measure of risk is far and away the most heavily weighted technical tool that I use. It is the underlying factor that has enabled me to limit my risk, minimize my losses, and maximize profits. It provides me an objective framework to help me concretely measure risk and reward, guiding me toward prudent weighting of my stock and index portfolios. In the context of the current market, for example, I am short OTC stocks and long the deep cyclicals, largely because the statistics guided me to the best overall risk-reward approach in both arenas.

With this in mind, let me explain in more detail how the life expectancy distributions are derived and implemented.

MARKET LIFE-EXPECTANCY PROFILES

As anyone can tell by looking at a year-to-year chart of the Dow Industrials, one way to make money is simply to take a traditional buy-and-hold approach. Many investors and portfolio managers take this approach, while attempting to further enhance returns through careful stock selection. Without a doubt, considered from a long-term perspective, this is an effective investment strategy. But money managers who consistently produce superior returns focus less on the long-term trend, and more on the intermediate-term trend. In a bull market, for example, they attempt to be 100 percent long in the early portion of a bull market intermediate uptrend, reduce exposure prior to a secondary correction, go short or remain on the sidelines during the correction, and go fully long once again near the correction bottom.

One of the greatest strengths of market life-expectancy distributions is the degree to which they enhance the trader's ability to move in and out of the market with changes in the intermediate-term trend. Consider bull market secondary corrections as a case in point.

First, a reminder on definitions. A *correction* (also known as a secondary reaction) is an important intermediate-term price movement moving in the direction opposite to the major long-term trend; "intermediate term" means lasting weeks to months. In my classification system, 95 percent of all corrections are longer than 14 calendar days in duration, and 98 percent have a minimum extent of 20 percent of the previous primary move. A common term for that is *retracement*. Percentage retracement means that, for example, if you have a 500-point bull market intermediate swing on the Dow, and if in the ensuing correction the Dow sells off 300 points, then there has been a 60 percent retracement of the intermediate move. During corrections, it is more useful to think in terms of retracement than in absolute percentage changes because it keeps you in perspective of what is happening in the market, as you will see shortly.

Table 9.1 summarizes the extent and duration of all bull market secondary corrections in the history of the Dow Industrial and Transportation averages since 1896. Note that tabulations are ranked in numerical order, and you can easily see that the distributions take on a "bell-curve" shape, as depicted in Figure 9.1.

A close examination of the data in Figure 9.1 shows that the "life expectancy" profiles of the two averages display normal bell curve distribution. Further study shows that the distributions of the S&P 500 or any other major average correlate with similar consistency. In other words, market moves do indeed have a tendency to fall within a statistically predictable life span.

Making use of this idea is a simple matter of arithmetic—of calculating your odds at any given point. With respect to the Dow Industrials and Transportations, for example, life expectancy data show that 68 percent of all bull market secondary corrections retrace between 25 percent and 75 percent of the previous primary upswing, over a corresponding period between 16 and 79 days. Only 22.7 percent of all bull market corrections in history have retraced more than 75 percent, and only 17 percent have lasted more than 100 days. So, if the market is in correction

Table 9.1 Extent and Duration of Bull Market Secondary Corrections, Dow Jones Industrial and Transportation Averages, 1896 to February 1991

Extent (%)				Duration (Calendar Days)			
Industrials	Transports	Industrials	Transports	Industrials	Transports	Industrials	Transports
1. 16.5	18.0	45. 46.0	50.1	1. 7	9	45. 45	49
2. 17.8	18.4	46. 48.9	51.7	2. 9	11	46. 45	51
3. 20.7	21.1	47. 49.6	53.0	3. 10	13	47. 47	52
4. 21.1	23.7	48. 49.8	53.2	4. 11	13	48. 49	55
5. 23.2	24.8	49. 52.4	53.8	5. 14	13	49. 49	55
6. 23.4	25.0	50. 52.6	54.3	6. 14	14	50. 51	57
7. 23.7	25.0	51. 54.0	55.5	7. 14	14	51. 51	59
8. 23.7	25.1	52. 54.8	55.8	8. 15	15	52. 53	59
9. 24.2	25.5	53. 56.0	57.9	9. 17	16	53. 54	61
10. 24.4	26.7	54. 56.2	58.0	10. 18	16	54. 55	61
11. 25.2	27.6	55. 57.3	59.6	11. 19	18	55. 55	61
12. 25.4	28.8	56. 60.0	60.3	12. 19	19	56. 55	62
13. 25.7	29.2	57. 60.8	60.8	13. 20	20	57. 56	63
14. 27.0	29.5	58. 61.1	61.8	14. 21	21	58. 57	64
15. 27.8	30.2	59. 62.8	62.7	15. 21	22	59. 58	65
16. 30.5	32.0	60. 64.9	64.0	16. 21	22	60. 59	68
17. 31.2	33.4	61. 65.3	66.4	17. 21	22	61. 60	69
18. 31.3	34.4	62. 66.2	67.7	18. 23	23	62. 61	69
19. 31.9	34.6	63. 66.7	67.7	19. 24	24	63. 61	70
20. 32.1	34.6	64. 68.8	68.7	20. 24	24	64. 62	70
21. 33.7	35.3	65. 71.9	68.9	21. 25	25	65. 63	73
22. 36.0	37.1	66. 72.2	72.0	22. 25	27	66. 66	75
23. 36.7	37.4	67. 72.2	73.4	23. 26	27	67. 66	77
24. 37.0	37.8	68. 74.1	76.8	24. 26	28	68. 67	81
25. 37.1	39.3	69. 74.6	77.1	25. 26	29	69. 72	82
26. 37.2	40.2	70. 74.9	78.3	26. 29	29	70. 77	85
27. 38.2	40.6	71. 76.9	83.8	27. 29	30	71. 78	96
28. 38.7	40.6	72. 78.0	84.6	28. 30	30	72. 89	98
29. 39.3	41.1	73. 79.7	84.9	29. 31	30	73. 95	103
30. 39.3	41.3	74. 80.4	87.2	30. 31	32	74. 98	106
31. 39.6	41.8	75. 82.7	88.3	31. 32	32	75. 102	112
32. 40.3	43.3	76. 83.5	90.3	32. 33	34	76. 104	113
33. 40.3	44.1	77. 89.0	90.9	33. 33	35	77. 108	114
34. 40.3	44.3	78. 89.7	92.7	34. 35	37	78. 111	119
35. 40.9	45.5	79. 89.8	93.2	35. 36	39	79. 113	126
36. 41.6	46.0	80. 91.3	94.0	36. 37	39	80. 117	129
37. 41.6	47.2	81. 100.7	103.2	37. 38	39	81. 139	140
38. 42.1	47.3	82. 107.7	110.7	38. 41	40	82. 161	144
39. 42.8	47.6	83. 113.7	112.4	39. 42	41	83. 173	175
40. 44.2	48.8	84. 116.9	122.0	40. 43	44	84. 178	201
41. 45.4	49.2	85. 120.1	128.4	41. 44	46	85. 190	214
42. 45.5	49.4	86. 135.0	163.8	42. 44	47	86. 196	216
43. 45.8	49.6	87. 194.2	173.4	43. 45	48	87. 201	245
44. 46.0	49.7	88. 246.0	227.9	44. 45	49	88. 209	613

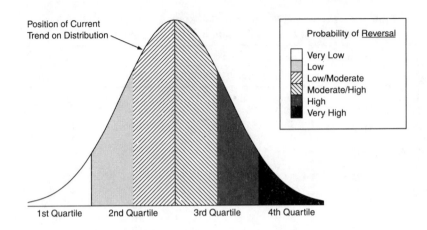

FIGURE 9.1 Composite frequency distribution for extent and duration in bull market secondary corrections.

and has retraced, on average, 75 percent of the previous primary upswing over an average period of 74 days, the historical odds of making money by going long at that point are 4.4 to 1 in your favor. Conversely, the historical odds of making additional money by being short in that context are 4.4 to 1 against you, providing, that it is a secondary downtrend and not the beginning of a bear market.

At every bull market top, there is always confusion among market analysts as to whether it is actually a top or just a correction. While there is no absolute way of knowing until either a bear market confirms or the correction ends, historical profiles of long-term trends can help you determine the probability of one or the other being the case.

Table 9.2 shows the extent and duration profiles for bull markets on the Dow Industrials and Transportation averages. Assume that a bull market in progress is 3 years old and has appreciated 115 percent from the previous bear market bottom. Now suppose that the market confirms in a secondary correction that has retraced 60 percent of the previous primary upswing over an average period of 58 days. Fundamentals aside, you can determine the odds that the market will continue in its downtrend based on the life expectancy profiles see Tables 9.1 and 9.2.

The formula is rather simple: merely compute the percentage of moves that ended before they reached the current extent, do the same for the

Table 9.2 Bull Market Average Extent and Duration Profiles, Dow Jones Industrial and Transportation Averages

Duration (Low-High Order)			Extent (Low-High Order)	
Period	Days	Years	Period	Percent
1939	164	0.45	1910–1912	22.9
1938	253	0.69	1960–1961	27.0
1960–1961	405	1.11	1947–1948	38.1
1947–1948	409	1.12	1939	38.6
1921–1922	452	1.24	1966–1968	42.0
1978–1981	472	1.29	1917–1919	49.0
1957–1959	606	1.66	1900–1902	51.7
1917–1919	670	1.84	1921–1922	52.7
1914–1916	674	1.85	1914–1916	67.8
1907–1909	684	1.87	1938–1939	70.4
1974–1976	684	1.87	1957–1959	71.5
1970–1972	686	1.88	1907–1909	77.5
1966–1968	787	2.16	1974–1976	78.6
1910–1912	799	2.19	1978–1981	81.3
1900–1902	813	2.23	1982–1983	87.7
1903–1906	844	2.31	1970–1972	95.1
1953–1956	952	2.61	1903–1906	100.1
1996–1999	967	2.65	1953–1956	102.0
1978–1981	1144	3.13	1962–1966	110.1
1949–1953	1295	3.55	1949–1952	128.1
1962–1966	1328	3.64	1996–1999	139.8
1942–1946	1482	4.06	1942–1946	160.9
1932–1937	1710	4.68	1923–1929	242.5
1984–1989	1923	5.26	1984–1989	245.7
1923–1929	2224	6.09	1932–1937	379.4

duration, average the two, and restate that average as a set of odds. In the preceding example, you would compute it the following way:

Probability that secondary correction will continue in:

$$\text{Extent} = (88 - 55)/88 = .37$$
$$\text{Duration} = (88 - 54)/88 = .38$$

or all samples minus number in sample divided by 88.

$$\text{Average} = .38$$

Odds: 1.63 to 1 against continuing correction

Probability that bull market has ended (and bear market has begun):

Extent   = 19/26 = .73
Duration = 20/26 = .78
Average = .76
Odds: 3.17 to 1 that a bear market has begun

This information actually provides you with a solid basis to pursue further risk-reward analysis of the market. For example, if the economy is strong, inflation low, interest rates low to moderate, and other fundamentals point overwhelmingly to a growing economy, then you would place the most emphasis on the odds against the correction continuing. If you were playing the short side, you might want to take some profits and scale down the size of remaining short positions, if not eliminate them.

If, on the other hand, the Fed was tightening credit and the economy was showing preliminary symptoms of recession, then you would want to weight the odds of a bear market more heavily. In that case, the next step would be to consider the intermediate downtrend not in terms of a secondary correction, but in terms of a primary downswing in a bear market. In this context, you would find that the probability of a continuing downtrend was much greater, and you would want to keep your short positions until the movement "aged" in the historical context of bear market primary downswings.

But what about cases where the statistics are indefinite? What about a case such as that illustrated in Figure 9.1 where the average extent and duration place the current correction at about the 40 percent point on the distribution? In such a case, the odds are slightly in favor of the current downtrend continuing—about 1.5 to 1 to be more precise. That's when the most emphasis should be placed on picking market segments and specific stocks that show strength (or weakness) relative to the market as a whole. We'll talk more about that in Chapter 10.

FOCUSING ON RISK

Perhaps the greatest single benefit of using statistical profiles is the focus they bring to risk-reward analysis. More specifically, they foster an attentive and objective focus on *risk*. When you picture an intermediate market movement traveling up along a bell-curve distribution of extent and duration, you are forced to realize that with each incremental shift on the distribution, the risk of losing money is increasing. When it reaches the mid-point, or median, of the distribution, you are placing a 50-50 bet based on history—the equivalent of a coin toss. Beyond that point, you are playing against the historical odds.

This perspective reinforces several important trading principles. First and foremost is to place as many odds in your favor as possible. Early in a bull market primary swing, for example, the odds heavily favor playing the broad market with as much leverage as possible; that is, with carefully selected options and futures. As the market matures toward middle age, more emphasis needs to be placed on economic considerations driving individual market segments and specific stocks. When the market ages beyond median levels, it's time to start thinking about diversifying stock portfolios into lower risk instruments or keeping a portion in cash, scaling down the size of positions as the market gets older and older.

This may sound like simple common sense, but evidently many people have difficulty following such a plan. Typically, at bull market tops, for example, the whole world is long, but there is a lot of "scared money" in stocks. Consequently, the market is ripe for a panic sell-off with news that would in other circumstances result in only a minor sell-off. Yet, each and every time there has been a panic sell-off, the historical profiles have acted as a caveat. The sell-off in 1929, for example, occurred after the longest bull market in history and after an unprecedented 11 primary upswings, or bull markets legs. Furthermore, the primary swing that preceded the October 29, 1929, panic had appreciated 29.9 percent over a period of 99 days, placing it well beyond median levels of the extent and duration distributions (yes, they would have worked then, too).

Similarly, preceding Black Monday (October 19, 1987), the market was in its seventh leg and had appreciated 26.9 percent over 96 days. Again, the bull market was aging and the primary upswing was well beyond median levels. On that basis alone, caution was warranted. In October 1989, the market was in its thirteenth leg and was the second largest and longest bull market in history. The primary swing had appreciated 24.4 percent over a period of 200 days, placing it well into the danger zone on the frequency distribution.

These are just a few examples of the many cases in history where market life expectancy distributions acted as an indicator of potential imminent death. They were major factors in my decision to be flat going into both the 1987 and 1989 crashes, and enabled me to focus enough on the downside potential to be short through both of them. The statistical profiles aren't the same as crystal balls, but they do act as concrete indicators of the risk inherent in the age of the market.

Not focusing on risk is the downfall of most traders. It is so easy to look at a chart and see nothing but room at the top. And when they're losing money, the top just seems to expand, giving those traders space to fill with idle hope. Market life-expectancy profiles provide a concrete and undeniable measure of risk that can prevent trading on hopes rather than facts.

CONCLUSION

While historical market life-expectancy distributions are not a guaranteed way to measure risk, they do lay the concrete foundation on which to build an entire system of keeping the odds in your favor. If you know the historical probability that the long-term and intermediate-term trends will continue or fail, you can then weight the probabilities using both fundamental and technical analysis. Furthermore, you can learn to put your main focus on risk and thus avoid giving back prior returns by trying to squeeze a few more percentage points out of an aged market.

In the next few chapters, I will demonstrate the technical principles that can be applied to help refine the odds established by historical comparisons. In particular, I will discuss my own technical method of identifying a change of trend, and integrate that method into an overall approach of trading only when the odds favor success.

Each market has its own median extent and duration profiles. The only way to learn what those profiles are is examine the historical data and do the work. I've written this chapter in order to show how to use these data. Unfortunately, I have these profiles only in terms of the stock market, and the numbers in my data bank are proprietary.

10

The Technical Principles of Market Analysis Applied

Definitions implicit in Dow Theory have allowed me to develop a simple set of technical tools that are so powerful I can acquire more information in a single glance at a chart than I could through days of studying market fundamentals.[1] In fact, several traders I trained in the mid-1980s traded solely on the basis of the technical principles, and with profitable results.

I use technical analysis as a basic building block in my approach to market analysis and to building a trading strategy. In the stock market, for example, I look at the charts of the major indexes to determine the general direction of price movements within various business sectors. I determine the direction of the trend, the "age" of the trend in terms of extent and duration in a historical context (as described in Chapter 9), and the strength of the trend as measured by volume relationships, momentum oscillators, and key moving averages (as defined in *Trader Vic—Methods of a Wall Street Master*). With this series of snapshots in mind, I then attempt to integrate economic fundamentals to form an accurate overall portrait of the general direction of stock prices, both as a whole and sectorwise.

Within this context of information, I may then take market positions on the indexes with futures or options, or I may decide to make specific stock selections that I think will move with the general trend, but to a greater extent and/or with lower risk. Often, I take positions in both the broader market and with individual stocks to limit risk while optimizing profit potential with leverage.

In this chapter, I will describe the fundamental technical principles I use to analyze and trade the stock, bond, and commodities markets. To some extent, this requires repeating material from my earlier book, but for the sake of economy, I must assume a general knowledge of simple technical tools. Then I will add another observation about determining when a trend changes.

Let me emphasize that I would never recommend trading based solely on technical information. Nor would I ever recommend trading without a few essential technical principles in your trading arsenal. The idea is to integrate knowledge gained through both fundamental and technical analysis with knowledge of market psychology to define the overall odds of success in any trade.

Remember the advice of George Soros, presented in Chapter 2: "The object is to recognize the trend whose premise is false, ride that trend, and step off before it is discredited." Obviously, to take that advice, you must first be able to identify a trend and the potential for a change in that trend. Also, to identify a trend driven by a false underlying premise, you must understand the broader, conceptual underpinnings of economics and market psychology. By combining empirical, technical knowledge with a conceptual understanding of economic and market fundamentals, you have all you need to fully understand the odds and trade only when they are in your favor.

DEFINING YOUR TERMS

The Three Trends

In analyzing market price movements, the first and most important fact to recognize is that there are three trends:

1. The short-term trend, lasting from days to weeks (usually 14 trading days or less).
2. The intermediate-term trend, lasting from weeks to months.
3. The long-term trend, lasting from months to years.

All three trends are moving all the time and may be moving in opposing directions. In general, the short-term trend is the province of what the Street calls traders, the intermediate-term trend is for speculators, and the long-term trend is for investors.

Whether your interest is in trading, speculation, or investment, it is vital to understand the nature and direction of the long-term trend. Understanding the nature of the long-term trend means understanding its source in the market's perception of economic fundamentals (whether true or not), its "age" in terms of extent and duration, the phase it is in (discussed below), and so forth.

Understanding the direction is a simpler matter, but it is nevertheless vital. Unless you are aware of the direction of the long-term trend, it is impossible to intelligently take anything more than a short-term position. Even then, your odds of success are greater if you understand the short-term trend within the context of the intermediate and long-term trends. For example, if you are short-term trading in a bull market primary swing, you are much more likely to see several up days or up weeks than down days or down weeks. Furthermore, as a rule, you are much more likely to see upside volatility driven by institutional program buying than downside volatility, except when the trend is ripe for failure.

The Four Phases of the Market

In any market—stocks, bonds, or commodities—the long-term trend is in one of four possible phases:

1. It is being accumulated (being acquired gradually by investors).
2. It is being distributed (sold gradually by investors).
3. It is trending up or down.
4. It is consolidating (adjusting after profit taking in a confirmed trend).

Technically, when a market isn't trending, it is drawing a line, which means it is in a process of consolidation, accumulation, or distribution. But technical analysis alone cannot tell you which until the trend continues (in the case of consolidation); until the line is broken on the upside, which means it has been in accumulation; or until the line is broken on the downside, which means it has been in distribution. Lines are formed in all markets, and are well-known technical tools. Probably the most important point to emphasize here is that in the stock market, lines must be formed and broken jointly on all related averages to be meaningful. That said, let me shift my focus to evaluating trends and changes of trends.

THE NATURE OF TRENDS AND CHANGES

No matter what form technical analysis may take, it is always based, at least implicitly, on the definition of a trend. And yet, in my library of almost 2,000 books on trading, I have never read one good, all-encompassing definition of a trend. Even the bible of technical analysis, *Technical Analysis of Stock Trends* by Edwards and MacGee,[2] never precisely defines what a trend is. Consequently, Edwards and Macgee, along with most other technical analysts, focus not on the *principles* of technical analysis, but on various technical tools, many of which become outmoded as they gain general acceptance, and therefore become self-defeating.

It is safe to say, however, that as long as there are markets, there will be trends. Therefore, there must be a precise definition of a trend that will stand the test of time. So the question becomes, what is genus and differentia of a trend; that is, what characteristic is common to all trends, and what distinguishes it from any other type of price movement?

A trend is a price movement—that's the genus, and needs no further explanation. But what is the essential difference between a trending market and a "choppy" market? The answer is so simple that it seems almost self-evident, and it can be described in purely technical terms.

For the sake of clarity, I have broken the essential definition into two components, one for an uptrend and one for a downtrend:[3]

Upward Trend: An upward trend is price movement characterized by a series of successive rallies that penetrate previous high points, interrupted by sell-offs or declines that terminate above the low points of the preceding sell-off. In other words, an uptrend is a price movement consisting of a series of higher highs and higher lows of gold (see Figure 10.1).[4]

Downward Trend: A downward trend is a price movement characterized by a series of successive declines that penetrate previous low points, interrupted by rallies that terminate below the high points of the preceding rally. In other words, a downtrend is a price movement consisting of a series of lower lows and lower highs of wheat (see Figure 10.2).

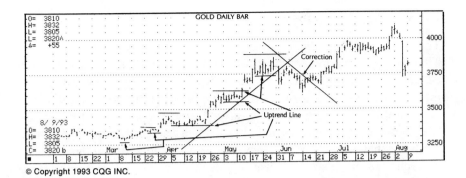

FIGURE 10.1   Upward trends and trend lines.

The beauty of a good definition is that it simplifies understanding and provides the basis for an expansion of knowledge. So it is with these definitions. They are completely general in that they apply to every market and to every kind of price trend. Moreover, understanding the definitions lays the foundation for a simple and consistent method of chart analysis that by its nature will always remain valid.

FIGURE 10.2   Downward trends and trend lines.

Drawing the Trend Line

The first step in technically evaluating a trend is drawing the trend line. This may seem simple, but just as very few people can give you a good definition of a trend, so very few can draw a consistently accurate trend line. My method of drawing a trend line is based directly on my previously stated definition. Even so, after trainees were given the definition, not 1 of 39 could consistently draw a correct trend line without further explanation. Rather, they would draw lines that *approximated* the trend but that also gave false signals in terms of potential changes of trends.

The following method (described in *Trader Vic—Methods*), provides consistent and accurate results and never gives false signals:

1. Select the period of consideration: the long term (months to years), the intermediate term (weeks to months), or short term (days to weeks).
2. For an uptrend within the period of consideration, draw a line from the lowest low, up to the highest minor low point preceding the highest high such that the line *does not pass through prices in between the two low points.* Extend the line upward past the highest high point. It is possible that the line will go through prices past the highest high point. In fact, this is one indication of a possible change in trend, as will be discussed in the following section (see Figure 10.1).
3. For a downtrend within the period of consideration, draw a line from the highest high point to the lowest minor high point *preceding the lowest low* such that the line does not pass through prices in between the two high points. Extend the line past the lowest high point downward (see Figure 10.2).

The beauty of this technique is that it provides an absolute means by which to evaluate whether a trend might change or has changed. In other words, if you use this method to draw a trend line on a chart, as prices go up or down, the necessity to draw the trend line differently will indicate the change in trend.

THE 1-2-3 RULE

For a trend to change, three events must occur:

Change of Trend Criteria

1. The trend line must be broken—prices must cross the trend line drawn on the chart.
2. Prices must stop making higher highs in an uptrend, or lower lows in a downtrend. For example, in a uptrend after a minor sell-off, prices may rise again, but fail to carry above the preceding high point or barely break the high and then fail. The converse would happen in a downtrend. This is often described as a "test" of the high or low point, and usually, but not always occurs when a trend is in the process of changing. When it doesn't occur, price movements are almost always driven by important news that causes prices to gap up or down and move erratically with relation to the "normal" price movement.
3. Prices must go above a previous short term minor rally high in a downtrend, or below a previous short-term minor sell-off low in an uptrend.

At the point where all three of these events have occurred, there exists the equivalent of a Dow Theory confirmation of a change of trend. Either of the first two conditions alone is evidence of a *probable* change in trend. Two out of three events *increases* the probability of a change of trend. And three out of three *defines* a change of trend.

To watch for a change of trend on the charts, all you have to do is translate these three events into graphical terms. The first step is to draw the trend line as described earlier. Then you draw two horizontal lines, as shown in Figure 10.3. In a downtrend, draw one line through the currently established low point and a second horizontal line through the immediately preceding minor rally high. For an uptrend, draw one horizontal line through the currently established high point and the second through the immediately preceding minor sell-off low.

If prices cross the trend line, mark the chart with a circled 1 at the point of crossing, as shown in Figure 10.3. If prices test the preceding

FIGURE 10.3 Charting the 1-2-3 rule.

high or low—that is, if they approach, touch, or slightly break the horizontal line corresponding to the current high or low and then fail to carry through—mark the chart with a circled 2 at that point. If prices carry through the line corresponding to the immediately *succeeding* sell-off high or low, mark the chart with a circled 3 at that point. If two out of the three conditions are met, there is a strong chance that a change of trend is in process. If all three conditions are met, then the trend change has occurred and is most likely to continue in its new direction.

THE 2B INDICATOR

Refer back to the second requirement of a change of trend: that prices must stop making higher highs in an uptrend, or lower lows in a downtrend—usually called a "test" of high or low point. Note that a test is not a *necessary* part of a change of trend. When the market forms a line, for example, you may never see a test. Instead, the market will waver in a range, break the trend line, and then eventually either move above or below the range of the line to establish a new high or low. However, when a test occurs, it *usually* signals a forthcoming change of trend. In fact, there is a special case of a test that I call the 2B indicator.

Look again at criterion 2. Note the statement that sometimes the test of the previous high (or low) may actually break the previous high (or low) and then fail. This is a special case of a test (hence the name: 2B) and it is very significant: more often than not, it signals a change of trend. In evaluating the potential for a change of trend, I weight the 2B event more heavily than any other single criterion.[5]

The 2B Rule

In an uptrend, if prices penetrate the previous high, fail to carry through, and then immediately drop below the previous high, then the trend is apt to reverse. The converse is true for downtrends.

This observation holds true for all trend periods, as Figure 10.4 shows. If a 2B is to occur in a short-term trend (3–5 days), then after the new high is established, prices will usually fail below the previous high or low within a day or two. In an intermediate-term trend, the 2B often marks the beginning of a correction and usually occurs within 7 to 10 days after the new high or low is made. At major market turning points, the 2B usually occurs in more than 7 to 10 days.

I have never done a rigorous test to determine how often the 2B indicator accurately predicts changes of trend, and I don't need to. Even if it works just one in three times (and I'd lay money that it's more), I would still make money by trading on it, especially in the intermediate-term trend. The reason is that a 2B allows you to catch almost the exact top or bottom, and thus sets up a great risk-reward scenario. In an uptrend, for example, the ideal way to capitalize on a 2B is to sell on a stop when prices break below the previous high, as shown in Figure 10.5. After selling, you then put in a buy stop at the 2B high. When trading in the intermediate-term trend, this almost always sets up a reward-to-risk ratio of 5 to 1 or more. Even if you get whipped out two, three, or even four consecutive times, the one you catch will end up making you a bundle.

FIGURE 10.4   The 2B rule in three periods.

If you practice evaluating charts using the 1-2-3 and 2B criteria diligently, you will soon reach the point where drawing the trend line and the associated horizontal lines is unnecessary. Instead, you will soon find yourself thinking in terms of just 1-2-3: 1—a break in the trend line; 2—a test and failure of the previous high or low; and 3—the breaking of a previous important high or low. And, you will learn to watch for the potential 2B and understand why you should always use stops to limit losses when you trade based on it.

Trading on the 1-2-3 Criterion

In terms of trading on the basis of the 1-2-3 criterion, the best way is to trade before condition three is met. In Figure 10.6 for example, you see that the NASDAQ Composite Index underwent a classic 1-2-3 change of the intermediate trend. From a trading perspective, when prices broke the trend line at about the 640 level with significant volume, there was no

© Copyright 1993 CQG INC.

FIGURE 10.5   A 2B sell signal.

way to be sure that the trend would change. Nevertheless, it was a compelling short from a risk-reward standpoint. Let me evaluate that opportunity in detail from a purely technical standpoint.

Put yourself in the position of a trader on the day when the prices broke through the intermediate-term trend line at 640 (which, by the way, was a short-term 2B). If you assumed that the trend had changed and went short, then the market would prove you wrong if prices moved above the daily closing high of 644 (in round numbers). By setting a buy stop at 644, then your risk was 4 points above your entry point. In terms of potential reward, the market would prove you right at about 615, a full 25 points below your entry point. Thus, your risk reward ratio was 25 to 4, or 6.25 to 1 in your favor.

Given such a favorable risk-reward scenario, further technical analysis was obviously warranted. In this instance, the life expectancy profiles powerfully supported the assumption that the trend would change. As of the closing high of 644.92 on February 12, the NASDAQ composite had

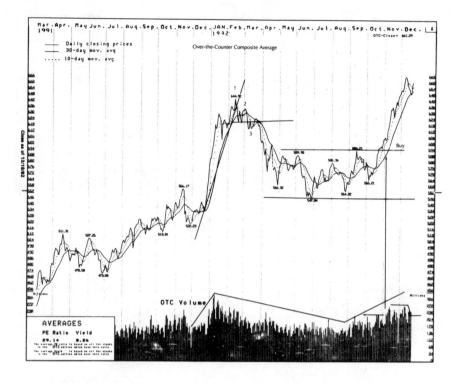

FIGURE 10.6 1-2-3 trading signals and OTC composite volume.

been in a sustained primary swing that appreciated 36.3 percent over 230 days. Only 21.4 percent of all bull market primary swings had been greater in extent, and only 22.1 percent had lasted longer. Based on this measure, the odds were 3.6 to 1 in favor of the OTC trend reversing. I realize you don't know these exact statistics, but if you're conscious of looking for the odds you will see them on the level of common sense, just as you know an old man from a young one.

If the fundamentals had been right, and they were, this information would probably have been enough to justify at least a small short position in the OTC market. But as I have said, it always pays to examine the odds from every possible dimension so you can more fully comprehend your chances of success.

When the Market Draws Lines

Before I discuss other technical tools that can supplement your decision-making process, it is necessary to point out the one case in which the 1-2-3 criterion is not the primary technical consideration. As discussed earlier, when the market is consolidating or distributing, it draws a "line." If the market is consolidating, then it will eventually "break out" above the range (on heavy volume if you're trading the stock market). If it is distributing, then it will "break" below the trading range on significant volume.

Unfortunately, from a purely technical perspective, there is no way to tell whether a market is consolidating or distributing until a break or breakout occurs. There is, however, a simple way to trade on a purely technical basis when the market is drawing a line. Basically, it's a two-step process (refer to Figure 10.6):

1. Draw horizontal lines corresponding to the highest and lowest points of the trading range.
2. If the market breaks out above the top horizontal line on heavy volume, buy the market with a sell stop at the point of the breakout. If the market breaks below the bottom horizontal line on heavy volume, sell the market with a buy stop at the point of the break.

This trading technique has several things in common with the 2B. Like the 2B, it applies to every market and to all three trends if you remove the volume observation. Also like the 2B observation, this method reflects what *usually* occurs. False breakouts and breaks will occur, possibly because this is a widely known technical tool, so you will sometimes get whipped out of your position; but the risk-reward scenario is usually quite good if you use your stops effectively.

Although this can be a powerful technical tool, it should never be used in a vacuum. The best way to avoid getting whipped out of your position is to have fundamental knowledge as to whether the market is consolidating or distributing. By fundamental knowledge in this case, I mean understanding the market psychology in the Soros sense.

I am speaking from a recent negative experience here. For virtually the entire last half of 1991, the market was drawing a line. I was convinced from a fundamental economic standpoint that the market was distributing, preparing for at least a major correction and possibly a bear market. What I failed to discount fully was that the market believed lower interest rates would push the market up. Thus, I shorted the market on the rally in November and caught a sharp sell-off in mid-November. But when the Fed lowered the discount rate a full point in December, I didn't feel the market would believe that another cut would change the fundamental weakness in the economy. Thus, I lost a significant portion of the gains I made by being short, and missed the spectacular December rally, which was a classic breakout on heavy volume.

SECONDARY TECHNICAL TOOLS

Volume Relationships

Although definitely a technical indicator, volume relationships are probably the least objective of the technical methods I use. Nevertheless, no trade should ever be made on the stock market without considering volume.

The reason I say that volume relationships are the least objective of technical tools is that there are no hard-and-fast rules. Instead, there is a set of general observations that must be interpreted in a specific market context. And, the only way to interpret them accurately is to watch the market every day to get a feeling for "normal" versus "heavy" or "light" volume. The following list gives general observations; I then demonstrate how I applied them in evaluating the NASDAQ scenario.

Important Volume Relationships

1. Volume tends to move with the trend; that is, in a bull market, volume tends to be heavier during rallies and lighter during declines; in bear markets, the converse is true (see the bottom portion of Figure 10.6). The exception is when the market is approaching a correction, which is covered by the next observation.

2. In an intermediate rally, bull or bear, a market that is overbought tends to lose volume on rallies and gain volume on

declines. Conversely, in an intermediate decline, an oversold market tends to gain volume on rallies and lose volume on declines.

3. Bull markets almost always end in a period of extraordinarily high volume (relative to previous periods) and begin in light volume. Stated differently, bear markets almost always begin with heavy volume and end on light volume.

Observation 3 bears closer scrutiny in light of the example shown in Figure 10.6. If you look at the volume section of Figure 10.6, for example, you will see a marked swelling of volume beginning in late January. This is particularly interesting because the OTC sector was far and away the top performer throughout 1991 and already enjoyed fairly good volume. If you now study volume relationships in the lower portions of Figure 10.7, you will see a significant difference in the patterns of volume on the Dow and Transports versus the OTC composite and the S&P 500. Specifically, the volume on the Dow and the Transports diminished significantly in February and March during the sell-off, while the OTC Composite and the S&P 500 remained high relative to preceding months.

This was a key reason I told my institutional subscribers in the February 20 issue of my investment advisory publication, *The Rand Monitor of Market Risk,* to "hold long positions in cyclical stocks, and move to minimum exposure in OTC and high-growth stocks." The OTC, the S&P 500, and several other indexes that had been the market leaders were showing classic technical topping action from virtually every aspect, and volume was confirming the action by being high both in the final rally and in the ensuing sell-off. The OTC market, in particular, was long overdue for at least a substantial correction, and in my opinion, was taking a leadership role in heading for a new bear market.

By the same token, the Dow and other cyclical indexes were showing bullish action, with volume diminishing on the downside and expanding on the upside. This factor weighed heavily in my decision to play the market both ways: long the cyclicals and short the OTC and growth stocks.

This brings me to another important, but secondary, technical principle of market analysis that few people apply to markets as a whole—relative strength.

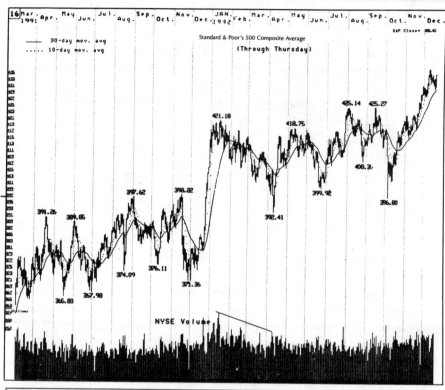

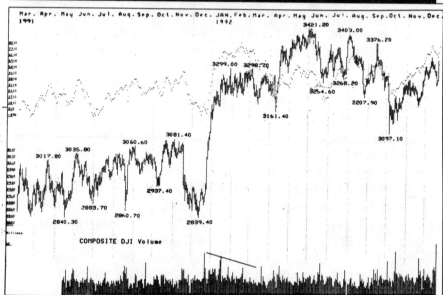

FIGURE 10.7 Volume patterns, Dow Jones composite, and Standard & Poor's 500 composite.

Relative Strength

As recently as 10 to 15 years ago, you could pretty much get a feel for "the market," referring to the stock market as a whole, by analyzing the Dow averages—the Industrials, Transportations, and Utilities. No more. As advances in information technology have made it possible to isolate and analyze different market segments, it takes a much broader view to understand stock price movements. In tracking the broader market, I watch no less than 18 indices, tracking the daily closings, extent, and duration of each. Using Dow Theory as the basis for analysis, I compare price movements, volume relationships, and breadth (the advance/decline ratio) to look at the similarities and differences among the many averages.

In a strong bull market, all the averages will move in the same direction. In an economy of mixed strength and weakness, such as the current one, some of the indices, such as the Dow Industrials and the XMI (Major Market Index), move together, while others lead or lag the other indexes. In other words, I look for relative strength relationships among the many indexes.

Robert Rhea alluded to the concept of relative strength with the phrase, "the habits of stocks and how they perform against one another." Although he was referring to individual stocks, it is now necessary to evaluate the habits of indexes and how they perform against one another. As I mentioned earlier, throughout 1991, the S&P 500 and the OTC indexes outperformed the industrial indexes and the broader indexes such as the Dow and the AMEX—they had greater relative strength. To project the future accurately, it is important to identify the relative strength of the different markets and the implications they have for trading.

To carry forward the analysis of the OTC market, it didn't take a genius to look at the charts throughout 1991 and determine that the OTC was the strongest market. But what is not intuitively obvious is that because it was the strongest market for so long and in a speculative environment, it would also be the market that would fail first and most swiftly in a marketwide downturn—if the shelves of a china cabinet collapse, the pieces on top are most likely to break.

The 200-Day Moving Average

Although it does not apply to the current example, another key technical indicator I watch is the 200-day moving average. It first caught my eye in

1968 when I read the results of a study by William Gordon demonstrating that by buying and selling the Dow Industrial stocks solely on the basis of the 200-day moving average, an investor would have achieved an average yearly simple return of 18.5 percent.

Using the 200-Day Moving Average

1. If the 200-day moving average line flattens out following a previous decline or is advancing, and prices break out through the moving average on the upside, then these events constitute a long-term buy signal, as shown in Figure 10.8.
2. If the 200-day moving average flattens out following a previous rise or is declining, and prices penetrate the moving average on the downside, these events constitute a major long-term sell signal.

The single biggest problem with the 200-day moving average is that it is such a heavily lagged indicator. As you can see in Figure 10.8, by the time the 200-day moving average indicated buying or selling on the Dow Industrials, most of the move was over. In addition, it is virtually worthless in protecting you from sudden crashes or minicrashes after a sustained, speculative market climb. For that reason, I use the 200-day moving average only as a supporting technical tool. If, for example, the OTC Composite index had, among everything else, also broken below the 200-day moving average, I would have been short the world on the OTC stocks in late March and early February. Instead, I only held a moderate short position.

Breadth and Momentum Oscillators

The final two indicators I use are breadth, or the advance-decline line (the A/D line) as it is sometimes called, and momentum oscillators.

The A/D line is simply a plot of the difference between the total number of advancing issues and the total number of declining issues. It is important because it is an indicator that compensates for virtually all stock averages being weighted. The Dow, for example, is an average of only 30 stocks, weighted to price. Sometimes, if a heavily weighted

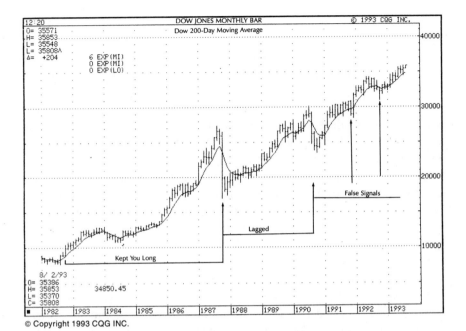

FIGURE 10.8 Signals of the moving average.

stock, like IBM, makes an unusually extensive move, it can throw off the validity of the average as an indicator of performance of industrial stocks as a whole.

As a general rule, the A/D line's daily movements follow the general direction of the broader averages, and when they don't, the discrepancy often signals a coming change in trend. In fact, I use it virtually like another average, applying Dow Theory principles in analyzing it versus other indexes. However, the daily A/D line only has to confirm the *previous* high (or low), not the high or low you're comparing it with. Also, the weekly A/D line should confirm your bullish or bearish convictions. For instance, the best technical indicator since the October 1990 low has been, without exception, the weekly A/D line. As another example, in March and April 1992, the Dow was making new highs, while the OTC Industrials, the S&P 500, and breadth were not. I viewed this situation as a possible divergence, indicating the possibility that the Dow might be approaching its top.

I always watch breadth closely, treating it as a near equivalent of any other stock index. I put secondary weight on a measurement derived from it, a momentum oscillator that measures the general upward or downward bias of the market as a whole. Every day, I keep a running, cumulative total of the daily difference of advancing minus declining issues for the previous 30 trading days on the NYSE. Then I divide the result by 3 to get the 10-day equivalent, net change, moving average breadth oscillator. It is quite often an effective measure of the intermediate term "overbought" or "oversold" condition of the market.[6]

As with the 200-day moving average, I use breadth and momentum oscillators as secondary, supplemental tools to augment more fundamental technical measures as the 1-2-3 criterion, the 2B rule, and the life-expectancy profiles in determining the overall odds of success. For example, in late February and early March, breadth was failing to make new highs and the overall market was in a mildly overbought condition according to my long-term oscillators. Thus, breadth was supporting my short position in the OTC market, and my oscillators were mildly supporting it. In net effect, the overall odds were in my favor, but not heavily enough to take an aggressive short position. At no time was more than 2 or 3 percent of my own or my clients' capital at risk.

A NEW EXCELLENT INDICATOR

I hope you feel that I've contributed some solid ideas and money-making suggestions in this book. Now I'm going to add one more: the 4-day rule. It is my favorite intermediate indicator of a change in trend, and I decided to share it because I feel some attachment to all the people who have read and commented on my previous book, *Trader Vic—Methods of a Wall Street Master.*

As usual, the discovery of this rule involved a great deal of painstaking work. I made a study of the Dow Jones Industrial average from 1926 to 1985, and measured every top and bottom in that time from an intermediate point of view. Table 10.1 shows the correlation of tops and bottoms with 4-day sequences (that is, 4 up or 4 down days in a row). Looking at all the data, I made two observations.

Table 10.1   1926–1985 4 Day Rule Samples (Intermediate Moves)

No. of Days	Frequency	Occurrence (%)	Composite (%)
69	2	0.9	90
56	1	0.4	90
53	1	0.4	89
52	1	0.4	89
50	1	0.4	88
48	1	0.4	88
45	2	0.9	87
40	2	0.9	86
38	2	0.9	85
36	1	0.4	85
35	3	1.3	84
34	1	0.4	83
33	1	0.4	82
32	1	0.4	82
31	2	0.9	81
30	3	1.3	80
29	1	0.4	79
28	3	1.3	79
27	1	0.4	77
26	1	0.4	77
25	4	1.8	76
24	1	0.4	75
23	2	0.9	74
22	3	1.3	73
21	1	0.4	72
20	1	0.4	71
19	4	1.8	71
18	5	2.2	69
17	2	0.9	67
16	5	2.2	69
15	4	1.8	64
14	10	4.5	62
13	4	1.8	57
12	8	3.6	55
11	2	0.9	52
10	7	3.1	51
9	3	1.3	48
8	6	2.7	46
7	5	2.2	44
6	5	2.2	41

Table 10.1   *(Continued)*

No. of Days	Frequency	Occurrence (%)	Composite (%)
5	9	4.0	39
4	6	2.7	35
3	10	4.5	32
2	5	2.2	28
1	56	25.0	25

No. of Days The number of days after the high or the low that the 4-day sequence began.

Frequency The number of occurrences between 1926 and 1985 that the 4-day sequence began a particular number of days after the high or low.

Occurrence The percentage of highs or lows that were followed by a 4-day sequence starting the given number of days after the high or low. Note that 10 percent of all intermediate moves had no 4-day sequences.

The Four-Day Rule

When the market has a reversal, in the form of a 4-day up or down sequence from a high or a low, after an intermediate move has taken place, the odds of the trend having changed is very high.

The first observation is that a 4-day sequence associated with an intermediate top or bottom almost always points you in the direction of the trend. As Table 10.1 shows, 25 percent of the intermediate highs or lows were immediately followed by a 4-day sequence in the direction of the new trend, 41 percent were followed by a 4-day sequence within 6 days, and 75 percent had a 4-day sequence within the first 24 days. Only 10 percent of the intermediate moves did not contain a 4-day sequence in the direction of the trend.

Take a look at Figure 10.9, which is a weekly and daily chart of the S&P 500 Index. It bottomed on October 9, 1992, at 402.66. The next 4 days were as follows: 10/12 +4.78, 10/13 +4.86, 10/14 +0.70, and 10/15 +0.23. That's 4 days up in a row, signifying a *bottom*. The market was also up on October 16, but that is not important. If this is a true low, it should never trade below the low of 10/9/92 for many months, and therefore you can use that as your stop.

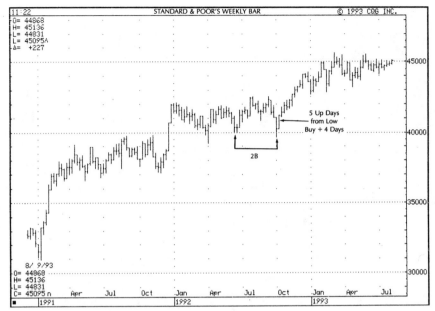

© Copyright 1993 CQG INC.

FIGURE 10.9   The four-day rule (S&P 500).

This 4-day rule works well with commodities as well, but I don't have a statistical breakdown for those occasions as I do for the Dow Industrials. Figure 10.10, a daily chart of the September Japanese yen, contains two excellent examples of the 4-day rule.

The second observation is another twist on the same tool:

Four-Day Corollary

After a long move of intermediate proportions, when you have a 4-day (or longer) sequence *in the direction of the trend,* the first day in the opposite direction often signifies the top or bottom and a change in trend.

© Copyright 1993 CQG INC.

FIGURE 10.10   The four-day rule (Japanese yen).

Figure 10.11, a daily chart of the Dow Transportation Average, illustrates this second observation beautifully. After a long uptrend, and 5 days up in a row, the first downday signified an intermediate top. You would short the first downday, and use the high of the 5-day sequence as your stop.

The reason this corollary works is that you have a climax over a series of days that is moderate, as opposed to a single-day climax top or bottom on high volume. Figure 10.12, September Silver, and Figure 10.13, S&P Index, are other good examples.

Watch for this 4-day phenomenon; the more you see it the more you'll realize how significant it is.

FIGURE 10.11   The four-day rule (Dow transportation averages).

CONCLUSION

In summary, I evaluate the market using three primary technical tools and several supplementary ones. I evaluate the market indexes in terms of the 1-2-3 criterion, the 2B rule, and the market life-expectancy profiles (described in the previous chapter). If the odds favor a change of trend with a net reward-to-risk ratio of 3 to 1 or more, I then look at volume relationships, the moving average, breadth, and momentum oscillators. If, after weighing all the odds, I find they are in my favor, then I take a position, sometimes on a purely technical basis. (Incidentally, there are many other good technical indicators that I have not touched on. A good

FIGURE 10.12   The four-day rule (silver).

current book that will give you a historical synopsis of all the important ones is *Trading for a Living* by Dr. Alexander Elder. I recommend it.)

Let me emphasize, however, that the times I take a purely technical position are rare. I have seen too many traders with tattered shirt cuffs and poorly fitted suits to put that much faith in technical analysis. Nevertheless, it is an invaluable tool in terms of concretely measuring the odds of success on any trade, and I think anyone who ignores technical principles in an overall approach to market analysis and forecasting is foolish.

The key is to pick as primary technical tools those that have stood the test of time, like the 1-2-3 criterion, and then to supplement them with secondary tools that work well over a significant time period. But, because every good tool will eventually gain market recognition, it will also become invalid. Never get married to one technical indicator as the end-all of end-alls, or you will end up losing money. I have!

Throughout this discussion, I've been referring the OTC example in terms of analyzing the broader market. As those of you who are experi-

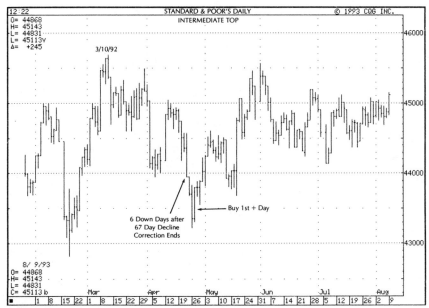

FIGURE 10.13   The four-day rule (S&P index).

enced know, however, there isn't an OTC Index actively trading today. Rather, a position must be taken in stocks and stock options. So, what is the next step? How do you select stocks or options to take your position and increase your odds of success?

Basically, you go through the same process, adding a few more technical measures to put even more odds in your favor, which is the subject of the next chapter.

11
The Principles of Technical Analysis Applied

Let me tell you the story of Mr. Carmine Grigoli, the strategist for First Boston Corp. In the first half of 1991, he was looking for the stock market to make new lows below the 2365 low set in October 1990. Instead, the market went to 3188 by the end of the year. According to the Dick West's market letter, March 5, 1992, his answer for this phenomenon was "I think most clients felt that I was right on the fundamentals. It was the implication it held for the market that was wrong." I can feel for Mr. Grigoli, because we have all made the same mistake, especially when we really know the fundamentals. But what is critical is the sentiment, not the fundamentals. Sentiment is shown by what people believe to be correct, not what actually is true. Where money goes scores the game, because the game of markets never ends even though players sometimes drop out, whether by choice or by necessity.

By their nature, markets can be wrong too, since they are merely a group of individuals who are trying to discount future events. A lot of very smart people got buried in the last half of the 1980s, because real estate, which was "never supposed to drop in value," did. And that brings us to this chapter on charting and interpreting technical analysis, or price changes.

In *Trader Vic—Methods of a Wall Street Master,* I revealed two methods of catching the changes of trend, and I named these methods 1-2-3 and 2B. They are summarized only briefly in the preceding chapter, because

I did not want to repeat myself here. If this question of technical analysis is important, you should consult that earlier book.

I've been asked, probably a thousand times, to explain specific price action or to recommend what to do with a specific stock. In this chapter I will show you how I look at charts. I use commodity charts for examples, so that I won't be accused of choosing charts that fit my principles. These are all the most widely followed commodities in the nation. In simple terms, I'm going to take a chart and analyze it according to my principles, and tell you what I see and how I interpret it. And I'll add a few new insights that I didn't discuss in my first book. I call them the *gap rule* and the *high-low 3-day rule*.

The gap rule is simple; when you have a gap *above* or *below* a trend line, it indicates an important change (news and/or fundamental) and points to a change of trend. Under this rule, you no longer need a test or a 2B. The gap must break the trend line, however, to make this rule valid. I will point this rule out as it occurs in the charts.

The high-low 3-day rule uses the intraday high and low of the preceding three days. When a reversal occurs, to the extent that it goes above or below a three-day high or low, you go long or short. You use the high or low of the third day as your stop, and if that stop is hit, you then reverse your position. I'll point this rule out in the charts as well.

Please note that these two rules can be used only in conjunction with another confirming principle.

CHART ANALYSIS

September Oats (Figure 11.1). In a downtrend since December with a low in February, followed by a rally and test in March. Here there was a 2B (new low that didn't follow through) when a new low was made at 133.0. You would buy the next day's close of 135.25 and use 132.75 as your stop. You could then add to your position above the March rally highs. Notice that it didn't trade below those March highs once it broke out—a great sign!

The top gave you no sign technically, so here is our first example of the new 3-day rule: After a large move (subjective), sell when the market breaks below 3 days of previous daily lows *and the trend line.*

The low came in June with another 2B on the break of the first 2B in March. You know you're looking at a valid 2B when it breaks the previous lows by only one day. Use the new 2B low as your stop.

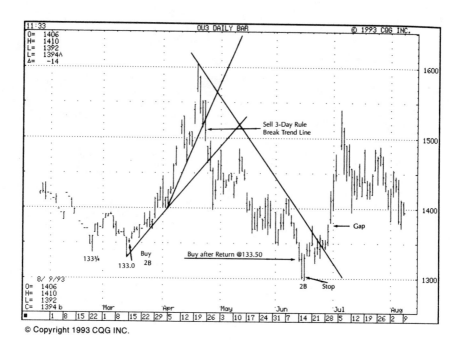

© Copyright 1993 CQG INC.

FIGURE 11.1 September oats.

Standard & Poor's Monthly Cash (Figure 11.2). As I write this, you would sell when the long-term trend line, drawn from the 1990 lows, breaks. This trend line is currently around 432.30, which is also the April 1993 low. Strong support would then be found around 332.00, or 100 points (handles) lower.

FIGURE 11.2   Standard & Poor's monthly cash.

Platinum Weekly Spot Month (Figure 11.3). A great 2B buy signal in January 1993 at 339.0. The low was 335.50 after taking out the low at 338.50. You would buy on the way up, and use 335.00 as your stop. It was followed by a great sale at 399.50, after taking out the high in June 1992 at 400.00.

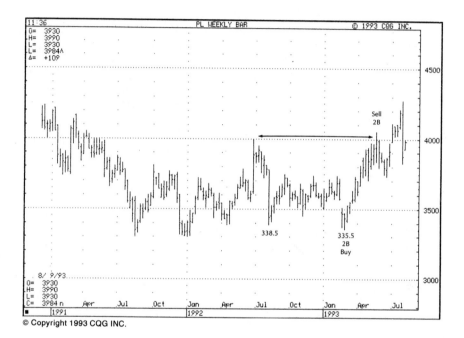

FIGURE 11.3   Platinum weekly spot month.

October Platinum (Figure 11.4). After the 2B sale at 399.50 you had a fake buy 2B in early June at 378.50 which you sold at 373.75 in late June. The hardest thing in trading is to reverse your position after getting whipsawed. I recommend you *double* your position on the second 2B buy after a whip. Make it pay double!

FIGURE 11.4   October platinum.

October Cotton (Figure 11.5). After the long rally from the lows in January, *sell* on the break of the previous 3 days' lows *and* the sell 2B. Buy in late April, and then resell when it takes out the initial 2B. Rebuy on the next 2B, and then sell because of the 3-day rule. A new signal is not in the works, as you remain short all the way down. You should always place stops above high and low of 2B's.

FIGURE 11.5   October cotton.

August Gold (Figure 11.6). Buy on the 2B in March. Add to the position on the gaps in March and April. Sell on the 2B in May, and then buy on the 2B in June.

FIGURE 11.6   August gold.

September Deutsche Mark (Figure 11.7). Buy in early March. You could have sold on the gap rule in early May, or where *sell* is indicated on the 1-2-3 and is breaking the 3-day lows.

FIGURE 11.7   September Deutsche mark.

August Pork Bellies (Figure 11.8). You could have sold on the day after the "1" because of the gap rule and breaking the 3-day lows, or sold on the day after "2" for the 3-day rule. You would then buy on the 2B in July, using 31.75 as your stop, also using the gap rule.

FIGURE 11.8   August pork bellies.

Dow Jones Industrials Weekly (Figure 11.9). Buy in late 1991 on 2B after Dow traded at 2839. Buy at 2861. Again, a similar 2B in late 1992.

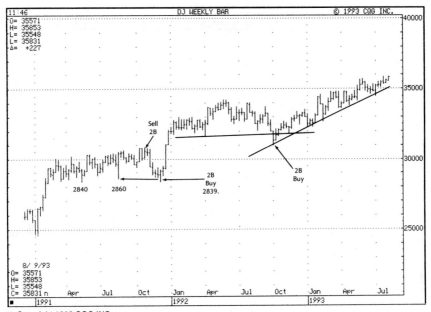

FIGURE 11.9   Dow Jones Industrials weekly.

December Wheat (Figure 11.10). Here you have a classic 1-2-3. Buy on the gap opening, with a stop if it fills the gap. You would have sold at 328 2B.

© Copyright 1993 CQG INC.

FIGURE 11.10   December wheat.

September Treasury Bills (Figure 11.11). Sell on the 2B in late April, and then on breaking the minor low on the 1-2-3. Buy on the 2B in June.

FIGURE 11.11   September treasury bills.

Natural Gas Weekly (Figure 11.12). Buy on 2B in January 1992. First sell occurs in September on the 2B from the December 1990 highs. Cover when the downward trend line is broken. Sell again on the next 2B.

© Copyright 1993 CQG INC.

FIGURE 11.12   Natural gas.

British Pound Weekly (Figure 11.13). Buy in March on 2B. Sell at the highs on the 2B from February, add on gap rule position, and if you're George Soros, make a billion dollars!

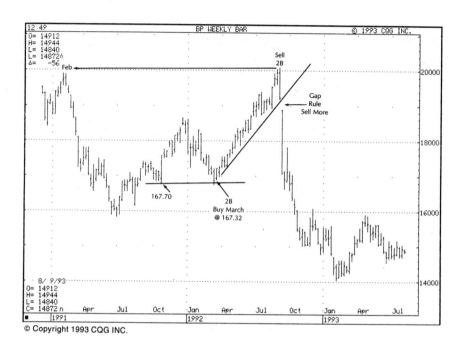

FIGURE 11.13   British pound.

September Bonds (Figure 11.14). Buy on the 2B in early April. Sell on the 2B in mid-April. Buy on the 2B in May, which you get whipsawed on. Remember, buy *double* on the second 2B. You'd still be long as of the end of August 1993.

© Copyright 1993 CQG INC.

FIGURE 11.14   September bonds.

December Corn (Figure 11.15). This chart started with a false 2B in March, which you are stopped out of with a small loss in April. Then there was another 2B around 250. You'd go short on the gap the following day—it also traded below the lows of the three previous days. You'd then buy on the 2B in early May, and go short on the 2B 3 days later. You'd then go long with the 2B in June, from which a perfect 1-2-3 is formed. Finally, you'd go short on the 2B on the last day of the chart.

© Copyright 1993 CQG INC.

FIGURE 11.15   December corn.

November Soybeans (Figure 11.16). Soybeans have been in an up-trend since October 1992 with various corrections. You had one false 2B buy signal in June. Then the rains came, and the time to be long in size was June 16, 1993, because you had a 2B with dramatic fundamental support—floods. You also had a gap the following day, trading above the highs of the previous 3 days. You should have added to your position at point 1. At point 2, you broke above the previous minor and *intermediate* highs and should have added to your position again. Sell 2B at July top and go directly to Paris.

© Copyright 1993 CQG INC.

FIGURE 11.16   November soybeans.

September Orange Juice (Figure 11.17). You had a minor 2B buy in February, and a minor 2B sell in March. You then had a breakout gap and a 1-2-3 buy! In April you had a sell gap breaking the trend line, a clear sell signal. You would then repurchase on the buy gap in May. You do not sell on breaking the trend line in June, as it was not a 1-2-3 situation. You'd still be long.

© Copyright 1993 CQG INC.

FIGURE 11.17   September orange juice.

Value Line Cash Weekly and Daily (Figure 11.18). You got a 2B buy on the weekly chart in October 1992. You could have shorted the market on the 3-day rule in February 1993 (see daily chart), and repurchased on the same rule. You then had a 1-2-3 sell and a 2B buy in late April. You sell on the 2B in June. The 3-day breaking low rule is not applicable because the move was not long enough or large enough to be valid.

© Copyright 1993 CQG INC.

FIGURE 11.18   Value line cash.

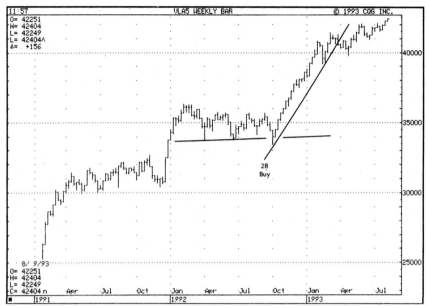

© Copyright 1993 CQG INC.

FIGURE 11.18   *(Continued)*

Standard & Poor's 100 (OEX Index) (Figure 11.19). Easy sell on June 1, 1993 from a 2B. Stay short, and lower your stop from the June 1, 1993 high to the June 29, 1993 minor high of 418.55. Rebuy on 2B in July.

FIGURE 11.19   Standard & Poor's 100.

Japanese Yen Weekly and Daily (Figure 11.20). The weekly chart gave you a simple buy in June at 70.41. You had a whipsaw from a short at 79.13. You would then rebuy at 79.14 on the way up after making a low at 70.31 in July, and resell on January 20 at 81.13, or one tick below high of 81.14. You then had an easy 2B buy in April followed by a 2B sell in October and a 2B buy in January 1993.

Now switch to the daily chart, with a great uptrend in force. You had a 2B sell in March. Note this key point: you only had a one-day follow-through. That's a bad sign—you could have covered and gone flat. Regardless, you go long, breaking above the mid-March high. You'd then sell on the breaking 3-day lows rule in June and wait to buy at new highs, while *waiting* for a 1-2-"3" sell which would be complete only when breaking the June low at 89.41. You'd presently be flat!

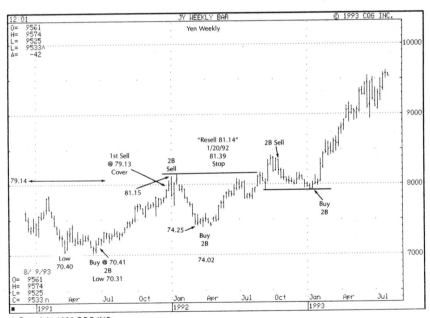

© Copyright 1993 CQG INC.

FIGURE 11.20   Japanese yen.

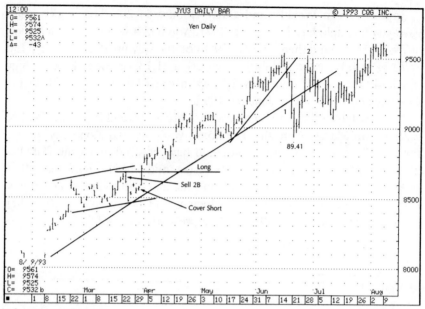

FIGURE 11.20   *(Continued)*

Commodity Research Bureau Index Cash (Figure 11.21). You had a common 1-2-3 correction. Buy on the 2B in May, sell on the following 2B, and then follow the 1-2-3 buy signal.

FIGURE 11.21 Commodity research bureau index cash.

Relative Strength of December Wheat, December Corn, and November Soybeans (Figure 11.22). Notice that Wheat failed to get above the highs of January–March, while Corn and Soybeans did. This tells you that Wheat is the weakest of the three. Corn then made new lows from January, while Soybeans didn't. This tells you Soybeans is the strongest of the three, followed by Corn and then Wheat. One common strategy is to sell the weakest and buy the strongest as a spread. This was also pointed out by a 2B in late April. *Always* buy the strong and sell the weak.

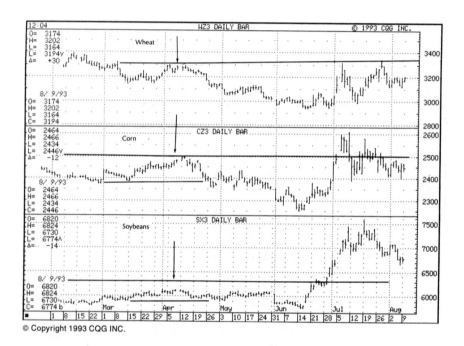

© Copyright 1993 CQG INC.

FIGURE 11.22   Relative strength of three commodities.

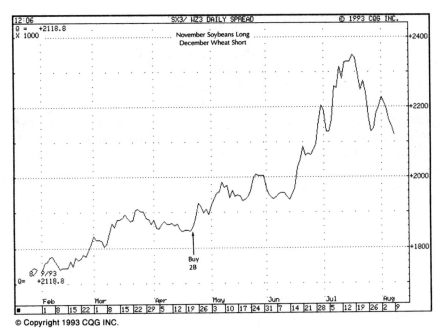

© Copyright 1993 CQG INC.

FIGURE 11.22   *(Continued)*

Lumber Weekly and Daily (Figure 11.23). Lumber gave you a buy signal with a typical 1-2-3 formation on the weekly chart. You could also have used the 3-day buy rule on the daily chart. The only sale was on a gap breaking the trend line (daily chart), which created a minor but important 1-2-3. What makes this 1-2-3 important is that the gap and test-break of the minor low came after a *big move*. The longer and bigger the (up) move, the more important a minor (sell) 1-2-3 becomes. Otherwise, this chart was very straightforward: Buy at the low, sell at the high. If you had used the 3-day rule as a system, you would have made $15,000 per contract from January to June. I do *not* use it as a system, however; I always integrate it into other rules.

FIGURE 11.23   Lumber.

© Copyright 1993 CQG INC.

FIGURE 11.23 *(Continued)*

Nikkei Cash (Figure 11.24). This was a classic 1-2-3 buy, followed by a long rally from a long bear market.

© Copyright 1993 CQG INC.

FIGURE 11.24   Nikkei cash.

PART THREE
OPTIONS TRADING

12
Options: The Key to Triple-Digit Returns

A lot of floor traders, especially the younger ones, love to write naked options. "The fools," they say, speaking of the options buyer, "they just keep giving me their money, and I keep selling 'em options that end up expiring worthless." For 11 months of the year, they can report a 90 percent success rate writing options, but in the last month, seemingly out of nowhere, the market moves 10 percent and they find themselves shelling out a lot more money than they had made, or even going completely broke.

The consensus on Wall Street is that buying and selling options is the riskiest game in town. The odds are against you, the "experts" say; not only do you have to be right about price changes, but you must have nearly perfect timing. These critics sometimes quote a 1960 SEC (Securities and Exchange Commission) study that showed over 85 percent of people who bought options lost money. However, this study evaluated only a single quarter, and it was an extremely dull period at that.

Admittedly, making money trading options is more challenging than with stocks, bonds, and other instruments. Nevertheless, they always have been my favorite trading instruments. I began my trading career in options. In January 1968, I went to work as an options trader at Filer Schmidt & Company, "making the middle," as we called it, by brokering options over the counter. By March 1968, I was managing my first hedge fund: Using a $50,000 options portfolio, I hedged a $1 million long equities portfolio. I began to grasp the ultimate profit potential of trading options.

Used correctly, options offer several major advantages over other market instruments:

1. They enable you to absolutely limit your risk (downside) while maintaining or increasing your potential (upside).
2. They enable you to command large quantities of market assets with only a small amount of capital; that is, they provide optimum leverage.
3. They allow you to design a flexible trading strategy with minimum risk.
4. In the event of dramatic market volatility, premium in options can sometimes move faster and to a greater extent than the price movement of the underlying instrument, so the probability of earning superior returns is greater.

The only catch is, you have to know which options to buy and when. In this chapter I hope to shed some light on just that.

LIMITING RISK

Before I began my trading career, I played a lot of poker. I read every book I could find on the subject and learned that poker isn't a game of luck, but one of both risk and odds management. Leaving bluffs aside, if you bet or call only when the odds are in your favor and plan your bets so that you stay at the table, you will make money over time. That doesn't mean you'll win every hand, far from it. But if you always keep the odds in your favor and scale your bets accordingly, you will come out a winner in the long run.

The same is true in trading options. To be successful, you can't just sit down, place your bet, and leave the rest to lady luck. You have to know the odds, and you have to develop a betting strategy. In terms of identifying the odds, all the principles I've outlined in this book apply, including the market life expectancy profiles.

As an example, let me use the current market situation. As of this writing (June 1993), we are in a bull market. An intermediate up leg, which began on October 9, 1992, is in place. On that date, the Dow Industrials closed at 3136.58, while the OEX (S&P 100 Index) closed at

368.57. It is important to understand that this intermediate trend can only end when a secondary intermediate correction kills it. This correction is called secondary because it is *against* the long-term trend currently in existence. You can normally expect a secondary correction in a bull market to correct between one-third and two-thirds of the previous up move (in this case the up move that started on 10/9/92). If you look back at Table 9.1 (in Chapter 9), you'll note that the *median* corrections last 47 days, and correct 48 percent of the previous move (averaging the Dow Industrials and Transports).

For example, in June 1993, you could have made a strong fundamental and technical case that the market is topping. The uptrend has been in force for 235 days (10/9/92–6/1/93), making it the longest up move without a secondary correction since the second leg of a bull market, which lasted from September 30, 1982 to June 1, 1993. Under that criteria, this is a very *old* move that was ready to die at any time. The numerous other fundamental and technical signs of a top aren't specifically important for this discussion, so let's just say you believe the market was ready to move down, and you decide to short the market. The question then becomes, "How should I do it?"

You could short stocks on 50 percent margin. You could sell the S&P futures and risk the market exploding in your face and absorbing unlimited risk if you're wrong. Or, you could buy equity or stock index puts to absolutely limit your risk while retaining the profit potential. Obviously, from a risk-reward standpoint, the options are the best bet.

But which ones do you buy? When trading options, you must always remember that the *critical* questions are by how much and over what period of time will the market move (in this case, sell off)? Your choice of options should be determined primarily by the answers.

With that in mind, given the current example, I feel the S&P's largest 100 industrials or the OEX Puts are the place to be. The OEX Index rallied from 368.57 on October 9, 1992, to a closing high of 420.63 on June 2, 1993, which is a 14.2 percent appreciation. We've already decided that the odds favor a sell-off, so we must now determine what extent to expect during the next 30 days or monthly change. Corrections or declines usually last 45 days (see Table 9.1) and the bulk of the decline comes in the first 30 days so its best to buy one month options and then roll out.

Table 12.1 analyzes the Dow Jones Industrials for each month since January 1939, showing the likelihood in percentage terms of what you

Table 12.1   Dow Jones Industrials—Monthly Volatility Comparisons, January 1939–May 1993

This table shows the percentage change of the Dow Industrials in any monthly period. It divides the monthly movements into five time periods of about 126 months each, and then shows the distribution by percentage of the moves in each time period. By studying this table, you can see the amount of volatility in each time period, and also build a deep understanding of what you can expect a future range of movements to be. For instance, if you average the movements for the last 54 years, you'll see that a monthly move will fall into the 0.0%–1.9% range about 42.1% of the time. Since January 1984, the incidence was even a little higher, 45.1%. This can be used if you sell naked options and want to figure your odds of success. You should note that from January 1973 to date, the volatility has picked up in the 8%–9.9% and 10.0%+ categories, while falling in the 4%–5.9% area. What it means is the likelihood of the market moving further in a given month, once it has moved 4.0%–5.9%, has increased. Obviously, there are many other observations you can make on your own.

Percentage Moves Between	1/39–6/49 (%)	7/49–6/62 (%)	7/62–12/72 (%)	1/73–12/83 (%)	1/84–5/93 (%)
0 to 1.9	38.9	35.2	47.6	43.9	45.1
2 to 3.9	25.4	38.4	21.4	25.0	21.1
4 to 5.9	21.4	19.2	21.4	14.4	16.8
6 to 7.9	9.5	4.8	7.2	7.6	8.0
8 to 9.9	2.4	2.4	1.6	3.0	6.2
10+	2.4	0.0	0.8	6.1	2.7

can expect the market to move. Since 1984, the market, 54.9 percent of the time, has made moves of at least 2 percent and has made moves of at least 4 percent more than a third of the time. This distribution has been fairly consistent since 1939, but I'm specifically focusing on the last column since the current climate of program-driven trading has come into play during that time. While the long-term effects of such programs are questionable, they can certainly affect the market in the short run. So, our game plan should be to buy puts that will break even or make a some sort of profit should the market sell off as little as 2 percent in 30 days.

With the OEX closing at 420.63, the OEX *July 415* puts closed at 4⅞. These options are 1.3 percent "out of the money" and have 44 days left before they expire. A sell-off of 2 percent would bring the OEX to

412.22. At that level, these 415 puts would probably be trading around 4½ or 5, depending on how volatile the market is and how long the 2 percent sell-off takes. On the other hand, if the market sells off 4 percent in 30 days, the OEX will be at 403.18, and the 415 puts will be worth a minimum of 11¾—more than double your original cost! In addition, Table 9.1 shows that the median corrections are 48 percent of the previous move. In this example, that would be a 6.8 percent sell-off, putting the OEX at 392.08 and making the puts worth almost 23 each, or almost 5 times your original cost.

These July puts are also ideal since the 44 days to expiration almost meets the median duration of corrections shown in Table 9.1. Your investment in this trade should be no more than 3 percent of your capital. For example, if you have $100,000, then you should buy 6 puts for $487.50 each. With the puts struck at 415, this investment of $2925 is the same as being short $246,075 worth of the OEX Index (almost 2.5 times your total capital) 2.5 percent below the market.

If the market stayed the same over the next 30 days, or went up, the loss would be small. I have a hard-and-fast rule never to put more than 10 percent of my risk capital in any given options position. In fact, I rarely go as high as 10 percent; 1 to 3 percent is a typical position for me, and I recommend only 2 percent to 3 percent to most traders. However, when I feel certain the market is going to move in a major way, as was the case just prior to Black Monday and also before the October 1989 minicrash, I go up to as high as 10 percent.

I keep my options trades small because that reduces the number of times I have to be right to win. By trading only when the odds are in my favor, by limiting my trades to opportunities with a 5-to-1 payout or better, and by keeping the bets relatively small, I only have to be right 1 in 4 times to stay ahead of the game. If I get hot, I make a lot of money. If I hit 1 in 4, I stay ahead of the game. And if I only hit 1 in 6 or so, I still have plenty of capital left to stay in business.

As it turned out the OEX dropped to 406.50 on July 7, 1993 and rallied back. You could have easily sold them with a small profit anytime thereafter. So, although a real correction never took place it was a fair and profitable trade.

Just prior to the New Hampshire primary in 1992, for example, I was talking to an investor who had caught the entire move in the biotech and drugs stocks throughout 1991. He had amassed a very large portfolio and asked me what I thought about the downside potential. I explained to him that I was starting to get bearish on that stock segment, and that I thought the market could plunge as much as 5 or 10 percent if President Bush lost to Patrick Buchanan in the first primary. After listening to all my reasoning, he asked me to hedge his 2.8 million long portfolio, and wrote me a check for $75 thousand to do so. I hedged his entire portfolio to the tune of $2 million in stocks and $4 million in OEX puts, not even using the full $75,000.

Well, Buchanan made a good showing, but he lost, and the market barely blinked, selling off only 20 points on the day of the election. But because I bought puts on specific stocks I was bearish on anyway, and because I sold nearly the entire portfolio as soon as the election results proved me wrong, I ended up making him a little over $25 thousand in a couple of days. I managed the odds, putting as many of them in my favor as possible, and even though my hypothetical scenario didn't materialize, I made money on all but 1 of 15 total positions. If, on the other hand, Buchanan had won due to a protest vote, I think the market would have sold off at least 5 percent, and I would have made him a real bundle. That's why I like options.

Options also occasionally allow you to risk a little bit of money to make a lot when you really don't have much going for you. It's like bluffing in poker. For example, in early March 1992, coffee made a 17-year low, trading down to 66.25 on the May futures. Technically, the chart looked terrible. Fundamentally, the picture wasn't any brighter. And yet, as I said on my 900-number phone consultation service, "There isn't any reason to buy May Coffee, but when you break a 17-year low, you've got to take a shot that it'll bounce back." I recommend buying the May 80 calls, which were then $75 each. About a week later, the May coffee futures were at 71.50, and the options were at $243. Luck? Some! Intuition? Sure! A gamble, but a gamble I could afford. I put one-quarter of one percent on that play, just on a hunch.

Let me hasten to add that buying those coffee options was a direct violation of one of my trading rules: "Never buy just because the price is low, never sell just because the price is high."[1] But gambling on a hunch is OK as long as you take a very small risk, can afford and even have fun losing the money, and don't make it a habit. If you make a habit of playing the long shot, then you'll always end up busted.

Trader Vic's Rules for Options Trading

1. Keep trades small: 2 to 3 percent of your risk capital.
2. Trade only when the odds are in your favor.
3. Trade only when the potential payout is at least 5 to 1.
4. Never buy just because the price is low; never sell just because the price is high.

I don't mean to suggest you concentrate only on options and ignore other financial instruments. In a sustained intermediate-term market movement, every portfolio should include positions with stocks that move ahead of the market. But near market turning points, especially volatile market turning points, there is no better way to maximize profit and minimize losses than with options. The reason is leverage.

LEVERAGING MARKET PSYCHOLOGY

From the outset, my approach to options trading hasn't followed traditional patterns. Between 1966 and 1968, there were perhaps 15 or 20 options firms on Wall Street and each dealer operated more like a used-car lot than a typical financial market as we know them today. Pricing was established virtually on a one-on-one basis, and many dealers attempted to make money by finding gullible buyers who would pay too much. These dealers didn't really concern themselves with the action of the market, they just worked the spread, buying and selling options to take advantage of the price differential between the bid and the offer. Not surprisingly, many of those dealers failed; after all, leaving the customers feeling ripped off doesn't do much to help build a long-term clientele.

As I explained in *Trader Vic: Methods of a Wall Street Master,* the process worked like this:

> When Joe Options buyer called Typical Options Company for the price of an OXY (Oxidental Petroleum) 6 and 10 call, there was no guarantee that he could buy the contract at the quoted price. Further, he may have called another dealer or two and found a 20–30 percent price difference either way! The

dealer would quote the buyer a "workout" price of, say, $225 per contract, and then try to find a seller bidding $150 to $175. Once found, he would turn the contract over to his buyer and "make the middle." If he couldn't find a seller at a reasonable price, then Joe was out of luck and he received a "nothing done."[2]

I did quite well horsetrading like this (and actually trading options and stocks) for several years for other firms. But as I observed the operations of different options dealers, I saw an opportunity to take a different approach by becoming a true market maker. With a few partners, I opened Ragnar Options Corp. in mid-1971. By this time, I had become a good tape reader and had a handle on how to read market trends. So instead of just horsetrading, we also traded options on our own account. The firm policy, which was revolutionary at the time, was to offer what we called "reasonable firm quotes" for any given option, meaning that we guaranteed our customers they would receive an option at the quoted price. If we could find the same option at a cheaper price, we would still make the middle. If we couldn't, we wrote the option ourselves. Our business really took off. When we opened Ragnar, we were the 27th firm in the business; six months later, we were the highest-volume OTC options dealer in the world.

We maintained a strong enough position in the market to buy several seats when the Chicago Board Options Exchange (CBOE) made options fungible in April 1973. It was at this point that the nature of the business started to change rapidly. Most firms had statisticians, mathematicians, and economists who priced options according to volatility and time-decay models, the most popular of which was the Black and Scholes model. From the outset, I disagreed with the concept of using mathematical models for options pricing, and at Ragnar, we continued pricing according to supply and demand considerations mixed with my estimate of the likely market trend.

The reason I disagree with mathematical modeling is that it cannot account for the single most important factor of options pricing, which I call the psychological premium component. If the price of an option is $300, for example, that premium reflects the option writer's judgment of worthwhile risk-reward based on which way and how fast the person believes the price of the underlying instrument will move. Once you buy the option, the passage of time will, in general, cause premium decay. But if there is any significant volatility in the underlying instrument at all, the price fluctuates rapidly, and time premium becomes less important. Market psychology drives the price more than time does, which is why mathematical models fail. You can't make money predicting the past.

When I trade options, I consider time, but not in the same way as many other options traders. Instead of thinking of options as consisting of price premium and time premium, I think of them as the right to trade pure leverage over a given period of time. If the economic fundamentals, the life expectancy profiles, the technicals, and the market's predominant psychology all favor the likelihood of a dramatic down move within a few days, I'll buy out-of-the-money puts that are very close to expiration.

Let's say, for example, that on March 3, 1992, I was convinced that George Bush was going to lose all of the upcoming primaries, with dramatic effect on the market. The OEX was at 384.65 at the time, and I could have bought a March OEX 380 put for 3⅛. What this means, in effect, is that for $312.50, I would have held claim to a $38,465 asset for a few weeks—that's 121-to-1 leverage. If I were right about the primaries and the market tumbled, then I would be able to sell the puts or exercise them for cash, gaining the full benefit of controlling the asset with less than a 1 percent outlay. To put it another way, if I was managing a $1 million portfolio, then I could short or hedge nearly 400 percent of the portfolio value for a little over $32 thousand.

Of course, the leverage does you no good unless there is price volatility. For this reason, I didn't make a lot of money trading options through most of 1991. For the entire year, the economic fundamentals were terrible. In several cases, both the statistics and the technicals favored a downturn of substantial proportions. The market had been going up in anticipation of a recovery, but the recovery didn't come. And yet, stock prices held in a 5 percent trading range near the highs for most of the year.

I knew that lower interest rates were dominating market thinking. I was also way ahead of the market in realizing that lower interest rates would not lead to a quick and strong recovery. What I didn't realize was how long market participants would cling to their faith that the Fed could work miracles. Time after time, poor economic data came out, the market would trickle down, the Fed would ease, and the market would rally again. Finally, in November, it looked as if the market had lost faith when the market broke through its October lows, giving a Dow Theory bear market call. I shorted size with options into the early December rally, expecting the market to break back down into a continuing bear market primary downswing. Then the Fed, in an unprecedented move, cut the discount rate by a full point in mid-December (a 22 percent cut, the largest percentage cut in history), and the market rocketed up 10 percent in just two weeks. It was the first time in history that Dow theory gave a false bear market call, and my options were virtually worthless in a matter of days.

This experience served to remind me of an old quote, the source of which I can't remember: "The market can behave irrationally much longer than your net worth can last." In other words, it does no good to be "ahead of the market" in terms of economic fundamentals if you can't translate the knowledge into catching changes in price trends. Even if the odds are in your favor, you need to keep a finger on the pulse of market psychology, and to do that, you must ride the technical trend established by the predominance of market opinion. The market's perception of the future is what drives prices, not the facts. Not weighing that simple fact has cost me more money than any other single factor in my career.

UNDERSTANDING THE INSTITUTIONAL PSYCHOLOGY

The fact that Dow Theory gave the first false bear market signal in the 96-year history of the averages also served to drive another point home. Since 1982, the market has become institutionally driven, which has major implications for gauging the predominant market psychology. Hundreds of thousands, perhaps millions, of individual judgments have been replaced by the judgments of a few scores of institutional money managers, most of whom operate on the same information and react similarly. Consequently, most volatile price moves in the market are driven by obvious news. For example, if most institutional money managers are of the mind-set that lower interest rates will lead to recovery, then if the Fed lowers interest rates, stock prices will rise. If you understand how the institutions will respond to news, and if you can anticipate the news, then you can anticipate the price movement. Therefore, you have to be a combination psychologist/news forecaster to play the options market effectively.

The institutional mentality has also had a dramatic effect on options pricing, especially the index options. For example, on January 16, 1991, just prior to the outbreak of the Persian Gulf War, I had become an intermediate-term bull, expecting a bear-market rally. The OEX was at

295, and I wanted to buy the February 305 calls. They were priced at 5¾! I remember thinking, "They've got to know something," the "they" meaning institutional managers. That was an exceedingly high price for options with one month to go, being 10 points out of the money, so I passed. I also felt that the war would begin Friday night, with the markets being closed the following day. I guessed wrong. War broke out Wednesday night, and it became obvious that the allied forces had established immediate air superiority. The market rallied 150 points the following day, and I would have doubled my money had I decided to pay the exceptionally high premium.

By contrast, on March 3, 1992, the OEX cash index was at 384.65, and the March 395 calls were at 1⁵⁄₁₆—more typical numbers. I wasn't a bull at that point, and neither were the institutional managers, but you can see what a dramatic effect psychology has on options pricing.

Institutional managers generally prefer index options over individual stock options for use in hedge, arbitrage, and program strategies. Since the institutions trade such huge quantities of assets, and because such a high percentage of investment now stems from institutional accounts, the demand for options on individual stocks has dropped, and they are often relatively cheap. It's a simple supply-demand relationship—diminished demand means cheaper prices. But cheaper prices don't necessarily mean less volatility. Consequently, I have shifted my emphasis to trading individual options as opposed to index options, with very positive results, as was the case just prior to the New Hampshire primary, as described earlier.

Using the technical methods described in Chapter 11, you can pick stocks that tend to move with the market, but with greater volatility. Then, among those stocks, you can pick those with a liquid options markets and achieve even better returns than you would by trading the index options. In effect, you can follow the trends established by the large institutions but achieve superior returns by buying leverage at a discount.

In general, however, options are not good for following established and generally recognized trends. To maximize your returns with them, you really have to be just ahead of the market, and you have to have a very good idea just how far ahead you are. You have to buy options at the right time when nobody wants them, and sell them back when everybody else does. It goes right back to the idea of the Soros opportunity—ride the tide of false opinion and get out just before the opinion changes. Options are the perfect vehicle to do just that.

REFINING TIME CONSIDERATIONS

By applying all the principles I've outlined so far, you can usually project a scenario of *what* will occur with a fairly high probability of being correct. But to capitalize on "the what" with options, you also have to know "the when." In some cases, this isn't too difficult. For example, when James Baker announced in October 1987 that he was going to "let the dollar slide" against the deutsche mark and the yen, it didn't take a genius to figure out that the market would sell off. When the market is behaving "normally," however; that is, when there are no extraordinary conditions, world events, breaking stories, and so forth, it can be very difficult to project the timing of market movements.

Suppose, for example, that the market is behaving normally, and you are interested in either writing or buying a call 2 percent out-of-the-money, expiring in two weeks. What are your odds of success?

As I've already mentioned, one of the best tools for determining odds in such a case is to use the market life-expectancy profiles. But you can do much better than that by taking the same concept underlying the profiles a step further. Table 12.2 shows a compilation of the absolute values of the biweekly percentage changes in the Dow Jones Industrials from January 1939 to February 1992. A quick look at the table will show you that of the 1,379 samples, only 591 (43 percent) moved 2 percent or more in a two-week period. Therefore, the odds are 1.3 to 1 against you if you buy the call and 1.3 to 1 for you if you sell the call—not good odds either way in my book.

This assumes you are in a "normal" market that is moving typically by historical standards. If the market is one week into a consolidation period, your odds in buying the call are much worse. If the market has been in a 5 percent range for six months and there is a strong likelihood that the Fed is going to ease, your odds are much better. You get the idea.

Now let's say that the market is stable, drawing a line, no news is imminent, economic indicators are mixed, the Fed's hands are tied with respect to easing—there is virtually no evidence that the market will move as much as 5 percent in the coming two weeks. According to the table, 94 percent of all two-week moves since 1939 have been less than 5 percent. The odds of success in writing a call 5 percent out-of-the-money are 15.7 to 1 in your favor.

You can use these kinds of statistics to evaluate pricing as well. Suppose, for example, that the market is flat and there are two weeks to go

Table 12.2   Dow Jones Industrials—Absolute Biweekly Percentage Changes,
January 1939–January 1992

This is simply a two-week (Friday to Friday) percentage change of the Dow
Industrials from January 21, 1939 to November 15, 1991, listed in low-high order.
The percentage move of occurrence 688 (the median occurrence) is 1.71 percent.
Use this to compute if a current straddle or other option combination is cheap or
not in relation to this 54-year history of volatility.

1	0.00	2	0.00	3	0.01	4	0.01
5	0.02	6	0.02	7	0.02	8	0.02
9	0.02	10	0.03	11	0.03	12	0.03
13	0.03	14	0.03	15	0.03	16	0.03
17	0.03	18	0.04	19	0.04	20	0.05
21	0.05	22	0.05	23	0.05	24	0.05
25	0.06	26	0.06	27	0.06	28	0.06
29	0.06	30	0.06	31	0.06	32	0.07
33	0.07	34	0.07	35	0.07	36	0.08
37	0.08	38	0.08	39	0.08	40	0.08
41	0.09	42	0.09	43	0.10	44	0.10
45	0.10	46	0.10	47	0.10	48	0.11
49	0.11	50	0.11	51	0.12	52	0.12
53	0.12	54	0.13	55	0.13	56	0.13
57	0.13	58	0.13	59	0.13	60	0.13
61	0.13	62	0.13	63	0.13	64	0.13
65	0.14	66	0.14	67	0.15	68	0.15
69	0.15	70	0.15	71	0.16	72	0.16
73	0.16	74	0.16	75	0.16	76	0.17
77	0.17	78	0.17	79	0.18	80	0.18
81	0.18	82	0.19	83	0.19	84	0.19
85	0.19	86	0.19	87	0.20	88	0.20
89	0.20	90	0.20	91	0.20	92	0.21
93	0.21	94	0.21	95	0.21	96	0.21
97	0.22	98	0.22	99	0.22	100	0.22
101	0.22	102	0.22	103	0.22	104	0.22
105	0.22	106	0.23	107	0.23	108	0.23
109	0.23	110	0.23	111	0.24	112	0.25
113	0.25	114	0.25	115	0.25	116	0.25
117	0.25	118	0.25	119	0.26	120	0.26
121	0.26	122	0.27	123	0.27	124	0.27
125	0.27	126	0.27	127	0.28	128	0.29
129	0.29	130	0.29	131	0.29	132	0.29
133	0.29	134	0.30	135	0.30	136	0.30
137	0.30	138	0.30	139	0.30	140	0.31
141	0.31	142	0.31	143	0.31	144	0.32
145	0.32	146	0.32	147	0.32	148	0.33
149	0.33	150	0.34	151	0.34	152	0.34

Table 12.2   (Continued)

153	0.35	154	0.35	155	0.36	156	0.36
157	0.36	158	0.36	159	0.36	160	0.36
161	0.36	162	0.36	163	0.36	164	0.37
165	0.37	166	0.37	167	0.37	168	0.38
169	0.38	170	0.38	171	0.38	172	0.38
173	0.38	174	0.38	175	0.39	176	0.39
177	0.39	178	0.39	179	0.39	180	0.40
181	0.40	182	0.40	183	0.40	184	0.40
185	0.41	186	0.41	187	0.42	188	0.42
189	0.42	190	0.43	191	0.43	192	0.43
193	0.44	194	0.44	195	0.45	196	0.45
197	0.45	198	0.45	199	0.46	200	0.46
201	0.46	202	0.47	203	0.47	204	0.47
205	0.47	206	0.47	207	0.47	208	0.47
209	0.47	210	0.48	211	0.48	212	0.48
213	0.49	214	0.49	215	0.49	216	0.49
217	0.50	218	0.51	219	0.51	220	0.52
221	0.52	222	0.52	223	0.52	224	0.53
225	0.53	226	0.53	227	0.53	228	0.53
229	0.54	230	0.54	231	0.54	232	0.55
233	0.55	234	0.55	235	0.55	236	0.56
237	0.56	238	0.56	239	0.56	240	0.56
241	0.56	242	0.57	243	0.57	244	0.58
245	0.58	246	0.58	247	0.58	248	0.59
249	0.59	250	0.59	251	0.59	252	0.59
253	0.59	254	0.59	255	0.59	256	0.59
257	0.60	258	0.60	259	0.60	260	0.60
261	0.60	262	0.60	263	0.60	264	0.60
265	0.60	266	0.60	267	0.61	268	0.61
269	0.61	270	0.61	271	0.62	272	0.62
273	0.62	274	0.62	275	0.62	276	0.62
277	0.62	278	0.63	279	0.64	280	0.64
281	0.64	282	0.64	283	0.64	284	0.65
285	0.65	286	0.66	287	0.66	288	0.66
289	0.66	290	0.66	291	0.66	292	0.66
293	0.67	294	0.67	295	0.67	296	0.67
297	0.68	298	0.68	299	0.69	300	0.69
301	0.69	302	0.70	303	0.70	304	0.70
305	0.70	306	0.70	307	0.70	308	0.71
309	0.71	310	0.72	311	0.72	312	0.73
313	0.73	314	0.73	315	0.73	316	0.73
317	0.73	318	0.74	319	0.74	320	0.74
321	0.75	322	0.75	323	0.75	324	0.75
325	0.75	326	0.75	327	0.75	328	0.76
329	0.76	330	0.77	331	0.77	332	0.77

Table 12.2 *(Continued)*

333	0.78	334	0.78	335	0.78	336	0.78
337	0.79	338	0.79	339	0.79	340	0.80
341	0.80	342	0.80	343	0.80	344	0.80
345	0.80	346	0.80	347	0.80	348	0.80
349	0.81	350	0.81	351	0.81	352	0.81
353	0.82	354	0.82	355	0.82	356	0.83
357	0.83	358	0.83	359	0.83	360	0.83
361	0.83	362	0.83	363	0.83	364	0.84
365	0.84	366	0.84	367	0.85	368	0.85
369	0.85	370	0.86	371	0.86	372	0.86
373	0.86	374	0.86	375	0.86	376	0.86
377	0.87	378	0.87	379	0.87	380	0.87
381	0.87	382	0.88	383	0.88	384	0.88
385	0.88	386	0.89	387	0.89	388	0.89
389	0.89	390	0.89	391	0.89	392	0.89
393	0.90	394	0.90	395	0.90	396	0.90
397	0.90	398	0.91	399	0.91	400	0.91
401	0.92	402	0.92	403	0.93	404	0.93
405	0.93	406	0.93	407	0.93	408	0.93
409	0.94	410	0.94	411	0.94	412	0.95
413	0.95	414	0.96	415	0.96	416	0.96
417	0.96	418	0.96	419	0.97	420	0.97
421	0.98	422	0.98	423	0.98	424	0.98
425	0.98	426	0.98	427	0.98	428	0.99
429	0.99	430	0.99	431	0.99	432	1.00
433	1.00	434	1.00	435	1.00	436	1.00
437	1.00	438	1.01	439	1.01	440	1.01
441	1.01	442	1.01	443	1.02	444	1.02
445	1.02	446	1.03	447	1.03	448	1.04
449	1.04	450	1.04	451	1.04	452	1.04
453	1.05	454	1.05	455	1.05	456	1.05
457	1.06	458	1.06	459	1.06	460	1.07
461	1.07	462	1.07	463	1.07	464	1.08
465	1.08	466	1.08	467	1.08	468	1.09
469	1.09	470	1.09	471	1.09	472	1.09
473	1.10	474	1.10	475	1.10	476	1.10
477	1.10	478	1.11	479	1.12	480	1.12
481	1.13	482	1.13	483	1.13	484	1.14
485	1.14	486	1.15	487	1.15	488	1.15
489	1.15	490	1.15	491	1.16	492	1.16
493	1.16	494	1.16	495	1.16	496	1.16
497	1.17	498	1.17	499	1.17	500	1.17
501	1.18	502	1.18	503	1.19	504	1.19
505	1.19	506	1.19	507	1.20	508	1.20
509	1.20	510	1.20	511	1.20	512	1.21

Table 12.2   *(Continued)*

513	1.21	514	1.21	515	1.21	516	1.22
517	1.22	518	1.22	519	1.22	520	1.23
521	1.24	522	1.24	523	1.24	524	1.24
525	1.24	526	1.25	527	1.25	528	1.26
529	1.26	530	1.26	531	1.26	532	1.27
533	1.27	534	1.27	535	1.28	536	1.28
537	1.28	538	1.28	539	1.29	540	1.29
541	1.29	542	1.30	543	1.30	544	1.31
545	1.31	546	1.32	547	1.32	548	1.32
549	1.32	550	1.33	551	1.33	552	1.33
553	1.33	554	1.34	555	1.34	556	1.35
557	1.35	558	1.35	559	1.35	560	1.35
561	1.36	562	1.36	563	1.36	564	1.36
565	1.36	566	1.36	567	1.37	568	1.37
569	1.37	570	1.37	571	1.38	572	1.38
573	1.38	574	1.38	575	1.39	576	1.39
577	1.39	578	1.40	579	1.40	580	1.40
581	1.41	582	1.41	583	1.41	584	1.41
585	1.41	586	1.41	587	1.41	588	1.41
589	1.42	590	1.43	591	1.43	592	1.44
593	1.44	594	1.44	595	1.44	596	1.45
597	1.45	598	1.45	599	1.46	600	1.46
601	1.46	602	1.46	603	1.47	604	1.47
605	1.47	606	1.48	607	1.48	608	1.48
609	1.48	610	1.48	611	1.49	612	1.49
613	1.52	614	1.50	615	1.50	616	1.50
617	1.50	618	1.51	619	1.51	620	1.52
621	1.53	622	1.53	623	1.53	624	1.53
625	1.53	626	1.54	627	1.54	628	1.54
629	1.55	630	1.55	631	1.55	632	1.55
633	1.55	634	1.55	635	1.56	636	1.56
637	1.56	638	1.57	639	1.57	640	1.58
641	1.58	642	1.58	643	1.59	644	1.59
645	1.59	646	1.60	647	1.60	648	1.60
649	1.61	650	1.61	651	1.61	652	1.61
653	1.61	654	1.62	655	1.62	656	1.62
657	1.63	658	1.63	659	1.64	660	1.64
661	1.64	662	1.64	663	1.64	664	1.64
665	1.65	666	1.65	667	1.65	668	1.65
669	1.65	670	1.66	671	1.66	672	1.66
673	1.66	674	1.66	675	1.66	676	1.67
677	1.67	678	1.67	679	1.67	680	1.68
681	1.68	682	1.69	683	1.70	684	1.70
685	1.70	686	1.70	687	1.71	688	1.71

Table 12.2 *(Continued)*

689	1.71	690	1.71	691	1.71	692	1.72
693	1.72	694	1.72	695	1.72	696	1.72
697	1.72	698	1.73	699	1.73	700	1.73
701	1.73	702	1.74	703	1.75	704	1.75
705	1.75	706	1.75	707	1.76	708	1.77
709	1.77	710	1.77	711	1.77	712	1.77
713	1.77	714	1.77	715	1.78	716	1.78
717	1.79	718	1.79	719	1.79	720	1.80
721	1.80	722	1.80	723	1.80	724	1.80
725	1.81	726	1.82	727	1.82	728	1.82
729	1.82	730	1.82	731	1.82	732	1.83
733	1.84	734	1.84	735	1.84	736	1.84
737	1.85	738	1.85	739	1.86	740	1.86
741	1.86	742	1.86	743	1.86	744	1.86
745	1.86	746	1.87	747	1.88	748	1.88
749	1.88	750	1.88	751	1.88	752	1.89
753	1.89	754	1.89	755	1.90	756	1.91
757	1.91	758	1.92	759	1.92	760	1.93
761	1.94	762	1.94	763	1.94	764	1.94
765	1.95	766	1.95	767	1.95	768	1.96
769	1.96	770	1.96	771	1.96	772	1.96
773	1.97	774	1.97	775	1.97	776	1.97
777	1.97	778	1.97	779	1.98	780	1.98
781	1.98	782	1.98	783	1.98	784	1.98
785	1.99	786	1.99	787	1.99	788	2.00
789	2.00	790	2.00	791	2.00	792	2.00
793	2.00	794	2.00	795	2.01	796	2.01
797	2.01	798	2.02	799	2.02	800	2.02
801	2.03	802	2.03	803	2.03	804	2.03
805	2.04	806	2.04	807	2.04	808	2.04
809	2.04	810	2.05	811	2.05	812	2.05
813	2.05	814	2.06	815	2.07	816	2.07
817	2.08	818	2.08	819	2.09	820	2.09
821	2.09	822	2.10	823	2.11	824	2.11
825	2.11	826	2.11	827	2.12	828	2.12
829	2.13	830	2.13	831	2.13	832	2.13
833	2.13	834	2.13	835	2.13	836	2.14
837	2.14	838	2.14	839	2.14	840	2.14
841	2.14	842	2.14	843	2.15	844	2.15
845	2.15	846	2.15	847	2.15	848	2.16
849	2.17	850	2.17	851	2.17	852	2.18
853	2.18	854	2.18	855	2.18	856	2.18
857	2.18	858	2.19	859	2.19	860	2.20
861	2.20	862	2.20	863	2.20	864	2.20

Table 12.2   (Continued)

865	2.21	866	2.21	867	2.22	868	2.23
869	2.23	870	2.24	871	2.24	872	2.25
873	2.25	874	2.25	875	2.26	876	2.26
877	2.26	878	2.26	879	2.27	880	2.27
881	2.28	882	2.28	883	2.28	884	2.29
885	2.29	886	2.29	887	2.29	888	2.30
889	2.30	890	2.30	891	2.30	892	2.31
893	2.31	894	2.32	895	2.32	896	2.32
897	2.33	898	2.33	899	2.34	900	2.34
901	2.34	902	2.34	903	2.35	904	2.36
905	2.36	906	2.37	907	2.37	908	2.38
909	2.38	910	2.38	911	2.38	912	2.39
913	2.39	914	2.39	915	2.40	916	2.40
917	2.40	918	2.41	919	2.41	920	2.42
921	2.42	922	2.43	923	2.44	924	2.45
925	2.46	926	2.46	927	2.46	928	2.47
929	2.47	930	2.47	931	2.48	932	2.48
933	2.48	934	2.49	935	2.50	936	2.50
937	2.51	938	2.51	939	2.51	940	2.51
941	2.51	942	2.51	943	2.52	944	2.52
945	2.53	946	2.53	947	2.53	948	2.53
949	2.54	950	2.54	951	2.54	952	2.54
953	2.54	954	2.56	955	2.56	956	2.57
957	2.58	958	2.60	959	2.60	960	2.60
961	2.60	962	2.61	963	2.61	964	2.62
965	2.62	966	2.63	967	2.64	968	2.64
969	2.64	970	2.65	971	2.65	972	2.65
973	2.65	974	2.66	975	2.66	976	2.66
977	2.68	978	2.68	979	2.68	980	2.69
981	2.69	982	2.69	983	2.70	984	2.70
985	2.71	986	2.71	987	2.71	988	2.71
989	2.72	990	2.73	991	2.73	992	2.73
993	2.74	994	2.74	995	2.75	996	2.75
997	2.75	998	2.77	999	2.78	1000	2.79
1001	2.79	1002	2.79	1003	2.79	1004	2.79
1005	2.80	1006	2.80	1007	2.80	1008	2.81
1009	2.81	1010	2.81	1011	2.82	1012	2.82
1013	2.83	1014	2.83	1015	2.83	1016	2.84
1017	2.84	1018	2.84	1019	2.85	1020	2.85
1021	2.86	1022	2.87	1023	2.87	1024	2.87
1025	2.87	1026	2.88	1027	2.88	1028	2.89
1029	2.89	1030	2.89	1031	2.89	1032	2.90
1033	2.92	1034	2.92	1035	2.93	1036	2.93
1037	2.93	1038	2.93	1039	2.94	1040	2.94

Table 12.2 *(Continued)*

1041	2.94	1042	2.95	1043	2.95	1044	2.95
1045	2.96	1046	2.96	1047	2.96	1048	2.97
1049	2.97	1050	2.98	1051	2.99	1052	2.99
1053	2.99	1054	2.99	1055	3.00	1056	3.00
1057	3.00	1058	3.00	1059	3.01	1060	3.01
1061	3.02	1062	3.04	1063	3.04	1064	3.04
1065	3.04	1066	3.05	1067	3.05	1068	3.06
1069	3.06	1070	3.06	1071	3.06	1072	3.07
1073	3.07	1074	3.07	1075	3.07	1076	3.08
1077	3.08	1078	3.08	1079	3.08	1080	3.09
1081	3.10	1082	3.10	1083	3.11	1084	3.11
1085	3.12	1086	3.12	1087	3.12	1088	3.13
1089	3.13	1090	3.14	1091	3.14	1092	3.14
1093	3.15	1094	3.15	1095	3.15	1096	3.16
1097	3.16	1098	3.17	1099	3.17	1100	3.18
1101	3.21	1102	3.23	1103	3.23	1104	3.24
1105	3.25	1106	3.25	1107	3.27	1108	3.27
1109	3.28	1110	3.29	1111	3.29	1112	3.30
1113	3.30	1114	3.30	1115	3.30	1116	3.31
1117	3.31	1118	3.32	1119	3.32	1120	3.32
1121	3.32	1122	3.32	1123	3.33	1124	3.34
1125	3.35	1126	3.40	1127	3.40	1128	3.40
1129	3.41	1130	3.41	1131	3.41	1132	3.41
1133	3.42	1134	3.42	1135	3.42	1136	3.42
1137	3.43	1138	3.44	1139	3.44	1140	3.44
1141	3.45	1142	3.45	1143	3.46	1144	3.46
1145	3.46	1146	3.46	1147	3.47	1148	3.47
1149	3.47	1150	3.47	1151	3.49	1152	3.49
1153	3.49	1154	3.50	1155	3.51	1156	3.51
1157	3.52	1158	3.52	1159	3.53	1160	3.56
1161	3.57	1162	3.58	1163	3.59	1164	3.61
1165	3.61	1166	3.61	1167	3.62	1168	3.64
1169	3.64	1170	3.65	1171	3.66	1172	3.67
1173	3.67	1174	3.68	1175	3.68	1176	3.68
1177	3.68	1178	3.69	1179	3.69	1180	3.70
1181	3.70	1182	3.71	1183	3.73	1184	3.74
1185	3.77	1186	3.78	1187	3.79	1188	3.80
1189	3.81	1190	3.81	1191	3.83	1192	3.84
1193	3.84	1194	3.85	1195	3.87	1196	3.87
1197	3.88	1198	3.88	1199	3.88	1200	3.88
1201	3.88	1202	3.90	1203	3.91	1204	3.92
1205	3.92	1206	3.94	1207	3.95	1208	3.97
1209	3.97	1210	3.98	1211	4.01	1212	4.02
1213	4.02	1214	4.02	1215	4.03	1216	4.03

Table 12.2   (Continued)

1217	4.04	1218	4.04	1219	4.07	1220	4.07
1221	4.07	1222	4.08	1223	4.08	1224	4.09
1225	4.09	1226	4.10	1227	4.11	1228	4.11
1229	4.16	1230	4.17	1231	4.18	1232	4.21
1233	4.23	1234	4.27	1235	4.27	1236	4.28
1237	4.28	1238	4.30	1239	4.30	1240	4.31
1241	4.32	1242	4.33	1243	4.34	1244	4.35
1245	4.35	1246	4.36	1247	4.39	1248	4.40
1249	4.40	1250	4.42	1251	4.42	1252	4.42
1253	4.43	1254	4.43	1255	4.44	1256	4.45
1257	4.45	1258	4.47	1259	4.48	1260	4.48
1261	4.48	1262	4.51	1263	4.53	1264	4.54
1265	4.55	1266	4.63	1267	4.64	1268	4.64
1269	4.65	1270	4.65	1271	4.66	1272	4.67
1273	4.67	1274	4.68	1275	4.68	1276	4.69
1277	4.70	1278	4.72	1279	4.72	1280	4.73
1281	4.77	1282	4.81	1283	4.81	1284	4.81
1285	4.83	1286	4.85	1287	4.86	1288	4.86
1289	4.88	1290	4.88	1291	4.89	1292	4.91
1293	4.91	1294	4.92	1295	4.93	1296	4.94
1297	4.98	1298	4.99	1299	5.00	1300	5.04
1301	5.13	1302	5.16	1303	5.16	1304	5.21
1305	5.21	1306	5.22	1307	5.23	1308	5.30
1309	5.31	1310	5.36	1311	5.45	1312	5.50
1313	5.53	1314	5.54	1315	5.54	1316	5.56
1317	5.61	1318	5.62	1319	5.70	1320	5.72
1321	5.77	1322	5.82	1323	5.89	1324	5.94
1325	5.98	1326	6.02	1327	6.03	1328	6.03
1329	6.05	1330	6.05	1331	6.07	1332	6.09
1333	6.12	1334	6.20	1335	6.22	1336	6.24
1337	6.27	1338	6.29	1339	6.31	1340	6.39
1341	6.42	1342	6.44	1343	6.46	1344	6.47
1345	6.67	1346	6.69	1347	6.69	1348	6.76
1349	6.77	1350	6.82	1351	6.85	1352	6.85
1353	7.02	1354	7.13	1355	7.23	1356	7.35
1357	7.51	1358	7.53	1359	7.57	1360	7.58
1361	7.67	1362	7.67	1363	7.74	1364	7.77
1365	7.96	1366	8.25	1367	8.27	1368	8.60
1369	8.99	1370	9.14	1371	9.16	1372	9.23
1373	9.40	1374	10.18	1375	10.37	1376	10.83
1377	11.80	1378	20.78	1379	21.41		

before expiration. You are considering writing naked straddles (a call and a put at the same strike price and the same expiration) to make some money. The OEX is at 381, so you get the market on the 380 straddles in the near month. They are at 5⅞. Should you write the straddles?

A price of 5⅞ translates to a 1.54 percent move on the index. By looking at the table, you can quickly calculate that approximately 55 percent of all two-week moves since 1939 have exceeded 1.54 percent in extent, so the odds of success are against you as a straddle writer at that price, and only slightly in your favor as a buyer. With those kinds of odds, I wouldn't participate on either side of the trade unless there were extraordinary circumstances.

The scenario just prior to the Persian Gulf War presented circumstances that could have lured me into a trade in which the historical odds were marginal at best. Fear dominated the marketplace. People were talking about $100-per-barrel oil. I felt confident that we would win the war and win decisively, plus the market was technically set up to rally. I wanted to buy calls 10 points out of the money with just one month left on them. In effect, I wanted to bet that the market would move more than 3.5 percent within one month, and I was counting on psychological factors to move options prices dramatically in the process.

Unfortunately, the fear translated to extraordinary premiums, and I would have had to risk almost 2 percent of the potential move to make the bet. I just couldn't justify the play in risk-reward terms. Had the options been at 2½ or 3 instead of 5¾ to 6, I would have played it in size.

Hopefully, these examples illustrate what a powerful basis the extended statistical profiles provide for trading options. Not only do I have these numbers compiled for biweekly moves, but I also have them for the weekly and monthly moves. I use them regularly in developing my options strategies, both for timing and for pricing.

EMERGING TRENDS IN MARKET VOLATILITY

When you're in the business daily for almost 30 years, you develop a feel for market volatility. For several years now, there has been no doubt in my mind that institutional dominance has changed the nature of market volatility, especially on an intraday basis. But when I got these numbers on percentage moves compiled, I began to wonder just how much, if any, market volatility had changed.

A cursory examination of the monthly data combined with my prior knowledge of market history made one fact abundantly clear: the decade of the 1930s was anomalous; that is, it was full of 10-percent-plus moves unmatched by any period prior or before. That's why I use only the data starting from 1939. I broke the data down into five periods and compared the distribution of percentage moves in the five periods. The results are summarized in Table 12.1.

Actually, I was surprised by the consistency of the results with one significant exception. From 1982 to 1992 (see Table 12.2), the percentage of two-week moves in the 3- to 4-percent range dropped, on average, 5.2 percent from the previous periods. The percentage of moves in the 7- to 8-percent range rose, on average, 4.7 percent. Obviously, there has been a shift in volatility from the lower range to the higher one. What is surprising about this is that the shift is so focused, so well defined between these two ranges. You would think that better information dissemination combined with institutional dominance in the market would translate to a general shift toward greater percentage volatility. Well, it doesn't, except intraday and in this particular range. This just bears out Dow Theory's premise that manipulation is possible only in the short term.

STRATEGIC PLANNING WITH OPTIONS

Up to now, I've been speaking mainly about using options to capture volatile moves within a relatively small time frame. But one of the beauties of options is that you can develop strategies for almost any market if you use them right. Let me take a recent example as a case in point.

1991 was a year for stock pickers until the market took off and rallied approximately 10 percent across the board in the last two weeks of December. For the two months after that, it traded in a narrow range, with the exception that the Over-the-Counter Market (OTC) and secondary sector started a slow-moving correction. By March, the S&P 500 had corrected 37 percent of the previous *intermediate* up move, while the Dow was still making new highs. In other words, the market was a mixed bag. The various indexes weren't trending together, making it hard to trade on the broader market. In this kind of mixed but relatively stable environment, you can use options to make some consistent income with very low risk.

During March 1991, the market was choppy with a mild bullish bias, and I thought it would remain stable for several weeks. In this scenario, a strategy I have used successfully is to sell naked straddles surrounded by wings. The OEX cash index was at 383 and a fraction. The April 385 calls were at 5⅜ and the puts were at 6⅞, making the one-month straddles worth 12¼. Since I thought the market was going to remain stable, I sold the straddles. To protect myself from unexpected events, for each straddle, I bought a 400 call at ⅞ and a 375 put at 2¼, making my net premium 9⅛. These are the wings.

Table 12.3 shows a breakdown of all monthly moves on the Dow since May 1982. As you can see, the median *monthly* move is 2.2 percent, and 59 percent of all monthly moves since 1982 have been less than 3 percent. If the OEX moves up the median level of 2.2 percent to 391.4 by expiration, I will probably have to pay about 7½ to buy the calls back, but I will still net about 1⅝ on the deal. If it moves up higher than that, I'll lose some money, but I won't be killed because of the hedge provided by the 400 call. Furthermore, in general, the premium will erode more quickly on the straddle than it will on the wings, which works in my favor. The same thing applies on the downside. But if the market behaves as I expect it to, staying in a 1- to 2-percent range, then I'll lock in a nice little profit. I make money even while the market virtually sits still.

That isn't a great trade, but it isn't bad either. The risk is very low, the chances for reward are good, and the leverage is excellent. The average investor will have to put up about $2 thousand in margin for each set of straddles and wings of this type. A profit of just $200 per setup makes for a handsome 10 percent return in a month—not bad for a flat market.

This is just one example of many possible applications to use options for strategic trading. They can also be used for hedge, arbitrage, and insurance purposes not just in the equities market, but in the futures as well. Too many books have been written on various options strategies for me to go into more specific details.

CONCLUSION

Options are, many say, the riskiest game in town. Certainly they are by far the most challenging, flexible, and potentially profitable financial instruments available. But if you trade them prudently, if you apply sound

Table 12.3   Dow Jones Industrials—Absolute Monthly Percentage Changes,
May 1982–June 1993

This table shows the distribution of monthly moves in the Dow Industrials in low–high order. Only data since May 1982 are used in this table since that is when the S&P futures began trading. The median percentage move listed is 2.2 percent. Less than 4 percent of the time will the market end the month more than 10 percent from where it began the month.

0–1%	1%–2%	2%–3%	3%–4%	4%–5%	5%–6%	6%–7%	7%–10%	10+%
1 0	31 1.0	64 2.0	79 3.0	92 4.0	1 5.0	12 6.1	20 7.1	28 10.0
2 0	32 1.0	65 2.1	80 3.0	93 4.0	2 5.2	13 6.2	21 7.5	29 10.6
3 .1	33 1.0	**66 2.2**	81 3.0	94 4.0	3 5.3	14 6.2	22 8.0	30 11.4
4 .1	34 1.1	67 2.3	82 3.3	95 4.1	4 5.4	15 6.2	23 8.2	31 13.8
5 .1	35 1.3	68 2.3	83 3.4	96 4.5	5 5.4	16 6.3	24 8.5	32 23.2
6 .2	36 1.3	69 2.3	84 3.4	97 4.5	6 5.4	17 6.4	25 8.7	
7 .2	37 1.3	70 2.4	85 3.5	98 4.7	7 5.5	18 6.8	26 9.0	
8 .2	38 1.4	71 2.4	86 3.5	99 4.8	8 5.6	19 6.9	27 9.7	
9 .3	39 1.4	72 2.5	87 3.6	00 4.8	9 5.7			
10 .3	40 1.4	73 2.5	88 3.8		10 5.7			
11 .4	41 1.4	74 2.5	89 3.9		11 5.9			
12 .4	42 1.4	75 2.7	90 3.9					
13 .4	43 1.5	76 2.8	91 3.9					
14 .4	44 1.5	77 2.8						
15 .4	45 1.5	78 2.9						
16 .5	46 1.5							
17 .5	47 1.5							
18 .6	48 1.5							
19 .6	49 1.5							
20 .6	50 1.6							
21 .6	51 1.6							
22 .6	52 1.6							
23 .7	53 1.7							
24 .8	54 1.7							
25 .8	55 1.7							
26 .8	56 1.7							
27 .8	57 1.8							
28 .8	58 1.8							
29 .9	59 1.8							
30 .9	60 1.9							
	61 1.9							
	62 1.9							
	63 1.9							

principles of money management, trade only when the risk/reward ratio is highly in your favor, and execute your trades with diligence and patience, then in all likelihood you will be profitable over the long term. I can say, conservatively, that at least 40 percent of all the returns I've made in my life have been with options.

Remember these critical points:

1. High premiums always indicate impending news.
2. Never use more than 3 percent of your capital to trade one option position.
3. Always know the odds and risk/reward ratio of your trade.
4. Do not use models that are typical.
5. Writing options will make you money most of the time, but you will lose in the long run.
6. Build a strategy that limits risk but has a risk/reward ratio of at least 3 to 1, with 5 to 1 preferred.

The key to my success is focusing on risk with a combination of economic and fundamental analysis and statistical life-expectancy profiles. When you use these tools, you can play the odds effectively and end up winning.

13

A Professional Method of Day Trading*

Lorenzo Ghiberti, the fifteenth-century sculptor, had all the character traits necessary to be a great day trader: dedication, focus, concentration, determination, and willpower to complete a task. Ghiberti spent 48 years sculpting four bronze doors for the Baptistery of San Giovanni in Florence, Italy. Imagine working on a single project for 48 years. With no one to talk to for most of the day, the painstaking work would seem endless.

In many respects, the willpower and mind-set of a trader is not too different from that of a master sculptor. Both work alone, in focus, concentrating on minor detail, forming the details in their minds, then bringing it forth. They are both very individual, solemn businesses, and the results are rather slow and plodding, yet they can add up to a masterpiece.

As I began to watch the ticker tape at Filer Schmidt & Company in 1968, I became in effect a day trader, and I remained one for the next 18 years. By 1986, I had developed an amazing pace: 30 trades a day in the S&P futures. I also developed high blood pressure, so I switched to trading the intermediate trend. After all, it's not a meaningful accomplishment to become the richest man in the cemetery. In 1987, I made only 5 trades, made 168 percent on my capital, worked out with a personal trainer five days a week, and got my health back to normal!

---

* This chapter is dedicated to Howard Shapiro who was the best day trader I ever knew.

Where is the moral of the story? Well, after the Gulf War in January 1991, the stock market turned into the dullest market in the past 97 years (see Chapter 7), and intermediate market trading became next to impossible. So, I went back to day trading for a while. In this chapter, I hope to add some insight to this very difficult, very intense business.

THE PSYCHOLOGICAL REQUIREMENTS

Overall, day trading has always been very easy for me, because I have a personality trait that lends itself to this particular business, and that is the ability to take losses and never let it bother me.

Most people hate to be wrong. No one I ever knew relished saying, "You know, I'm dead wrong in this." Ego is the killer here; ego in the psychological sense, rather than in the philosophical meaning, is the opposite of self esteem. Ego (or false pride) says (subconsciously) "I can never be wrong, or make a mistake, because I am great. If I do make an error in judgment, I will not be respected." But human beings are not gods, and traders are not omniscient; they *must* be wrong sometimes. To be unwilling to accept this would be illogical.

To be a day trader you need self-esteem, the healthy sense that you are competent and worthy. If you don't feel confident with your own judgment, you can't execute your trades properly. In order to trade, you must be able to take losses, thousands of them, and yet come back and trade again with confidence. Just remember: Don't let ego (false pride) take the place of self-esteem.

Ideal day traders are deeply introspective, and know who they are as deeply as possible. To be a successful day trader means to be real and honest with yourself at all times. Without the ability to be honest with yourself, forget this chapter—you cannot day trade. You must be at a stage where you do not try to lie to yourself. The simple fact is, you *will* lose sometimes. You don't have to rationalize it away; you don't have to hide behind typical defense mechanisms. Just stand up and say "I'm wrong." This admission does not mean that you are stupid or incompetent. Being wrong is part of this business, and a part of life. In day trading, you are your only enemy; you are your own boss, and you determine your own destiny.

THE KNOWLEDGE REQUIREMENTS

With this background in mind, let me tell you about some knowledge you'll need to acquire. Begin by buying a copy of Yale Hirsch's yearly *Stock Trader's Almanac.* The information it contains about the nature of the market is superb. In the late 1960s and early 1970s, I made a living just by reading this book. The introduction of program trading into the markets has changed things somewhat, but many of the facts Yale Hirsch publishes are important and recurring. You must have this information even to begin making decisions, in the same way you must know the alphabet in order to read.

What I'm going to do in this chapter is teach you how to day trade by predicting the pattern of the market. If you have listened to any of the messages on my 900-number phone line, you understand my technique of calling the markets. The basic concept is this: Know what is *supposed* to happen, and then if it doesn't happen, you'll know immediately that you are wrong and must make adjustments. For instance, you may plan to go on a picnic tomorrow and the weatherforecaster says it is going to be sunny, fine. You plan the picnic, but when you wake up the next morning, it is raining. You wouldn't say, "It's not raining" and go outside to lie on the grass. What you would do is say, "It's raining—the weatherforecaster must have misread the satellite pictures—so I'm going to change my plans and go to a movie." Again, the key to trading is to know in advance what is supposed to happen, so if it doesn't you can adapt to the situation quickly!

Your prediction should be based on the following ingredients:

1. Knowledge of the trend in the long, intermediate, and short term.
2. A feel for and understanding of the economic news of the day.
3. Knowledge of the seasonals (knowing what happens at each time of the year), which you can obtain from the *Stock Trader's Almanac.*
4. Grasp of the technical considerations, such as option expirations, program trading clues, chart patterns, institutional money management biases (i.e., end-of-quarter markup), earnings reports, and Mutual fund outflows or inflows of public cash.
5. Awareness of pending political changes.

6. Ability to interpret Fed policy meetings, and their market interventions which all have a meaning.
7. Being well read in all the current themes worldwide, such as the state of the European economies. Read *Barron's* and *The Wall Street Journal* (especially the editorials in both), *New York Times* and *Washington Post* (skip the editorials in both), *Forbes, Fortune, Investor's Daily, London Times, The Economist, Newsweek, Business Week,* and *Institutional Investor Magazine.*
8. A healthy mental attitude, free of outside pressure.
9. Good physical condition—fit, awake, alert.
10. Focused, observant, intense attitude and deep concentrated thought about all the markets and how they relate.

In *Trader Vic—Methods of a Wall Street Master,* I had a chapter of rules called "There Must Be Fifty ways to Lose Your Money." Some of these rules apply only to floor traders. Since I trained many people for work on the floors of exchanges, I made them aware of these important rules, which I had printed up on cards. (For an in-depth explanation, see *Trader Vic—Methods.*) Here is a somewhat different list of rules I keep in front of me at all times when trading:

Traders' Commandments

1. Do not overtrade.
2. Do not take a loss home.
3. Never add to a bad trade.
4. Never let a profit become a loss.
5. Always figure your stop loss before you initiate a trade.
6. Don't be a one-way trader. Be flexible.
7. Add to profitable trades when appropriate. The best time to buy or sell is after consolidations and a break above or below range prices.
8. Concentrate on one pit, if you're on the floor.
9. Learn the quirks of all traders and brokers.
10. Try to avoid trading in the middle of the session unless the market is active.
11. Never leave the floor or your machine without a stop loss order entered for every position.

---

12. Be cautious when you buy rallies or sell breaks while initiating a new trade.
13. Stifle your emotions, including fear, greed, hope, pride of opinion, anxiety, recklessness, and happiness.
14. Have patience.
15. Cut your losses and let your profits run.
16. If you are not sure, don't trade.

DAY TRADING, STEP BY STEP

Now that you are prepared to trade, the first thing you must do is forecast what is supposed to happen throughout the day. After 28 years in the business, this comes to me from my subconscious *after* I've read the papers and posted my charts: the high, low, and close of the Dow, S&P, Transports, and A/D line. I do this first thing in the morning, and I'm finished by 5:30 A.M.

After you look at how the world markets are trading, including the overnight trading of U.S. bonds and stocks, and look over today's news, especially the news that will affect the markets during the next several days, you can make a prediction. This is very important. When inflation is the watchword, economists make their estimates *several days before,* so if the key number is coming out in several days you must focus on what economists are going to project. If that number is coming out within five days, follow the *opening* of the markets very carefully, and especially look for *gaps* at the opening; they are signs of the economists' projections, and how they're estimating the numbers.

You now are ready to make a call. Bonds have traded overnight, but the news for the day has not been released yet. It usually starts coming out at 8:30 A.M. New York time. My first call of the day on my 900-number is around 8:50 A.M.; by then I have a feel for bonds, the news, and the momentum of overnight stocks. When I call the market, all that I have discussed is integrated into a whole, and I put myself on the line every day.

My calls are made at 9:00 A.M., 12:00 noon, 3:00 P.M., and 5:00 P.M. weekdays. There is also a longer, intermediate-term-oriented message at 5:00 P.M. on Sundays. When I'm dead wrong, or when the markets are extremely volatile, I make short updates at 10:30 A.M. or 1:30 P.M.. Here is a sample morning call:

Monday Morning Call, 9:00 A.M., July 12, 1993

Bonds are up on the −0.2 percent to −0.3 percent projections on the PPI coming out tomorrow. This is fully discounted. Bonds, currently +3, should be somewhere between +8 to −2 on the day. At +16, profits should be taken, since these projections were known last Thursday. Stocks will follow bonds today. The pattern will be a flat-to-up opening, a rally, sell-off, and a rally on the close. Net a mixed-to-up day. Gold slightly higher after profit taking on Friday, which had nothing to do with the PPI or CPI numbers. Gold should trade at $400 after Wednesday, and currently is trading at $394. Soybeans will trade lower on a break in the weather. Don't sell weakness; hold for a rally. We have over a 100-point profit on Soybeans, from 615 to 717. I'll let you know what to do at 12 o'clock.

Having a blueprint like this for the day is critical, because if something happens in opposition to your prediction, it is a *signal* that something is wrong. Perhaps there is a "program trade," or you're wrong in your interpretation of the news, or you underweighted the importance of some legislation. The point is, you must know *in advance* what all this is going to mean; the fact that the reverse is happening is very valuable for turning a loss into a profit. A simple slogan I've used throughout my career is: "When something is supposed to happen and doesn't, reverse your position immediately."

Let me reference this to discussing the opening of the S&P futures. This is a critical part of the day. The most important ingredients in your profit mix are: (1) the opening range, and the direction prices take immediately after the opening; (2) whether the opening is above yesterday's close, and (3) whether it is higher than yesterday's high or lower than yesterday's low.

Knowing nothing else, if the market trades above the opening range today, you should buy with a stop one tick below the high of the range. For example, if the market closed at 450.00 yesterday and today's opening range is 450.00–450.25, you should buy at 450.30 with a sell stop at 450.20. However, you should only use that sell stop to go flat, not to initiate a short position. If the market breaks the high of the opening range and starts to trade higher after a gap, it is possible you have seen the lows of the day. It is especially significant if the opening tick is the low of the day initially; that can mean a strong upday will follow (the opposite is true for downdays).

As a trader, you must also know that your job is to buy and sell, not to hold. When trading the S&P futures, a key point to take a partial profit (meaning you must trade at least two contracts) is one point (one "handle") above the opening price, or in this case 451.00. At that price, you sell one-half your position. Why? Because this is what traders on the floor do. It's a tacit agreement of the inner circle.

If there is a gap, and it is going to reverse, it will do so 10 to 15 minutes after the opening 95 percent of the time. Please believe me on the odds, they are real. If the market continues in the direction of the gap after 10 to 15 minutes, it is a strong sign that the move will continue for the rest of the day, closing in that direction as well. Even if the market reverses after the 10 to 15 minute period, if it fails to fill the gap, odds are that the market will close in the direction of the gap. This also applies to stocks and other commodities.

Let me pause a minute. The opening and the action following it takes up about half an hour. The normal movement after that usually is strictly trader or "local" oriented, where one market keys off another based on some news, statement, or internal development, fundamental or technical. An example would be the typical action in the bond market. When bonds move, stocks move, and then gold moves, then the CRB Index, and then other commodities. Of course, there are limits to these movements; they may not move at all, but most of the time there is some minor interrelated impact. The fundamentals to these relationships are important to understand, and they are explained indirectly throughout this book and my previous one, *Trader Vic: Methods*. The more you can understand macroeconomic events, the more money you will make. A typical daily pattern is:

> From 10:00 A.M. until 11:45 A.M., the markets are quiet and usually focus on any Fed action, which usually comes around 11:40 A.M.. Most Fed action is anticipated and not unusual, but traders must be alert for that 1 percent of the time when the action sends signals of a critical change in policy. From 11:45 A.M. to 2:30 P.M., the stock market tends to remain quiet, and generally chops up and down. After 2:30 P.M., stay awake—most moves begin to show themselves here.

H-hour begins at 3:10 P.M.. Whatever direction the market takes at this time will follow to the close about 80 percent of the time. Here again, watch for a move after 3:10 P.M.; then watch for a reversal. If it goes the other way and back through the prices set at 3:10 P.M., it indicates an even bigger move in that direction. Please note this is a general pattern not a "sun will rise in the east" phenomena.

You should also keep in mind that during most days the S&P futures have four distinct movements: (1) the opening and contraopening move; (2) a choppy one-direction move from 10:00 A.M. to 12:00 noon; (3) a choppy move in the opposite direction between 12:00 noon and 2:30 P.M.; and (4) the close, usually in one direction. The key word here is *usually*. All things being equal, you have to expect what "usually" happens and adjust to all the contingencies. Most other commodities have the same trading pattern as well, except that the times must be adjusted for each commodity due to different trading hours (see Figure 13.1).

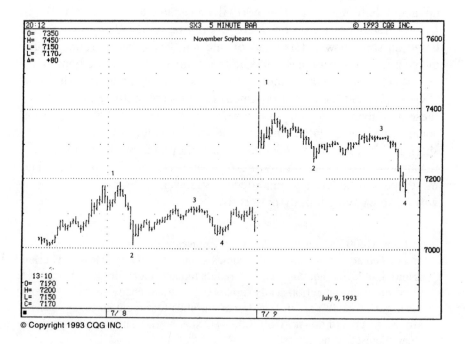

© Copyright 1993 CQG INC.

FIGURE 13.1   Moves per day.

SHORT-TERM TRENDS

Throughout this book, I have emphasized using historical studies to guide you, with odds to make the best speculations. This policy must be integrated into an overall approach, so as not to weight one aspect of trading too heavily. Knowledge of all the ingredients I've mentioned should be blended to assure a more consistent result.

To achieve this integration, you must be aware that trading within a day is part of the short-term trend, meaning one that lasts from days to weeks and almost never more than 14 days. Any longer than that and you are dealing with the intermediate-term trend, or weeks to months. The short-term trend is often thought to be an irrational aberration, impossible to predict. Wrong!

Today's action can give you a big clue and edge on the next day. Figure 13.2 shows the actual way a real-life example works. The idea is to trade the day within the context of what the short-term trend should be!

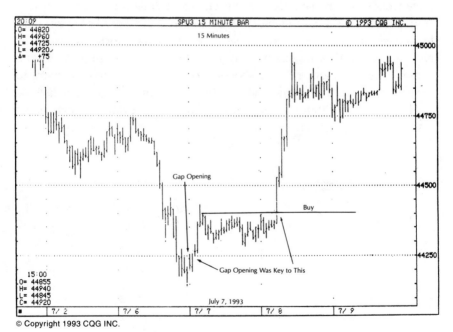

© Copyright 1993 CQG INC.

FIGURE 13.2   Standard & Poor's futures.

In Figure 13.2 the September S&P Futures (15-minute chart) traded in an unusual manner. In this example, it is implicit that stocks *follow* bonds, but on July 7th bonds were down yet the S&P futures gaped up at the opening, which is a tell tale sign of *"unusual."* This had to do with July 13th and 14th forecasts that were coming out on July 7th of the producer and consumer price index.

The question should immediately strike a trader—why are stock futures up and bonds down? The fact you don't know is not critical but the reality that the gap was not filled from the July 6 close was a very bullish sign. It led to the ability to predict the July 8th pattern of *up.* As you can see on the chart, the market was telling you on the 7th that something positive was happening because stocks should have followed bonds down for the day.

If the short-term trend is up, you can estimate what the next day will be like *until it isn't anymore.* In other words, you can predict what is supposed to happen tomorrow, and if that fails to happen, you know that a change is probably occurring that will affect the short-term trend. This applies exactly the same way when short-term trends change to intermediate trends and intermediate trends change to long-term trends.

In Figure 13.3, I have included daily patterns, composed of open-high-low-close, that tell you a great deal about what the short-term trend is, and what the following day will be like. Please study these patterns and commit them to memory. The short-term trend usually moves contra to the intermediate-term trend and usually lasts from one to three days.

Here is a list of items you can use to interpret the daily action. Using a simple scoring system, each item would be worth one point.

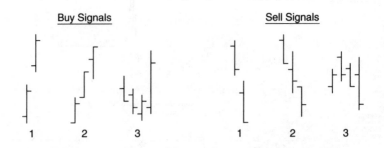

FIGURE 13.3   Buy and sell signals.

Did the stock or commodity. . .

1. Make a higher high or lower low than yesterday?
2. Open up or down on the day?
3. Close up or down on the day?
4. Close in the upper 50 percent or the lower 50 percent of today's range?
5. Close above or below today's open?
6. Make a higher low or a lower high than yesterday?
7. Close above yesterday's high or below yesterday's low?

You would score a point for each item that is bullish, and subtract one for each that is bearish. To clarify, the bullish sides of the items are:

1. Making a higher high than yesterday.
2. Opening up on the day.
3. Closing up on the day.
4. Closing in the upper 50 percent of the range.
5. Closing above the opening.
6. Having a higher low than yesterday.
7. Closing above yesterday's high.

When you get all seven items going in the same direction, the next day is 90 percent likely to trade above the high of that day, and 80 percent of the time will close above the close. If you wish, you could play with these items and build a trading system out of it. I have done this, but I am not selling you a system. I am trying to show you how to integrate bullish or bearish observations into a method of forecasting the next day with a high degree of probability. This is only one valid observation, however; there are obviously many others (see Figure 13.4).

The best way for me to describe the thought process, so that you can observe and build your own predictions, is to use the metaphor of *The Magnificent Seven.* In this classic Western starring Yul Brynner and Steve McQueen, farmers in a Mexican village hire Yul and six other professional gunfighters to protect them from bandits. As the selection process takes place, one of the villagers looks at a man with a huge scar on his face and says "He must be tough. Just look at the scar on his face."

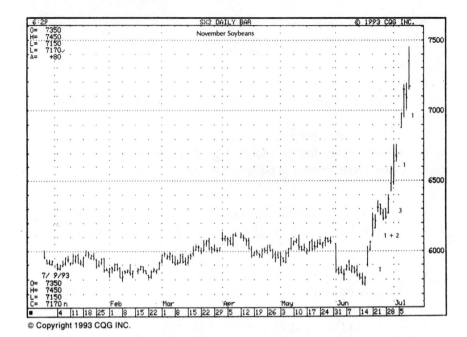

© Copyright 1993 CQG INC.

FIGURE 13.4   Buy signals.

Another man says, "No, you want the man who *gave* him that scar, not him." Yul turns and says, "Now you're learning!"

You must study and observe the recurring winning patterns. I can't give them to you because I don't know them all, and they change to a degree with each commodity or stock, but I am trying to teach you what to look for and how to begin.

ANALYZING A TREND

The best way to test theories, as we have seen throughout this book, is to do a study as far back as you can. Here is a critical and powerful example:

Trading within the Intermediate Trend

By knowing the direction of the *intermediate-term trend,* the trader can use this information to trade within the short term or minor trend. This works on everything that moves.

Essentially, this comes down to a question of knowing the daily odds. For example, during an intermediate-term uptrend in the stock market, the daily odds are as follows:

No. of Downdays	Odds of Next Day Being Up
1	60.0 percent
2	85.9 percent
3	94.4 percent

Simple, but how did I get these odds? To find these numbers, first you must classify the intermediate moves. As an example, note the numbers in Table 13.1. You then measure each sequence of up- and downdays for intermediate up moves in bull markets and corrections. For bear markets, you measure the downday sequences for bear markets and bull market corrections. I've given you the totals and the way I measured them to find the pertinent data. I did the work first by hand, and then later by computer. The classifications are done by Dow Theory standards.

For these studies, I used the Dow Industrials, since they go back to 1897. However, this study covers the period since 1926 because I was relating it to a system on the S&P futures which began in 1926. I used the Dow instead of the S&P because I already had the data, and the moves correlate almost perfectly. The variance is insignificant.

What does all this tell you? As much as you can observe. For one example, look at the totals for "Bull Market Intermediate Upmoves." Most of the time, if the intermediate trend is up in a bull market, you can expect a 3-day upmove with a mean percentage gain of 2.068 percent. When the market then sells off, you would expect only a 1.666 percent decline. Also, you can expect many more 1-day declines in an uptrend (1,042 occurrences) versus 1-day upmoves (692 occurrences). But in an upmove

Table 13.1   Analyzing Intermediate Moves

Dow Industrials Bull Market Intermediate Moves

Decline (Bottom)	7/31/23	86.91
Advance	8/29/23	93.70
Decline	10/27/23	85.76
Advance	2/6/24	101.31
Decline	5/20/24	88.33
Advance	8/20/24	105.57
Decline	10/14/24	99.18
Advance	3/6/25	125.68
Decline	3/30/25	115.00
Advance	2/11/26	162.31
Decline	3/30/26	135.20
Advance	8/14/26	166.64
Decline	10/19/26	145.66
Advance	10/3/27	199.78
Decline	10/22/27	179.78
Advance	5/14/28	220.88
Decline	6/18/28	201.96
Advance	11/28/28	295.62
Decline	12/8/28	257.33
Advance	2/5/29	322.06
Decline	5/27/29	293.42
Advance (Top)	9/3/29	381.17

Dow Industrials Bear Market Intermediate Moves

Advance (Top)	9/3/29	381.17
Decline	10/4/29	325.17
Advance	10/10/29	352.86
Decline	11/13/29	198.69
Advance	4/17/30	294.07
Decline	6/24/30	211.84
Advance	9/10/30	245.09
Decline	12/16/30	157.51
Advance	2/24/31	194.36
Decline	6/2/31	121.70
Advance	6/27/31	156.93
Decline	10/5/31	86.48
Advance	11/9/31	116.79
Decline	1/5/32	71.24
Advance	3/8/32	88.78
Decline (Bottom)	7/8/32	41.22

Table 13.1   *(Continued)*

Bull Market Intermediate Upmoves
Sample Analysis of One Move

Date Begin: 3/30/26   Date End: 8/14/26   No. of Days: 113
Dow Begin: 140.46   Dow End: 166.64   No. of Pts.: 26.18
% Change: 18.6%

Mean Upmove: 2.05%   Mean Downmove: −1.21%
Median Upmove: 1.74%   Median Downmove: −.99%
Mean Updays: 3.04   Mean Downdays: 1.73
Median Updays: 3   Median Downdays: 1

Upday Sequences:

No. of Days	No. of Times Occurred	Median % Move
1	6	.28
2	4	1.13
3	6	1.56
4	4	1.77
5	2	2.27
6	0	N/A
7	1	6.13
8	1	4.49

Downday Sequences:

No. of Days	No. of Times Occurred	Median % Move
1	15	−0.79
2	5	−1.68
3	0	N/A
4	1	−2.8
5	1	−2.77
6	1	−1.89

Totals: All Bull Market Intermediate Upmoves from 1926 through 1985

Upday Sequences:

No. of Days	No. of Times Occurred	Median % Move
1	692	0.39
2	530	1.06
3	349	1.72
4	168	2.29
5	114	2.82
6	61	2.90
7	31	3.46
8	21	4.07

Table 13.1   *(Continued)*

No. of Days	No. of Times Occurred	Median % Move
9	12	3.30
10	7	4.96
11	2	2.83
12	1	8.23

Downday Sequences:

No. of Days	No. of Times Occurred	Median % Move
1	1042	−0.33
2	523	−0.83
3	214	−1.45
4	86	−1.87
5	35	−2.36
6	19	−2.59
7	3	−3.12
8	0	N/A
9	1	−3.05

Bull Market Corrections
Sample Analysis of One Move

Date Begin: 8/14/26   Date End: 10/19/26   No. of Days: 53
Dow Begin: 166.10   Dow End: 145.66   No. of Pts.: −20.44
% Change: −12.3%

Mean Upmove: 1.05%   Mean Downmove: −1.92%
Median Upmove: .92%   Median Downmove: −1.71%
Mean Updays: 1.69   Mean Downdays: 2.21
Median Updays: 2   Median Downdays: 2

Upday Sequences:

No. of Days	No. of Times Occurred	Median % Move
1	6	0.71
2	5	1.29
3	2	0.91

Downday Sequences:

No. of Days	No. of Times Occurred	Median % Move
1	5	−0.58
2	5	−1.84
3	2	−2.40
4	0	N/A
5	2	−4.58

Totals: All Bull Market Corrections from 1926 through 1985

Table 13.1   *(Continued)*

Upday Sequences:

No. of Days	No. of Times Occurred	Median % Move
1	233	0.43
2	142	0.95
3	52	1.64
4	14	1.77
5	18	2.25
6	6	1.89
7	2	1.48
8	0	N/A
9	1	8.27

Downday Sequences:

No. of Days	No. of Times Occurred	Median % Move
1	195	−0.43
2	117	−1.15
3	90	−1.94
4	61	−2.89
5	29	−3.09
6	11	−4.21
7	7	−4.08
8	2	−7.56

Bear Market Intermediate Downmoves
Sample Analysis of One Move

Date Begin: 9/3/29	Date End: 10/4/29	No. of Days: 27
Dow Begin: 381.17	Dow End: 325.17	No. of Pts.: −56.00
% Change: −14.6%		

Mean Upmove: 1.08%	Mean Downmove: −2.89%
Median Upmove: .96%	Median Downmove: −3.00%
Mean Updays: 1.42	Mean Downdays: 2.12
Median Updays: 1	Median Downdays: 2

Upday Sequences:

No. of Days	No. of Times Occurred	Median % Move
1	5	0.67
2	1	2.10
3	1	1.65

Table 13.1   *(Continued)*

Downday Sequences:

No. of Days	No. of Times Occurred	Median % Move
1	3	−1.23
2	4	−3.00
3	0	N/A
4	0	N/A
5	0	N/A
6	1	−5.03

Totals: All Bear Market Intermediate Downmoves from 1926 through 1985

Upday Sequences:

No. of Days	No. of Times Occurred	Median % Move
1	421	0.47
2	202	1.11
3	84	1.79
4	36	2.14
5	19	2.64
6	6	2.24
7	2	2.84
8	0	N/A
9	0	N/A
10	1	5.59

Downday Sequences:

No. of Days	No. of Times Occurred	Median % Move
1	244	−0.04
2	218	−1.40
3	165	−2.23
4	72	−2.72
5	64	−3.55
6	29	−4.69
7	21	−5.68
8	10	−8.99
9	1	−4.37

Table 13.1   *(Continued)*

Bear Market Intermediate Corrections
Sample Analysis of One Move

Date Begin: 10/4/29   Date End: 10/10/29   No. of Days: 5
Dow Begin: 325.17   Dow End: 352.86   No. of Pts.: 27.69
% Change: 8.5%

Mean Upmove: 4.26%   Mean Downmove: −.21%
Median Upmove: 2.27%   Median Downmove: −.21%
Mean Updays: 2   Mean Downdays: 1
Median Updays: 2   Median Downdays: 1

Upday Sequences:

No. of Days	No. of Times Occurred	Median % Move
1	0	N/A
2	2	2.27

Downday Sequences:

No. of Days	No. of Times Occurred	Median % Move
1	1	−.21

Totals: All Bear Market Intermediate Corrections from 1926 through 1985

Upday Sequences:

No. of Days	No. of Times Occurred	Median % Move
1	231	0.51
2	205	1.14
3	120	1.73
4	61	2.10
5	43	2.84
6	22	3.12
7	5	2.19
8	6	3.47
9	2	2.44
10	1	4.62

Table 13.1   *(Continued)*

Downday Sequences:

No. of Days	No. of Times Occurred	Median % Move
1	339	−0.36
2	170	−0.74
3	76	−1.16
4	34	−1.89
5	19	−2.16
6	10	−3.39
7	4	−4.36
8	1	−4.58

you'd expect many more 2-, 3-, and 4-day up sequences; the percentages are all listed there.

One way to use this data in day trading is to set up an example. Assume an intermediate bull market uptrend is in force and that you have declines 3 days in a row for a loss of 1.666 percent. You can integrate this with the days' down odds I've given you (with 3 downdays, odds are 94.4 percent that the next day is up) and say that if you buy at the close of the third downday, you can expect to make an average percentage gain of 1.309 percent or a median change of 1.06 percent in 2 days. You could use these odds and numbers a hundred different ways.

All you need is imagination and time to go with the direction I'm showing you. Could I show you a system? Yes! But systems don't work all the time, and I don't use them as such. Any system I could give you might require changes by the time you read this book. Besides, for you to trade a system religiously, you must truly believe in it, and any system I offer here won't mean as much to you as one of your own creation. What I much prefer to give you, what I hope I *have* given you, is the big picture. *Good luck and leave scars!*

PART FOUR
A TRADER'S PSYCHOLOGY

14

The Character and Personality of a Trader

What does it take to be a successful trader? Experience? A good "feel" for the market? Mastery of analytical atechniques? All these are important, but reaching even the highest level of "facts and figures" expertise is not in itself sufficient. To achieve real success as a trader—no matter how you define "success"—you must have all the ingredients of a trader's psychology: good character, a certain personality type, and a particular way of thinking.

ACHIEVING REAL SUCCESS

To a large extent, this book, like most others that deal with the market, concentrates on the cognitive sphere: all the things we can know and understand with our mind. The preceding chapters concern themselves with concrete, rational, scientific ideas: techniques of technical analysis, basic economic principles, tables of illustrative data.

To be sure, these tools, and the mental acuity to apply them intelligently, are absolutely essential to success as a trader. But genuine success as a whole, integrated human being, takes more than a good brain. It also takes character.

Character is a function of a person's ethical and moral philosophy. Webster's dictionary defines it as "the complex of mental and ethical traits marking a person." Ethics are evident in the code of values that guide a person's actions and choices. Do you put your own interests and those of your family first, or are you more concerned with the well-being of others? Do you choose honesty over lying, integrity rather than hypocrisy, productiveness over idleness? Can you consistently weigh, based on some internal sense of right and wrong, justice versus mercy, rationality versus emotional whim, pride versus humility? The process of making those choices and decisions may be intuitive and hard to explain, but in all cases it begins with your own personal sense of morality and ethics— in other words, your character.

Personality, on the other hand, is how a person *behaves* as opposed to what that person *believes*. Again from Webster's: "(1) . . . the complex of characteristics that distinguishes an individual; (2) the totality of an individual's behavioral and emotional tendencies; (3) the organization of the individual's distinguishing character traits, attitudes or habits; (4) their disposition."

Do you have the type of character and personality necessary to be a successful trader? What are the ingredients of a healthy psychology? Can humans learn to change? These critical questions are extremely important to everyone in leading a happy and successful life, but they are even more critical to a profession that is one of the toughest on Earth.

The reason trading is so difficult is that you cannot lie, hide, feign, or rationalize failure. In the life of a trader, reality is what it is. *Or in Aristotelian terms, A is A!* If you are a lawyer and you lose a case, you can rationalize "the jury was biased." If you are a doctor and the patient dies, you can say "I did all that was humanly possible but it was in God's hands." In both cases, the professionals still get paid. However, at the end of the trader's marking period—be it a day, a month, a quarter, or a year—the "report card" will either show plus or minus capital. There are no excuses, because all that matters in this business is the bottom line. Traders don't get paid for failure.

Ayn Rand's great discussion on the trader principle includes this statement:

> The symbol of all relationships among [rational] men, the moral symbol of respect for human beings, is *the trader*. We, who live by values, not by loot, are traders, both in matter and in spirit. A trader is a man who earns what he gets and does not give or take the undeserved. A trader does not ask to be paid for his failures, nor does he ask to be loved for his flaws.[1]

This is the essence of the trading business. Understand it, accept it, or pass on this profession!

THE NEUROTIC TRADER

Whenever we move into areas like personality and character, we are dealing with questions of psychology. To put the matter in blunt, precise terms, you cannot be successful as a trader if you are psychologically unhealthy. Unhealthy people, neurotic people, want to duck from reality, and that is not possible in trading—not for long.

Rather than facing difficulties head on, neurotics want to escape them. That escape takes the form of alcohol abuse, drugs, overeating, promiscuity—anything that will make them feel better temporarily. In the world of trading, what we see most often is an unhealthy attraction to the thrill of gambling.

Neurotic traders use trading for the "high" it gives them. These people have a need to be always on the edge. They trade during the day, bet on professional sports at night, go the racetrack on weekends, and even plan their vacations around gambling. For them, the thrill is in the bet, not the outcome. Their mind is always on the next game, the next trade, wherever money can be won or lost. They have no goal beyond the moment. As we will see later on in this chapter, that is the underlying psychology of impulsive behavior, and it is the exact opposite of the healthy psychology of successful traders.

TWO PERSONALITY TYPES

The opposite of neurotic is what Karen Horney called "Wholehearted, or to be without pretense, to be emotionally sincere, to be able to put the whole of oneself into one's feelings, one's work and one's beliefs." These are truly profound words and I really suggest you memorize her thoughts, because they will be extremely important to you in every aspect of your life, not only trading, but especially your critical relationships . . . lover, spouse, family, children, and friends.

What are the personality traits of a successful trader? In outward style, there seem to be two opposite types. One is quiet, reserved, and not normally noticed at a gathering. The other is an extrovert, flamboyant, fun-loving eccentric; something of a renegade. But inwardly, they are alike. In college both types spent a lot of time at extracurricular interests, and both had irregular grades—A's in some subjects, C's in others. Usually they are neither loved nor hated, and they adapt to new people and events with ease. They are extremely determined and extremely individual, never asking for favors or help. They may ask your opinion and read many forecasters' views, but rarely act on anything but their own decisions. They are honest to the bone, living by their own wits and courage. Some are vocal and curse at losses or themselves, and sometimes yell and scream at executions; but generally, this is just an outlet for tension. All view profits and losses as their own responsibility, not anyone else's problem. The best ones are usually internal; they hold hurts within and force a smile when taking losses. Most pros talk about their losses, not their profits. They brag not about their winners, but how they lost.

People not cut out for trading will ask others for opinions, act on that information, and then blame the people giving the advice for the loss. These ineffectual traders never take responsibility for their own decisions, rationalizing away losses or blaming them on bad luck. They are always comparing themselves with others, are envious, do not look to improve through constant study of their mistakes. Indeed, they refuse to accept that they make mistakes at all!

A trader I know—call him John—was once sitting at a bar, talking to his friend Paul.

"Paul," he asked, "am I not a great trader?"

"You're good, John," Paul replied, "but not great."

"What do you mean? Last month I had 32 profitable trades out of 34, and lost only a thousand bucks."

This is rationalizing. It's also an example of the most common reason some traders are unsuccessful—the inability to take losses.

QUALITIES OF SUCCESSFUL TRADERS

So what exactly are the qualities that successful traders need? I've listed here the traits that I believe are important. I don't say much about them, because we all know what the terms mean, but this is far more than just a list of words. These simple words represent real principles for living.

In general, a successful trader has these character traits:

Judgment	Integrity
Courage	Loyalty
Self-criticism	Self-truthfulness
Commitment	Devotion to winning
Honor	Honesty

A trader's personality traits include:

Discipline	Passion
Concentration	Perfectionism—"Type A Personality"
Patience	Competition
Supreme desire to win	Intensity
Detachment	Inspiration

The *attitude* of a trader—part feeling, part action, and part beliefs—includes:

Self-esteem—the feeling you are good, able, worthy.

Optimism—never giving up and always seeing a positive future.

Trust—in your competence.

Flexibility—to change.

Perseverance—to study and learn constantly.

Admiration—to think highly of the success of others, rather than feeling envy.

Intelligence is also necessary—not merely a high IQ, but a sense of inner understanding. It includes:

Clarity—of purpose.

Wisdom—to observe objective relationships.

Imagination—to speculate what the future will be.

Creativity—to build a portfolio.

Certainty—to take a position!

(All the preceding traits, however, do *not* apply to locals, pit traders, specialists, and floor traders . . . only kidding!)

These qualities cannot be understood in a vacuum. The best way to see what you should be is to understand what not to be. Let me describe an "impulsive personality"—it's the opposite personality and character profile of a successful trader.

THE LESSON OF IMPULSIVE BEHAVIOR

Impulsive people have a way of understanding, and a mode of action, that, in comparison with normal deliberations and intentions, we would consider impaired. This impaired way of behavior shows itself as lack of control—acting on whim, giving in to temptation, doing what you have told yourself not to do. A person who decides to trade 10 contracts and then trades a 100 lot and says "I just did it—I don't know why" is acting impulsively.

All varieties of impulse, whim, or urge are essentially the same: a distortion of normal desires and wants, a sort of seizure that overrides good sense. Impulsive people are not self-confident but simply *hope* and *wish* for results. They have no long-term goals, only immediate urges. Their behavior is abrupt, immediate, and unplanned; the time between thought and execution is very brief. This is not to suggest that quickness in trading is a negative. To the contrary, it is essential to good traders, but the difference is in the size of commitment the person takes on the spur of the moment, and the existence (or absence) of an underlying plan.

The net outcome of unplanned behavior is that when failure occurs, the integrated process malfunctions and the person cannot accrue effective lessons from the loss. Without a plan, impulsive people can't develop sustained methods to determine what works and what doesn't. They can't understand why they failed, and they can't understand, as good traders do, that a failed plan is beneficial because it leads to avoiding the same mistakes in the future.

Lack of planning is only part of the problem. Impulsive people are also deficient in a certain method of thought process. Where normal people weigh, analyze, research and develop an initial impression, impulsive people guess and bet heavily, without much thought. They lack patience, concentration, the ability for abstraction, and reflective thought. Their judgment is often thought to be poor but what shows itself as "poor judgment" is really the result of character and personality, not intelligence.

It is also a question of integrity. A person of character has certain moral values that have been consciously thought out. Character means living your life in accord with highly developed principles, even though the consequences of those principles are intangible and invisible to others, and even though they are mainly for the long term. Impulsive people, in their thirst for immediate satisfaction, are hampered by integrity. For them, character gets in the way. For them, life is a series of temptations. These temptations always seem to be opportunities, but they inevitably lead to disappointment, frustration, and anxiety or depression, which in turn leads to all manner of neurotic, self-destructive behavior. If anyone confronts them, they will say "I can't stop it." In one respect they are absolutely correct: You can't stop what you don't want to stop.

To make things worse, impulsive people are handicapped by a lack of balance in their lives. They usually have no outside interests or indeed any goals beyond the immediate satisfaction of winning today. They don't give much thought to family, to friends, to community activities. Their ability to maintain rewarding personal relationships is shaky at best, and they have little or no involvement in cultural, intellectual, or ideological issues. Thus, when their work life starts to fall apart (as it usually does), they have nothing else to sustain them.

CONCLUSION

A thorough understanding of yourself is essential in trading. How you think, what you believe, and how you act out your life are critical parts of winning in trading and winning in life. Very few people understand, or are aware of, this subtlety in the trading profession. In other careers, you can get by; but in trading, you are quickly eliminated. The sad part is, most people have no idea why they have failed.

Epilogue
The Morality of Wealth

This book is an attempt to understand reality and truth in relation to financial markets. The best methods for doing so are hard work, objective study, and historical observation. In ending this book, I would like to put forth my personal views based on what I have learned in trying to understand how markets and the economy function, and how they move civilization through the ups and downs of recoveries and recessions.

The process is political. It is really a struggle of freedom versus the power to control in the name of some good cause. The reasons have been the nation, the poor, the common good, altruism, hunger, or any one of an unlimited number of human needs and desires. But it boils down to a desire for power and control by leaders over the people.

It isn't often you read about these topics in a book on trading, but realistically it should be included since capitalism is such an unusual occurrence in history. Capitalism existed in its purest form in the United States between 1776 and 1913, or a period of 137 years, until it officially ended with the adoption of the Sixteenth Amendment (the power to tax income at unequal rates) and the formation of central banking. Here is some basic information on the issue, and how it relates to you, the trader.

Most people pay little attention to their own psychological makeup. Your beliefs and why you hold them determine your actions. Your belief system plays a great role subliminally in how you trade and how you live. Strange as it may seem, you are being subconsciously programmed, by almost everyone, that "making money" is okay, as long as you don't make or keep too much! You are bombarded with news, movies, books, educators, religious leaders, and political preaching, telling you that helping others is the proper moral code of values to hold, at the expense of your own well-being. You can observe this in every area of your life. In films, the rich are portrayed as the bad guys, usually as businessmen committing white-collar crime. Although you'll enjoy the movies because of a star, humor, or good acting, the philosophical theme will be "the rich" and self-interest versus sacrifice. Self-interest and sacrifice are opposite moral concepts, and neither is exclusive. But which is primary and proper? This is a critical question to ask yourself, because your psychological views of money affect how you trade, and trading is all about creating wealth. The more you create, the better you do your job.

Morality is a code of values that guides your choices and actions. Individually, it pertains to how a person should live, whereas politics concerns itself with how society should function. Classically, religion provided the main code of ethics, which is outlined in the Ten Commandments. But there isn't a monopoly on morality. Since the late 1700s, the state or nation has been substituted for God. After World War II, morality came to be defined as the public good, in the form of welfare, or sacrifice to others in general. Almost never mentioned is self-interest.

Throughout the ages, most philosophers have despised wealth (perhaps because they were intellectuals and hated work, and consequently were poor). Karl Marx's mother has been quoted as saying, "If Karl would only stop talking about capital and go earn some." But of course he found a backer in Friedrich Engels. Ironically, Engels' father was a rich manufacturer, who supported his son and Marx. This faction also includes Jean Jacques Rousseau, who was the first environmentalist and originator of the welfare state, and Immanuel Kant, who supplied the ethical doctrine of sacrifice coined "altruism."

On the other side of the fence are a handful of philosophers and intellectuals who believed that creating wealth is not only acceptable but even "the good." The main ones were Adam Smith and John Locke. They created most of the ideas that were originally written in the U.S. Constitution. Jefferson paraphrases Locke in the Declaration of Independence.

Who is right and who is wrong? Is wealth good or bad? In answering this question, it is important to start with reality, or what is common practice? In other words, what does human nature tell us compared with what the philosophers, scholars, and theorists idealistically "wish and want" reality to be?

All humans hate poverty. We all work to escape it, and the insecurity it brings. The only question is which approach we should take in order to stop being poor and become better off. The normal person has no quandary in deciding whether to remain in poverty. The approaches are (1) welfare (you owe me all the basics of life—food, health care, shelter, clothing, and cable TV—without working, as a right because I am a human); (2) stealing or other illegal means; (3) inheritance, or the "lucky sperm" contest; and (4) hard work, the common sense method.

Hard work doesn't guarantee success, but it usually means a minimum form of security. All men and women prefer wealth to poverty, even those hypocrites who preach the contrary. Members of Congress, for instance, have given themselves a raise from $60,662 in 1982 to $130,000 in 1992, or a 141.3 percent increase. During the same period, the Consumer Price Index (CPI) only rose 41.9 percent . . . and yet many in Congress continue to claim that the policies of Reagan benefited only the rich.

The desire for wealth is fantastic, huge, constant, universal, dominant, and total. Most people work 8 or more hours a day, not including travel time, to make money beyond that needed for survival. The desire for wealth is a core need of men who want to use their success to attract women. Historically, women have wanted to marry successful men in order to have security when raising children. Today, society is changing; many women now have professional careers and help financially support their family, but they still generally opt for men with power, money, and at least equal financial status.

Those who preach altruism say we should go beyond the love of money to a higher morality (sacrifice). To them, I pose this question: By what standard do you judge this morality? The obvious universal standard for all human beings is life—*your life,* not the 5 billion other lives on the planet, nor those of animals, insects, and plants.

Your survival, values, goals, and life are the essence of why the creation of wealth is "the good." Your survival and goals determine your choices and actions, which is the reason you need an ethical code. Fulfilling the endless needs and desires of an unlimited number of strangers is an impossible morality to live by. The only code that is "fair" is mutual respect for each other's lives. Some religions preach that death is the goal of life. Christianity claims that the true moral goal of a lifetime is earning a place in heaven, and some Christians say that to attain this goal you must be poor, suffer, and atone for Adam's sin of eating the apple (from the tree of knowledge). This is not the way people really live, even those who are religious. Human nature and reality say,"That's a nice theory, but I reject it as a way of life, even if I believe in God."

You should live your life with your continued existence as a supreme (primary) value. You should not be sacrificed on the altar of society for people you don't know, or for causes a politician preaches while trying to get reelected. Ayn Rand said it best in the foreword to her novel *We the Living,* where she explained that the book's philosophical theme is the supreme value of your life, in terms of yourself. A young girl is sentenced to Siberia, and knows that she will never return. She voices this theme by saying: "There's your life. You begin it, feeling that it's something so precious and rare, so beautiful that it's like a sacred treasure. Now it's over, and it doesn't make any difference to anyone . . ." (Ayn Rand, *We the Living,* Foreword).

This is a great quote to help you understand why, at the drop of a hat, some people will send you off to a war you have no interest in, or take your tax money for a cause you never heard of. Politicians are indifferent to your life, but not their own. Did you ever hear a politician say "I believe we have to do something to stop this 500-year-old war in Bosnia! We need to send in troops, and I volunteer to be the first in line!" No, of course not! In that sentence, "we" really means me and you, but not them! Have you ever heard politicians offer to give up all their possessions and all their income, except for sustenance income, in order to sacrifice to help "the poor"? Did you ever hear them say, "Let me be an example"? No! The underlying reason they tell you how necessary it is for you to sacrifice for the nameless and faceless "poor," or "public good," is for their own power. To get elected, politicians need to spend your tax money to buy votes.

The Founding Fathers knew this scenario very well. Gouverneur Morris, a signer of the Constitution, said in a speech on August 7, 1787: "Give the vote to the people who have no property, and they will sell them to the rich who will be able to buy them." In 1993, the sequence works like this: A politician solicits campaign funds (in the millions) in return for creating a tax loophole, appropriation, grant, boondoggle, and so forth. The special interests comply smiling. The politician then hires a marketing team and a pollster, and is in business!

Isn't it self-evident that those who try to better themselves, and succeed, deserve the fruits of their labor? The concept of fairness cannot be defined objectively in terms of politicians taking money from some people by legal force, and giving it to others who bribe them with campaign funds to change the law to their benefit. Fairness is never mentioned in the Constitution; it is only used by politicians as the ultimate rationalization to take your hard-earned money and spend it to secure reelection, and with it the power, the perks, the $130,000 salary, the unspent campaign funds, and the retirement benefits.

From these facts, we must conclude that the creation of wealth from your own ability and work is the good and the *fair* way to live life. The founders of this country placed the eye of "Providence" on the back of the dollar bill (above the pyramid) because it means "active foresight accompanied with the procurement of what is necessary for future use," according to *Webster's New Universal Dictionary*. A politically free country exists to protect economic freedom and the property rights of the individual, not to redistribute wealth for personal power.

Perhaps some background on our Constitution will give you a better perspective on what our Founding Fathers thought was "fair." Article I, Section 9 states, "No capitation, or other direct, tax shall be laid, unless in Proportion to the Census or Enumeration herein before directed to be taken." In other words, there should be no direct taxes unless they are paid equally by everyone. Interesting that for 137 years, this was "fair," and tariffs paid for the needs of the country.

In 1913, the Sixteenth Amendment was passed, which allowed for "taxes on income, from whatever source derived, without apportionment among the several States and without regard to any census or enumeration." After passing this amendment, "fair" was a tax of 0.4 percent on a single person with an income of $5,000. Today's equivalent income after inflation would be $80,000, and the original 1913 tax on that $80,000 would be only $320. Today, an average family pays above $11,000. Again, interesting how "fairness" changes faster than the S&P futures, depending on which politicians are enacting policy.

Meanwhile, this loss of freedom is being expanded slowly along the lines of Fabianism: "the belief in slow rather than revolutionary change in government; relating to a society of socialists organized in England." For evidence, look at President Clinton's close friend Derek Shearer, who is an avowed Socialist although he now uses the term "economic democracy," since he says "you can't use the 'S' word." Shearer calls Bill Clinton "progressive," and says "Clinton believes in Activist Government." Isn't it telling that Shearer was appointed to be the Commerce

Department's Deputy Undersecretary for Economic Affairs? Or examine this classic statement by Secretary of Labor Robert Reich: "We must begin to celebrate collective entrepreneurship. We need to honor our teams more, our aggressive leaders and maverick geniuses less."

Today's political mentality is best summed up by Chairman of the House Ways and Means Committee Dan Rostenkowski, Democrat of Illinois, who said, "I'll do anything to go after the pocketbooks of those who have been enjoying themselves for the last decade." Contrast this with James Madison, the fourth President of the United States and the man called "Father of the Constitution," who wrote, "(The) chief object (of government is) to protect the separate and unequal faculties of acquiring prosperity," and you can see more than a slight change in the government's view of moral and political beliefs since 1913.

Weren't we taught by our parents that, within the boundaries of justice, hard work leading to prosperity was to be respected, and to be commended? But today, the political left denies that having to work is moral. They claim welfare is acceptable because everyone who is human deserves (tacitly) the right to have children; if a welfare mother wants to have 18 children, that's her right. If this is true, why restrict welfare to only the U.S. population? Why not the world?

Politicians' rationalizations are directed at the results of hard work, for the tax money. "You can't earn and keep too much," they say, because that would be greedy. The concept of greed is actually an anticoncept, because it can mean anything you want it to mean. Having two jars of peanut butter would be considered greedy from the point of view of a starving person. Really, the psychology of the term greed is used to attack only honest, successful people. For instance, you never read that a Mafia boss is greedy, only that he's a criminal. But a businessperson (who is rich) and commits a crime is greedy, not a criminal! This is political society trying to convince you to accept sacrifice, by making you feel guilty about your success. Think about these questions: Why isn't earning money legally and keeping it a moral good? Is Bill Gates greedy because he loves his work and still produces at age 37 instead of retiring? Does he work for the love of what he does or to make his seventh billion? What is immoral for the individual cannot be moral for society. It shows true hypocrisy for the political left to inhibit and criticize people for acquiring wealth, while at the same time doing all they can to expand the government's power in the name of helping people. Why are human beings bad if they gain control over material things they want or need? If a person wants to work 80 hours a week instead of 35, in order to earn money to eat in a fine restaurant and drive a Ferrari, why is that wrong? Why are the rich who work hard immoral, while individuals who produce nothing are virtuous?

These answers lie not in logic or misunderstanding but in ideology and psychology. In the latter, it is the resentment of the successful, and the desire to be the cause of their destruction, because the envious feel unable to equal their success. In the former, it is the egalitarian view that reality should change to make people what they never were—equal in their *desire* for work and success. The essence of the communists', socialists', collectivists', and liberal democrats' goal is the ethics of altruism, which is not the policy of being kind or nice to people in need, but rather the view that sacrifice for whatever cause sounds necessary is "the good," and living for your own self-interest is "the bad."

Please understand that self-interest does not mean at the *expense* of others. It does not suggest you should harm others. It does not imply that you would abandon your loved ones for your own satisfaction. It does not hint at taking advantage of others for your own gain. It means you have a right to live for yourself and are not obliged to be a slave for any cause, any time, any place. Ayn Rand said it best in *Philosophy: Who Needs It,* when she wrote:

What is the moral code of altruism? The basic principle of altruism is that man has no right to exist for his own sake, that service to others is the only justification of his existence, and that self-sacrifice is his highest moral duty, virtue and value.

This does not mean an ethical philosophy of being benevolent to people. It means you owe anyone your life if they need your help. Also, don't confuse this with choosing to give a dollar to a homeless person for a cup of coffee. Wrong or right, the question is do you *owe* every homeless person all your dollars to the point where you must become homeless yourself? The purpose of your life should not be slavery to others because they are in need. If you choose to help someone, fine; that is called *charity,* not a chattel on your being.

To be fair, let me quote a prime example of the opposite morality, so you can really see the contrast. From a *Playboy* interview with Fidel Castro in August 1985:

INTERVIEWER: . . . What still motivates Fidel Castro?

CASTRO: That's a very difficult question. Money does not motivate me; material goods do not motivate me. I think that personal self-lessness grows; the spirit of sacrifice grows; you gradually relinquish personal pride, vanity . . . all those elements that in one way or another exist in all men. . . .

If you do not guard against those vanities, if you let yourself become conceited or think that you are irreplaceable or indispensable, you can become infatuated with all of that—the riches, the glory.

Go back and read Rand's concept regarding your life as a supreme value, and you will understand why so many Cubans have attempted to escape to Florida. On the other hand, the former Soviet Union has had it with sacrifice and suffering, and the Russian people now want to copy the Japanese. In an interview that appeared in a Barcelona newspaper, Mikhail Fedotov, Russian Vice-Minister of Information and Press, stated [emphasis added]:

We have been educated in the belief that money was evil and the rich were bad, that the ideal was to toil for the state and that it would look after you. What we have to do now is to inform the people and have them convinced that *wealth is good,* that one has to be *selfish;* we have to create a society of *egoists* capable of working hard and observing the law. This way, we shall all profit. In Russia, we are 150 million invalids without the necessary consciousness to live a normal life.

The reason I have taken so much time to discuss this is that subconsciously you must know that making money is healthy, good, and the right thing to do. The amazing amount of guilt thrown at the U.S. population in the name of altruism is enough to make anyone feel nervous about succeeding. Being a trader is hard enough, but it becomes impossible when you worry about whether it is proper.

Another reason I've spent a great deal of time addressing this issue is because the United States is losing its preeminence as a free country every day. At this rate of decline of freedom, you may lose your ability to trade. High taxes, new laws, and political changes may someday make this profession obsolete. Understand that the business of trading is grounded in concepts and ideas. The ideas of the following men and women are completely opposite. They cover the whole spectrum of philosophical history, but you can only choose one side to accept as true:

Aristotle versus Plato
St. Thomas Aquinas versus St. Augustine
John Locke versus Jean Jacques Rousseau
Adam Smith versus Karl Marx
Thomas Jefferson versus Vladimir Lenin
Ayn Rand versus Immanuel Kant

In order to be a successful trader, you must be free to trade. In order to trade, you must understand and be able to defend yourself in the battle of ideas. Also you must feel that making money is perfectly moral, and the choice of how much to make is yours. Lastly, you must believe that you don't owe society your life, and that other people do not owe you theirs.

I cannot do justice to this concept in a single chapter on the ethics and psychology of wealth, but I hope I have stimulated you to think about some aspects of its importance, and have made you aware of the direction the United States is headed.

Capitalism was our original social system, but in 1913 it was changed to a mixed social system. The slow, but sure, destruction of capitalism into a combination of selective tenets from fascism, socialism, communism, and the welfare state is fact. The people responsible—politicians, journalists, professors, and lawyers—were certainly the primary beneficiaries of our original system. Yet the majority of these groups dispute the morality of wealth distribution based on personal initiative and its consequence: performance. I wish you all the freedom you can keep and the riches it can bring you.

Notes

Chapter 2

1. Ludwig von Mises, *Human Action* (3rd rev. ed., New Haven, CT: Yale University Press, 1963), pp. 10, 92. I highly recommend that anyone interested in learning more about the Austrian School read Thomas C. Taylor's *An Introduction to Austrian Economics* (Auburn, AL: Ludwig von Mises Institute, 1980). For further information, contact: The Ludwig von Mises Institute for Austrian Economics Inc., Auburn University, Auburn, AL 36849.

2. Victor Sperandeo, *Trader Vic—Methods of a Wall Street Master* (New York: John Wiley & Sons, 1990), p. 114.

3. The subjective nature of value and the fact that *differences* in perception of value drive the trade process seem to be simple concepts, but were in fact introduced and formalized by Ludwig von Mises. Adam Smith and the other classical economists thought that trade must be of *equal* value.

4. For a more complete discussion of the nature of wealth and a refutation of the commonly held economic belief that only the production of material objects increases net wealth, see *Trader Vic—Methods,* Chapter 9.

Chapter 3

1. Ludwig von Mises, *Human Action* (Chicago: Contemporary Books, 1966), p. 572.

2. Ludwig von Mises, *Human Action* (3rd rev. ed., New Haven, CT: Yale University Press, 1963), p. 398.

3. Ibid., p. 401. For a detailed explanation of the Austrian School Theory of Money and Credit, see *The Theory of Money and Credit,* translated by H. E. Batson (Indianapolis: Liberty Classics, 1981).

265

4. von Mises, *Human Action,* p. 418.

5. Ibid., pp. 416–419.

6. Ibid., p. 526.

7. Ibid., p. 527.

8. For a full discussion, see *Human Action,* pp. 534–586.

9. To those of you who read *Trader Vic—Methods of a Wall Street Master* (New York: John Wiley & Sons, 1990), please note that I was mistaken in saying that originary interest is a component of the gross market rate of interest. Rather, originary interest is the level to which net, real, interest always tends. The entrepreneurial and price premium components are not true interest rates, but discounting functions that depend on entrepreneurial risk and changes in the money relation, respectively.

10. von Mises, *Human Action,* 3rd rev. ed., p. 551.

11. For a full discussion of how this process works, see *Trader Vic—Methods,* Chapter 10.

12. It is possible that the increased demand for consumer goods could drive consumer prices up faster than in the capital goods market, resulting in forced savings that offset, to some extent, the upward pressure on producers' prices. In effect, originary interest would be lowered, and the pace of economic progress would be advanced. Eventually, however, prices for consumer goods rise to the point of causing a "flight to real values."

13. von Mises, *Human Action,* p. 559.

Chapter 4

1. von Mises, *Human Action,* 3rd rev. ed., p. 807.

2. John Maynard Keynes, *General Theory of Employment, Interest, and Money* (1st Harbinger ed., New York: Harcourt Brace, 1964), p. 95.

Chapter 7

1. Gordon A. Holmes, *Capital Appreciation in the Stock Market* (New York: Parket Publishing Company, 1969), p. 32.

Chapter 8

1. Irving Kristol, editorial, January 9, 1986, p. 28, *The Wall Street Journal.*

2. Robert Rhea, *Dow's Theory Applied to Business and Banking* (New York: Simon and Schuster, 1938).

3. The Barron's Index was discontinued in 1938. To maintain as much consistency as possible, I used the Industrial Production Index (1987 = 100) from 1921 to the present.

4. Op. cit., Rhea, p. 77.

Chapter 9

1. Robert Rhea, *Dow's Theory Applied to Business and Banking* (New York: Simon and Schuster, 1938).

Chapter 10

1. For a more detailed discussion of the merits and hazards of technical analysis as well as the specific technical methods I employ, see *Trader Vic—Methods of a Wall Street Master* (New York: John Wiley & Sons, 1990).

2. Robert D. Edwards and John Magee, *Technical Analysis of Stock Trends* (Springfield, MA: John Magee, 1966).

3. For a more complete discussion of my technical principles of market analysis, see *Trader Vic—Methods,* pp. 49–108.

4. When applied to the stock averages, all related averages must confirm the trend. If they do not, then a divergence exists—evidence of a possible change of trend.

5. For a detailed explanation of the causes of tests and the 2B pattern, see *Trader Vic—Methods,* pp. 81–84.

6. For a detailed discussion of the oscillators I use and how to calculate them, see *Trader Vic—Methods,* pp. 94–104.

Chapter 12

1. See Victor Sperandeo, *Trader Vic—Methods of a Wall Street Master* (New York: John Wiley & Sons, 1990), for further details on these trading rules.

2. Ibid.

Chapter 13

1. Yale Hirsch, *1993 Stock Trader's Almanac* (Old Tappan, NJ: Hirsch, 1993).

Index